Bennett's *New York Herald* and the Rise of the Popular Press

new york state
STUDIES

James Gordon Bennett. *Harper's Weekly*, July 10, 1858

Bennett's
NEW YORK HERALD

and the

Rise of the Popular Press

JAMES L. CROUTHAMEL

SYRACUSE UNIVERSITY PRESS

NATIONAL ENDOWMENT FOR THE

Humanities

*Open access edition funded by the National Endowment
for the Humanities/Andrew W. Mellon Foundation Humanities Open Book Program.*

This book is published with the assistance of a grant
from the Benjamin P. Atkinson Fund, Hobart and William Smith Colleges.

The paper used in this publication meets the minimum requirements
of American National Standard for Information Sciences—Permanence of Paper
for Printed Library Materials, ANSI Z39.48-1984. ∞™

For a listing of books published and distributed by Syracuse University Press,
visit www.SyracuseUniversityPress.syr.edu.

ISBN: 978-0-8156-2711-1 (paperback)
ISBN: 978-1-68445-004-6 (ebook)
DOI: https://doi.org/10.14305/sub.hobp.9781684450046

Library of Congress Cataloging-in-Publication Data.

Crouthamel, James L., 1931–
    Bennett's New York herald and the rise of the popular press /
James L. Crouthamel. — 1st ed.
        p.   cm.
    Bibliography: p.
    Includes index.
    ISBN 0-8156-2461-1 (alk. paper)
    1. Bennett, James Gordon, 1795–1872. 2. Herald (New York, N.Y. :
1835) 3. Journalism United States—History—19th century.
I. Title.
PN4874.B4C76   1989
071'.471—dc19   88-34305

Manufactured in the United States of America

*To my mother
and to the memory of my father.*

JAMES L. CROUTHAMEL is Professor of History, Hobart and William Smith Colleges. He has contributed articles to *Journalism Quarterly, Journal of Negro History,* and *New York History* and is the author of *James Watson Webb: A Biography.*

Contents

Preface

James Gordon Bennett did more than anyone else to establish an important American institution, the popular, cheap, mass circulation newspaper, and yet no good, scholarly study exists of Bennett and his paper, the *New York Herald*. This book is an attempt to fill that void.

The reasons for Bennett's neglect by historians seem clear. There are no surviving records for the *Herald* during Bennett's era, and his personal papers are sparse, most of them covering the period before the founding of the *Herald* in 1835. The evidence, then, must come primarily from a careful reading of the *Herald* itself. Reading over three decades of a daily that went from four closely printed pages to eight, and frequently twelve, with almost no graphic material to relieve the prose is tedious work; but sampling techniques, no matter how systematic, are no substitute. As a result, earlier studies of Bennett tend to be anecdotal and without much substance. Other evidence does exist, of course, especially the observations of Bennett's contemporaries about the man and his newspaper, and more indirectly, in the ways other newspapers borrowed the *Herald*'s style and techniques in trying to emulate its success. The *Herald*, however, is the primary source for this study. Bennett did not invent the cheap popular newspaper, but his innovations, through a combination of sensationalism, technological improvements, and comprehensive news coverage, made the *Herald* the most successful and widely circulated newspaper in mid-nineteenth-century America.

A subsequent generation of more famous yellow journalists, most notably Joseph Pulitzer and William Randolph Hearst, taking advantage of technical innovations in format (especially headlines) and in pictorial reproduction simply carried Bennett's techniques of sensationalism and popular appeal to new heights—or depths. But Bennett was the pioneer.

This book is not a biography of Bennett. Except on rare occasions he was guarded about his personal life, and there are no papers extant to illuminate the shadows. (In this respect, he was very different from his play-boy son and successor.) I therefore concentrate on the public Bennett, the editor and publisher, and the way he shaped the modern newspaper.

Even the public Bennett remains something of an enigma, an example of the paradox of the Jacksonian era, but this is why he is so fascinating. His editorials were notorious for their rhetorical extremism — strident, vituperative, and emotional — in behalf of politics that were basically moderate and balanced. He championed the masses and created a newspaper for them, but he was fundamentally a conservative. He claimed to be politically independent, above party, and yet he was constantly enmeshed in the party battles of the period.

He tended to form his public identity on the basis of negatives, Anglophobia, anti-Catholicism, and antiabolitionism in particular. He misled his unsophisticated readers with simplistic conspiratorial explanations of events and forces that greatly affected their lives. Many of his contemporaries envied his success but detested the means by which he achieved it. They respected his power, but they hated him.

Yet this rather unpleasant man seems to be almost a stereotype of the political culture of the period, exemplifying most of the traits Edward Pessen identified with the "new men of politics" in his *Jacksonian America*. The adjectives tumble from Pessen's pen: *opportunistic, pragmatic, self-made, materialistic, ambitious, shrewd, disingenuous, unprincipled, calculating, inconsistent, evasive, dissimulating, hypocritical, demagogic, conservative*. They all describe Bennett.

Were the readers of the *Herald* attracted by its breezy style and sensationalism, its news coverage, its editorials, its service advertisements, or a skillful mix of all? Because most copies of the newspaper were sold by newsboys rather than by subscription, no exact data exist on who read it and why; but one can exercise informed speculation. Bennett's remarkable success came because he created an attractive and useful product for which there was a widespread but untapped demand. The *Herald,* editorial columns aside, was the best *news*paper of its time, and it was written in a style that identified with rather than spoke down to its readers. The news was comprehensive and attractively packaged. News to Bennett was not merely what concerned merchants and politicians but the whole range of human activities: sex, crime and tragedy, society, medicine, religion, high culture and popular culture, and products. His advertisements were directed at ordinary readers and provided a valuable service. Priced cheap enough for most New Yorkers to afford, the *Herald* served up information that was useful, educational, and entertaining. Editorial policy seldom intruded into the mission of supplying news of a more accurate and comprehensive character than that provided by its competitors. Put off by the stridency of his editorials, however, his contemporaries did not always appreciate the value of his news coverage. Nor have many historians since then, preoccupied with mining the *Herald*'s editorials as a measure of "public opinion."

I have tried to look at the *Herald* as a whole, not simply as a carrier of editorials. It was not an "organ" of any party or faction; it spoke only for Bennett.

Many individuals and institutions have assisted me in completing this project. I have profited from discussions about Bennett in particular and newspaper history in general with the late J. Cutler Andrews, the late Holman Hamilton, George Juergens, Julian Rammelkamp, David C. Smith, the late Louis Starr, Wendell Tripp, and Bernard A. Weisberger. James Baughman provided encouragement over a long period, and David Schuyler gave support when I needed it the most.

Mary Lou Chilbert typed several versions of the manuscript with great skill, and I am grateful to my colleague William S. Atwell for instructing me in the mysteries of word processing.

Librarians at several institutions have been helpful, but I am especially indebted to the Concord, Massachusetts, Public Library for making the Frederic Hudson Papers available to me, and to the staff of the Warren Hunting Smith Library, Hobart and William Smith Colleges, for many kindnesses over many years.

The Faculty Research Fund of Hobart and William Smith Colleges provided grants for typing earlier versions of the manuscript.

I have also benefited from the excellent comments of the anonymous readers of the Syracuse University Press.

My greatest debts are to my colleague Daniel J. Singal for a searching critique of the manuscript, and especially to my wife, Marion Scott Remer, for an exhaustive criticism and for providing a warm and loving atmosphere conducive to scholarship. The manuscript is stronger for all the help that I have received; its weaknesses are my responsibility.

Geneva, New York   James L. Crouthamel
June 1988

Bennett's *New York Herald* and the Rise of the Popular Press

1

Learning Journalism

He arrived at the new five-story granite building at the corner of Fulton and Nassau streets at 7:00 A.M. The neighborhood was busy, with the post office, city hall, stock exchange, and many hotels nearby. HERALD BUILDING said the signs running the length and width of the building, and below that JAMES GORDON BENNETT. A visitor would no doubt have noticed Bennett, despite his careless dress. He was "a tall, slender man, well-formed," although he walked with a slight stoop, his movements abrupt and nervous. He wore his silver hair long and had a small chin beard. But it was Bennett's crossed eyes that would have first attracted the attention of a stranger.[1]

Bennett went directly to his second-floor office that summer day of 1845. Ten years after its opening there was a well-established daily routine at the *Herald.* His secretary had put the mail and newspapers on his desk marked for his attention. While breakfasting on tea and dry toast, the editor-publisher read and noted matters that he would pursue — on that morning, perhaps, an account of the expulsion of Cassius M. Clay's abolitionist organization and newspaper from Lexington, Kentucky, and an editorial from the local nativist *American Patriot* calling for the restriction of the political rights of immigrants. The first was worthy of a long editorial defending the mob; the second called for a shorter response supporting the political rights of the newcomers. Bennett next examined the overnight reports from Washington to see if there were any new developments in the combustible situation with Mexico (there were not) and, closer to home, reports from Delaware County of the grand jury investigation into the antirent violence there.

After dictating editorials to his stenographer, Bennett conferred with his managing editor, Frederic Hudson. During that week in August the paper was featuring a series about itself. Each day a woodcut of one part of its plant appeared on the front page and a story about the various

I

departments of the paper. No doubt Bennett scrutinized these carefully.

The editor and managing editor were almost alone on the second floor that morning. Most of the other thirteen editors and reporters were out on assignments in Wall Street, in the courts, at city hall, and in Brooklyn. They would come in later to write their stories, as would the theater and cultural critics who had been at their task late the previous evening. Others examined the exchange papers that were received daily, clipping enough short items to fill several columns of miscellany.

At noon Bennett received visitors for a short time — his gruff, impatient manner did not encourage small talk — but there were not many that vacation season because most of New York's important people were at Saratoga Springs (where the *Herald* kept a reporter). By about two o'clock the first of the material was ready for the compositors to set into type, and Bennett looked at it before starting his daily inspection of the plant.

He began his inspection in the basement, where twenty-two men operated the four two-cylinder flatbed presses, two for the twelve thousand daily *Herald*s and two for the twelve thousand weekly papers. One man wet the paper in preparation for the presses, eight men fed it into the machines, and eight more removed the printed sheets at the other end. A foreman and an engineer supervised the operation and ensured the steam supply from an engine below. Several others cut, folded, and counted the finished papers and then turned them over to a clerk, who distributed them, for cash, to the dealers and newsboys gathered outside. To cool the basement, a ditch covered with a grate ran the entire length of the building. That afternoon the pressroom was empty. In 1845 the presses started their daily run about two o'clock in the morning so the first *Herald*s were ready for distribution about four.

The mailroom was directly in front of the pressroom in the basement. Here six clerks sorted and routed the incoming mail and addressed the *Herald* to out-of-town subscribers, directing the paper to the proper railroad, stage, packet, or postal route.

Back on the first floor, Bennett entered the business office managed by his brother-in-law Robert Crean. The outside entrance to the building was on Fulton Street, and here the clerks took subscriptions and advertisements. The hundreds of ads, all of which would be termed "classified" today, ranged in August 1845 from help wanted to lost and found, from services such as dentistry and ophthalmology, French lessons, moneylending and daguerreotyping to commodities such as fishing tackle, needles, Aeolian harps, wigs, hats, paintings, hardware, and wine, to agricultural products like hemp seed, lard, wheat, and cotton. The largest number announced pharmaceuticals such as "diarrhoea cordial" and "Elixir of Love," medical treatises and treatments, and physicians who offered cures for "private diseases."

Back on the second floor, the four-room editorial department began to fill with reporters writing their stories. A large table in the center of the room held current books and periodicals; files of exchange papers were suspended from the walls. On that day the police court reporter featured an abortion case, which was also the subject of a short editorial. The money market column, entrusted to the managing editor's brother, Edward W. Hudson, discussed the annual foreign trade deficit, France's overseas trade, and a settlement that a bankrupt local bank had reached with its creditors. Another reporter was promoting the coming match between St. George's Cricket Club and the Cricketeers of All Canada.

Theater critics judged the performance of James H. Hackett at the Park Theatre in *The Merry Wives of Windsor,* the opening of Eugène Sue's *Mysteries of Paris* at the Bowery Theatre, the French opera *Ambassadress* at Niblo's, the "Infant Sisters" performing at Palma's Theatre, and the exhibition of the Mammoth Electrical Machine at Castle Garden.

Another reporter prepared the "Latest Intelligence" from the last evening's mail: cabinet discussions about Mexico, the nativist convention in Baltimore, and local politics in Philadelphia. A letter from Saratoga Springs was featured on the front page, and the leading local news story concerned appointments and removals at the custom house. Reporters in the commercial department wrote stories about the corn and cotton crops in the South and the sugar market at Havana and compiled lists of ship arrivals and departures and the registrants at the city's hotels.

This work was often routine without much glamour, and those who did it worked long hours for low salaries. They would have echoed the sentiments of a *Tribune* staffer who wrote a few years later:

> My work continues to be . . . not very inspiring. Shall I say it — there is drudgery connected with my work, a good deal of drudgery, a very little real hearty work, which leaves one better than it finds him. Drudgery in reading newspapers and scissoring them for things of no earthly interest to myself but of supposed interest to others; drudgery in looking over the telegraph & saying what shall be in this type & what in that; drudgery in fixing up other people's bad English & no apparent utility in either of these branches of labor; an occasional pleasure in turning a paragraph relative to the news, or "Ed. Head" as we call it, but oftenest drudgery therein also; and a climax of drudgery in hanging around the "forms", deciding what shall go in, out of several things.

On his way to the fifth-floor composing room, Bennett looked in on the book and job-printing departments on the third and fourth floors. The job presses had their own compositors and pressmen. Most of the handbills for New York's theaters were printed there.

The composing room was at the top of the building, lighted during the day through large windows and at night by one hundred gaslights. Here twenty men worked each day from ten o'clock one morning to two the next, with three hours off for meals. At one end of the room were the desks of the foreman and proofreaders. The compositors worked at their cases perpendicular to a long table that ran the length of the building and held the type forms. A good compositor could set seventy lines of type each hour, and in 1845, when two presses were used for the daily *Herald,* everything had to be set into type twice. The length of the paper was the equivalent in type to a 350-page octavo book. After the press run was completed, each piece of type had to be removed and returned to the proper case. The forms were carried to and from the basement pressroom by a dumbwaiter.

The inspection completed, Bennett went home to dine, usually alone. His wife, Henrietta, and four-year-old son, James, spent most of the year in Paris. After dinner Bennett returned to his office, sometimes looking in at the theater or opera on the way. He dictated any last-minute editorial changes and, after putting the paper to bed, went home to bed himself, almost always by ten o'clock.

The finished four-page *Herald* with its circulation of twelve thousand was in 1845 the most popular and profitable daily newspaper in the United States. Its niche was so secure that its success seemed almost inevitable. But Bennett was fifty years old, and his success had come very late, after many years of apparent failure.

All that is known about the early life of James Gordon Bennett is what information he was willing to disclose in a highly selective fashion. Bennett was born on September 1, 1795, in the highlands of Scotland and migrated to America in 1819.[2] He grew up in the tiny hamlet of Old Town in the village of Keith, Banffshire, about sixty miles north of Aberdeen. According to family tradition, the first Bennett (then Benoit) came to England from France with William the Conqueror. The Bennetts were relatively prosperous compared to their neighbors, and James's father was one of the few independent farmers in an area where nearly all the land was owned by the Earl of Fife. The Bennett house was large and comfortable and the family was well fed.

The Bennetts were different from most of their neighbors in another way: they were Roman Catholics, and this made them suspect in the community. Many of the harsher restrictions on Catholics had been repealed, but there was still an atmosphere of fear and superstition toward papists, and the elder Bennett was courageous to maintain his faith in a land that was so overwhelmingly Presbyterian. At the time James was born there were only twenty-five thousand Catholics in all of Scotland. He and his brother Cosmo were taught Catholic dogma and martyrology at home by their father, and grisly tales of persecution left James permanently prejudiced against the English.

He attended the public school each day as required by law. Latin and Greek were the basis of the curriculum; the Bible was the fundamental text; and the schoolmaster's rod was the main instructional tool. James was an apt pupil with a good memory, and he read many of the classics at Keith. Although he enjoyed swimming and outdoor games, he was a shy boy who took many solitary walks among the historic sites of Banffshire.

His father intended that James, the eldest son, should be trained for the priesthood at the Catholic seminary in Aberdeen. Therefore, at age fifteen, James was sent to Blair's College. The population of Aberdeen was forty thousand when he arrived, no doubt intimidating to the youth from Old Town with its 136 inhabitants. The college was small and undistinguished, but it had abler teachers than James's schoolmaster at Keith and the curriculum was broader—Greek, Latin, French, history, geography, bookkeeping, logic, church history, and science.

Bennett was an eager student, and he spent four happy years at the college, enjoying the atmosphere in which the teachers mixed in sports and play, reading widely in Burns, Smollett, Scott, Paine, Boswell, Rousseau, and Voltaire and sampling the world of letters through the *Edinburgh Review*. Lord Byron was a hero to Bennett and the other young would-be intelligentsia of Aberdeen. They belonged to a literary club that met in the Aberdeen grammar school, which Byron had attended.

Influenced by his reading in the rationalism of the Enlightenment, Bennett began to see shortcomings in the Catholic church, and after four years at the college he decided that he could not enter the priesthood. His crisis of faith could not be resolved, and he ended in a position of religious indifference. Eventually he developed a strong antagonism toward Roman Catholicism, blaming it for the death of his younger brother Cosmo at age twenty-three while undergoing the rigors of training for the priesthood.

When he left college in 1814, he had surely aquired an education equivalent to that in an American college. Little is known about the next five years of his life until he sailed for America in 1819, but he published his first article, an admiring piece about Napoleon, in a small Aberdeen periodical shortly after the Battle of Waterloo. He read philosophy and economics, including David Hume's *Treatise on Human Nature,* Adam Smith's *Wealth of Nations,* and Thomas Reid's *Inquiry into the Human Mind.* He probably also became familiar either directly or through the periodical press with other writers of the Scottish Enlightenment such as Lord Kames, Francis Hutcheson, Adam Ferguson, and Dugald Stewart. Scotland's universities surpassed Oxford and Cambridge during the late eighteenth century to make it the intellectual leader of the British Isles, especially in political economy. Bennett's reading was probably responsible for his interest in economic analysis and his support of laissez-faire economic doctrine. But though Adam Smith is evident in Bennett's later economic writings, he did not subscribe to the antislavery views of Smith and other leaders of the Scottish Enlightenment. His racist and proslavery opinions seem closer to those of Lord Kames and David Hume.

After leaving college, Bennett traveled extensively through Scotland, visiting many national shrines and especially the places described by Sir Walter Scott. Perhaps Bennett's father tolerated such prolonged aimlessness and continued to support his son in the hope that he would return to the Catholic faith. Bennett developed an interest in America during this time. The migration from Scotland to America was often at the rate of a thousand persons per week so this interest was not unusual. Books about America were very popular, and Bennett read Benjamin Franklin's *Autobiography* with great enthusiasm when it was published in Scotland in 1817, as well as three travel accounts that appeared in 1818.

According to Bennett, his decision to leave Scotland was made on an impulse. He met a friend on the streets of Aberdeen, learned that he was leaving for Halifax in April, and decided on the spot to accompany him. The family must have supported this whim and provided a small purse. On April 6, 1819, he sailed for America.

Bennett reached Halifax after a four-week voyage. The city of twelve thousand was undergoing a postwar boom, but Bennett saw it as merely a way station for points south. A rabid Anglophobe, he disliked the atmosphere of this loyalist stronghold and stayed only until he could earn enough as a schoolmaster to pay the passage on a schooner to Portland, Maine. He again taught school for a few months in the village of Addison. Although he admired the self-assurance of Maine's Yankees, then in the throes of the statehood movement, Boston and the scenes of Franklin's *Autobiography* beckoned. On New Year's Day 1820 he sailed to Boston.

Immediately on arrival, he visited and then revisited the famous revolutionary war sites he had read about. Then he searched for work and found a position as a clerk at Wells and Lilly, one of the leading publishers, printers, and booksellers of the city. Bennett worked diligently, learned much about publishing and printing, and came into contact with some of the literary, business, and political leaders of the city, while broadening his education by reading and attending public lectures. But as a clerk he left something to be desired. He was careless about his personal appearance and never mastered politeness; he asked too many questions and offered too much advice; his dry, cynical humor offended the customers. He was shifted to proofreading at Wells and Lilly, a position that had no contact with customers.[3]

After three years in Boston, Bennett moved to New York City. The reasons for the move are not clear — perhaps he felt the proofreading job was a dead end — but certainly there were greater opportunities in New York, a rapidly growing metropolis of 130,000 people. It was easier for a newcomer to win acceptance in this heterogeneous and cosmopolitan city than in staid Boston. Bennett frequented the coffeehouses in search of work and at one of them met Aaron S. Willington, publisher of the *Charleston* (South Carolina) *Courier,* who was in New York to buy presses, type, paper, and ink for his journal and to hire an editorial assistant. Bennett agreed to buy the supplies while Willington warmed himself in the coffeehouses. He must have done a satisfactory job and, probably because of his publishing experience in Boston, was offered the editorial position.

Bennett spent only ten months working for Willington on the *Courier,* but it was a pivotal part of his life. He decided to make journalism his career, and training on the *Courier,* one of the best newspapers in the nation, was invaluable. He also got a firsthand view of slavery and the South, toward which he developed a sympathetic feeling that was to last throughout his life.

The *Charleston Courier* was a commercial newspaper; thoroughness, accuracy, and moderation were its watchwords. It catered to merchants and planters eager for the latest cotton prices from England, and Willington put a premium on speed. In 1815 he had scooped every other newspaper in the country in printing the news of the Treaty of Ghent, which he obtained by rowing out beyond Charleston harbor to meet an incoming schooner. The *Courier* then obtained its own newsboat and made this a regular practice. With many packets sailing from Cadiz to Havana in the 1820s, news from western Europe often first reached the United States at Charleston.

Bennett's primary responsibility on the *Courier* was to translate the latest news from the Havana packets from Spanish and French. This news concerned not only Europe but also the Caribbean and Latin America, then in the throes of postrevolutionary disturbances. He developed an interest in and an expertise on Latin America which he never dropped. Later his *Herald* provided the most comprehensive and penetrating coverage of Latin America appearing anywhere in the press.[4]

Late in 1823 Bennett left the *Courier* and returned to New York, never explaining the reasons for his move.[5] In October he issued a prospectus for a "Permanent Commercial School" but was unable to raise the capital to open it. For the next four years, until November 1827, when he became an associate editor of the *New York Enquirer,* Bennett supported himself by free-lance writing, mostly for the party newspapers of the city. In 1825 he wrote for John Tryon's weekly *Courier* and for a few weeks he edited the sheet. By 1826 he was a regular contributor to the *Mercantile Advertiser,* a commercial paper that resembled Willington's, and he began to write for Thomas Snowden's *National Advocate,* the Tammany Hall organ. He specialized in economic analysis and created a stir by his factual reports of the fraud trials following the commercial crisis of 1825–26. These exposures of stock speculations stirred up resentment in some of New York's business circles.[6]

Soon after this Bennett became disenchanted with Snowden, who had endorsed John Quincy Adams's bid for reelection. Bennett returned to freelancing, assisting efforts to elect Andrew Jackson as president whenever he could. He made regular contributions to Mordecai M. Noah's *New York Enquirer.* Noah was a colorful and controversial editor and politician, a Jew who had written plays, tried to organize a Jewish colony on an island in the Niagara River, and served in minor patronage positions in New York. Since 1817 he had been an editor of Snowden's *National Advocate* but left the paper after a patronage dispute with Snowden and started his own paper, the *Enquirer,* in mid-1826.

Bennett and Noah were both ardent Jackson men, although they disliked each other personally. In the spring of 1827 Bennett persuaded Noah to allow him to write a series of humorous sketches for the *Enquirer.* The first, "Shaking Hands," appeared on April 27 and was the talk of the town, although the humor is very tortured for today's taste. The subject was forms of salutation around the world, and its freshness and impertinence created a demand for many extra copies. A second article, "Intemperance," had the same favorable effect on the *Enquirer*'s circulation. But Noah received so many indignant protests from subscribers that he halted the experiment.[7]

The *Enquirer* prospered as Bennett confined his contributions to more appropriate subjects. On the paper's first anniversary, Noah boasted a circulation of twenty-four hundred, very good for that time. The *Enquirer* resembled its contemporaries in the New York press. It was a commercial sheet, primarily offering news for merchants: ship arrivals and departures, market and financial conditions, the offerings of importers, and bank note values. Also like its fellows, the *Enquirer* had a political position — it supported Jackson. The paper contained four pages of six columns each, and pages 1, 3, and 4 were filled almost entirely with advertisements and legal notices. The news and editorials appeared on page 2, mostly short items clipped from other papers. Local news was slighted in favor of dispatches from Washington, Albany, and abroad. The *Enquirer* was dull by later standards but no more so than other New York newspapers.[8]

Bennett became an associate editor of the *Enquirer* in late 1827 after many months of irregular free-lancing. Since Noah did not relish the prospect of having the Scotsman around the office every day, he readily agreed to Bennett's suggestion that he cover the congressional session in Washington. For the next four years Bennett reported on politics and society from Washington, Albany, and Saratoga Springs. He became intimate with many of the leading political figures and was perhaps the most widely read political correspondent of the day.[9]

He had developed a distinctive style of correspondence patterned, he said, on the letters of Horace Walpole. His sentences were well constructed and rhythmical; his wit was sharp; his use of metaphor was effective. One day his pieces would be narrative, another day anecdotal, another analytical, and another moralizing. The reader never knew what to expect, and Bennett's unsigned pieces must have bolstered the *Enquirer*'s popularity.

The first of these pieces appeared on January 8, 1828, and described President Adams's New Year's Day reception at the White House. It was chatty, colorful, and ended on a critical note. A week later he discussed the alignment of forces in Congress over an issue involving slavery. The following week he was at a testimonial dinner for Jackson. The intimate details he provided of social life at the capital were especially popular with the *Enquirer*'s readers. But pro-Jackson politics was always in the background. Bennett brought to these partisan sallies an expertise gained from hard work and hours of research in the congressional library. His research proved, for example, that Jackson's spelling was no worse than that of the great men of the revolutionary generation.

During the summer of 1828 Bennett followed the politicians to the popular resort of Saratoga Springs, reporting the social life and gossip and making political predictions. In the fall he returned to Washington, and before Congress convened he filed a series of columns on political economy. He gloated over Jackson's election as president and described the inauguration at great length.[10]

The *Enquirer*'s leading rival was James Watson Webb's *New York Morn-*

ing Courier, a commercial paper that was also devoted to Jackson. Noah and Webb had quarreled, and Webb's *Courier* spent most of its editorial space during the 1828 election not campaigning for Jackson but campaigning against Noah, the regular Jacksonian nominee for sheriff. Webb organized an independent Jackson ticket to oppose Noah, and he injected anti-Semitism into the campaign. He was delighted when Noah was defeated, although his defection cost him the political advertising from Tammany Hall. But on national issues Webb and Noah saw eye to eye, being hostile to the Bank of the United States and protective tariffs and siding with Martin Van Buren against John C. Calhoun's wing of the Democratic party. The circulation of the rival papers was about equal in early 1829.[11]

Party leaders were disturbed by the competition between these two Jacksonian sheets that spent so much time attacking each other rather than the opposition. In the spring of 1829, when both Webb and Noah were in Albany seeking public printing contracts, the details of a merger were worked out. Bennett was also in Albany and was perhaps the first to suggest a union that would end the competition so that the new sheet could concentrate its fire on political opponents rather than fellow Jacksonians.[12]

Bennett was acting in his own self-interest in promoting the merger. He believed that the new paper would be unacceptable to the leadership at Tammany Hall, which distrusted Webb, and hoped that Tammany would ask him to start a new party organ in the city. He tried to undermine the newly merged paper, telling prominent New Yorkers that party leaders were dissatisfied with the merger and lacked confidence in Webb. When he failed to attract support for his own party paper, Bennett proposed that the local party appoint a political editor — himself, no doubt — to control the editorial policy of the *Courier and Enquirer.* Webb was aware of Bennett's scheming. He wrote to state party leader Azariah C. Flagg that "Bennett will never issue the first number of his paper." To check Bennett, Webb recommended to Flagg that the party issue a circular recommending the *Courier and Enquirer* to the party faithful.[13]

Bennett was without regular employment after the merger until September 5, 1829, when he joined the *Courier and Enquirer* as an associate editor. In the interim he probably lived off savings and occasional free-lancing and perhaps a retainer from Nicholas Biddle, president of the Bank of the United States. While still on the *Enquirer* staff before the merger, when the editorial policy of the paper was decidedly opposed to the bank, Bennett began sending reports to Biddle about banking conditions and sentiment in New York, explaining why so many of the New York banks were hostile to Biddle's institution. He left Biddle with the pessimistic impression that the Bank could not be rechartered in its present form.[14] Bennett reported to Biddle for several years, although in public he firmly opposed the bank's recharter.

Bennett served as an associate editor to Webb and Noah on the *Courier and Enquirer* for almost three years, a very important period in his development as a journalist. During these years the *Courier and Enquirer* was the best, the largest, and the most important newspaper in the nation, and Bennett deserves part of the credit for its success.

The immediate effects of the merger were beneficial. Advertising increased so much that a regular four-page supplement appeared each Saturday. With income from the combined subscription lists, the proprietors were able to buy a new printing press with a capacity of thirteen hundred sheets per hour in late 1829 and to house it in a new building. The day the new press was installed, the paper was enlarged from seven to eight columns and each page was lengthened by five inches. Daily circulation stood at four thousand, Webb claimed, *"which exceeds the united circulation of our morning contemporaries."* The new press was unable to keep pace with the circulation, and a faster press was installed in February 1830, which was also quickly outmoded. In January 1832 the *Courier and Enquirer* bought a new two-cylinder press with a capacity of two thousand sheets hourly.

Both physically and in circulation the *Courier and Enquirer* was the largest newspaper in the nation by 1832, netting the partners about $25,000 annually. Limitations in equipment to fold, cut, and print the paper forced expansion by enlarging the four-page sheet. An observer remarked in 1832 that the *Courier and Enquirer* "would almost serve a small man for a blanket."[15]

The paper's success was largely the result of Webb's news-gathering expertise, which Bennett, from his experience on Willington's *Courier,* must have encouraged. The enterprise started in a rivalry with the *Journal of Commerce,* another mercantile paper, to meet incoming ships outside New York harbor and remove the foreign newspapers and dispatches in their mailbags. By 1831 five competing schooners were engaged in this activity. Webb's boat cost about $5,000 annually to maintain, but it paid for itself, he claimed, in added subscriptions and the extras that were sold.

Webb also established an elaborate express system to bring Jackson's annual message to New York in December 1830. A pony express carried the document from Washington to Baltimore; from there a steamboat took it to Philadelphia, where it was transferred to another relay of express riders to New York. Here twenty-two compositors worked to produce an extra edition that sold for twelve cents — double the regular price. The time of twenty-seven and a half hours beat all rivals. The next year the *Courier* repeated its coup when its express delivered the president's annual message fifteen hours after its release.[16]

Bennett was partly responsible for the *Courier and Enquirer*'s success. Webb had been reluctant to hire him but was pressured to do so by the Jackson party's central committee in New York.[17] Webb, like Noah, then made the best of the situation by keeping Bennett on the move as a correspondent covering Washington, Albany, Saratoga Springs, and special events such as trials and conventions. Bennett's Washington correspondence dealt with a variety of political topics, always in a partisan fashion. When in the New York office, he wrote mostly about economic matters, especially banking. His political counsel was valuable to the partners because he knew personally so many important political figures.

One of Bennett's special assignments was a widely publicized murder trial in Salem, Massachusetts, in the summer of 1830. Joseph H. White, a wealthy retired sea captain, was beaten and stabbed to death. Eventually indicted were two of his heirs, John and Joseph Knapp, and George and Richard Crowninshield, brothers hired by the Knapps to kill Captain White while they stole his will so that he would die intestate and they would inherit part of his estate. Joseph Knapp confessed, and Richard Crowninshield committed suicide, leaving the Knapp brothers and George Crowninshield to stand trial.[18]

The New York press took considerable interest in the White murder, clipping stories from the Salem and Boston papers. The *Courier and Enquirer*'s coverage was typical, with grisly details of the murder and a lead editorial questioning Knapp's confession. Webb decided to send Bennett to Salem to provide his readers an exclusive account of the trial. Bennett first sent the paper a series of humorous travel letters from Boston, then went to Salem only to learn that the judge had died and the case was postponed for several weeks. He spent the time traveling in New England and sending more humorous filler to the paper.[19]

When the trial finally began in August, Bennett was one of a dozen special reporters there; the interest heightened when Daniel Webster arrived to assist the prosecution. Attorney General Perez Morton opened the prosecution's case with an attack on the press, questioning the propriety of the newspapers editorializing about the case. Bennett was enraged. "It is an old, worm eaten and Gothic dogma of the courts," he wrote, "to consider the publicity given to every event by the press as destructive to the interests of law and justice." If the publication of facts defeated justice, the best jurors would be those who were the most ignorant. "The honesty —the purity—the integrity of legal practice and legal decisions throughout the country, are more indebted to the American press than the whole tribe of lawyers and judges who issue their decrees. The press is the *living jury* of the nation."[20]

Initially, the court did not follow up Morton's admonitions, and Bennett was able to provide exciting coverage of the trial until August 10. On that day, the judge banned reporters from taking notes of publishing anything about the trial until its completion. Bennett exploded. In New York, he pointed out, "they 'order these things better,'" and put no restraints on the publication of testimony while a trial was in progress.[21]

As Bennett indicated, in the recent legislative session New York had passed a law stating that no court could punish for contempt a true, full, and fair report of a trial. Bennett's pieces publicized the problem, and eventually Massachusetts enacted similar legislation.[22] The ban had no effect in Salem, however, because the case went to the jury the next day. After a hung jury, the three defendants were tried separately and convicted. Bennett was again on hand, filing briefer reports unrestrained by the court, and noting that the public was losing interest in the murder.[23]

When he arrived back in New York, Bennett sent Nicholas Biddle an analysis of the political situation as he had observed it in his travels, especially attitudes in New England toward the Bank of the United States. These reports continued, along with advice about recharter.[24] As before, Bennett was sending confidential reports to the bank at the same time that the editorial policy of his paper opposed recharter. In late 1829 the *Courier and Enquirer* posed a series of damaging questions on the issue, furnished by Amos Kendall of Jackson's Kitchen Cabinet, which forecast Jackson's opposition to the bank in his annual message a week later.[25]

Bennett continued to write articles against the bank at the same time he was supplying Biddle with information and implying that he would support the bank if he were in editorial control of the paper. He would then be able to make it a "most useful engine" to forward useful measures. A month later he directly asked Biddle for $30,000 to buy half of the paper and again alluded to the probank stand he could then take. Nothing came of these overtures.[26]

Until 1831, the *Courier and Enquirer*'s opposition toward recharter was mild, and the pieces that Bennett wrote about the bank were approved by Webb and Noah.[27] Then on February 5, 1831, he wrote a slashing attack on the bank, describing it as a vast and corrupt political machine, buying and selling votes, bribing officials and editors, and "erecting within the states and the Union, a new general government—an Imperium in Imperia, unknown to the Constitution, defying its powers—laughing at its restrictions—scorning its principles—and pointing to its golden vaults as the necessary weapon that will execute its behests whenever it shall be necessary to carry them into action." These charges of political corruption were repeated a few days later, and in March Bennett called the bank a force for disunity in the nation.[28]

After this, the paper said nothing about the bank for a month. On April 9 the *Courier and Enquirer*'s position changed, and it supported a modified charter renewal. Bennett was silenced, and Webb made his own recharter views those of his newspaper.[29] What had caused the change? Bennett's negotiations to buy a share of the paper, for which he was unable to raise the money, resulted in the sale of a larger share to Noah on April 4, 1831. The money, however, had been indirectly furnished to Noah by the bank through Silas E. Burrows, a confidence man, speculator, lobbyist, and influence peddler. Burrows met Webb and Noah at Albany and loaned Noah $15,000, which he told the editors had come from his wealthy father. Unknown to them, he had received the money from Biddle, whom he had convinced that a loan to Noah would modify the *Courier and Enquirer*'s opposition to recharter. The resulting modification had led the New York City banks that opposed recharter to cut off Webb and Noah from their usual sources of credit there. The editors received two more loans from Biddle's bank in August and December, not knowing that the bank was the source of their earlier loan from Burrows. Their newspaper, in the meantime, had been almost silent about recharter.[30]

Bennett was muzzled on the bank issue, but Webb found other matters to keep his associate busy. That summer Bennett was sent on a tour of western New York, and he sent back to the *Courier and Enquirer* a series of descriptive "Letters from the Country." He traveled with Martin Van Buren a part of the way and kept a diary to record his impressions. Some of this information he passed on to Biddle, emphasizing that the bank was unpopular there because it was misunderstood and that probank sentiment did not have proper direction.[31]

He also reflected on his position on the *Courier and Enquirer*. The paper, he confided to Van Buren, was edited "without dignity" and could not "excite affection" in its readers. In his diary he indulged in self-pity: "I feel very unhappy in my present condition — what care I for the C. & Enquirer? What care I for money? What care I for peace and gratitude? Nothing — nothing did I say? Yes, I do care — I care much — I have endeavored to procure a high position in parties, and settle myself in life. . . . I have always failed. Why so?" But by the next day his mood had changed, and he sang the praises of the *Courier and Enquirer*.[32] It is clear that he chafed at the restraints Webb had placed on him and regretted that he had been unable to raise the money to buy into the paper when he had the opportunity.

With all the signs pointing to an early application by the bank for recharter in 1832 and of a possible congressional investigation that might divulge the bank's loans to the *Courier and Enquirer,* Webb pressured Bennett to put a signed statement in the paper on February 2, 1832, taking full responsibility for the antibank articles of 1831 and absolving Webb and Noah of blame. He did state the reason for his antibank position: it was a monopoly. "All banking institutions made exclusively by legislative acts, . . . are, to the extent of the privileges conferred on the few and denied to the many, infringements upon the natural rights of man."[33]

Except for this statement, Bennett wrote no more about the bank and devoted himself to other matters. He worked tirelessly to obtain the gubernatorial nomination for William L. Marcy instead of contenders backed by other Van Burenites in the state. On April 12, 1832, the *Courier and Enquirer* endorsed Marcy for governor after Bennett had pressured Webb for weeks. Marcy was nominated and elected. But some state party leaders resented Webb's and Bennett's interference.[34]

Webb had become antagonistic to the Albany Regency, the Jacksonian leadership clique at the state capital. Webb was an outsider, with no role in the decision-making process despite the circulation and influence of his newspaper. He retaliated with charges of corruption and mismanagement at Albany, which made it easier to break with the Jacksonians after the president's veto of the recharter bill in July 1832.[35] For his part, Bennett had confined himself to reports from Washington about nonbanking matters, the Jacksonian national convention in Baltimore, continuing to push Van Buren as the vice-presidential nominee, and other safe topics such as tariff reduction.[36] He must have become restive as Webb's antagonism to the party leaders at Albany increased. His own chances of political preferment were being damaged by his association with Webb.

Webb's newspaper remained silent on the bank question for about six weeks after Jackson's veto. During that time Webb received another loan from Biddle which enabled him to buy out Noah's share of the paper. On August 23, 1832, the *Courier and Enquirer* switched its political allegiance. The names of Jackson, Van Buren, and Marcy were removed from the top of the editorial column and replaced with the motto "Principles, not Men." A "Manifesto" signed by Webb asserted that the bank veto was the sole reason for deserting Jackson, and notice was given that Webb had bought out Noah because of their disagreement on the bank issue.[37]

Bennett quit the *Courier and Enquirer* immediately after it changed its politics. He was placed in a difficult situation. Having left Webb's paper because of his uncompromising Jacksonianism, Bennett now found himself under fire by the Jacksonian presses of the city because he contemplated establishing his own paper, and the columns of the Jacksonian *Standard* and *Evening Post* were closed to his attempts to defend his party regularity.[38]

In the next three years Bennett made two more ventures into party journalism. On October 29, 1832, he began publishing the evening *New York Globe*. About half the size of the mercantile papers, and cheaper, the *Globe* began as a campaign organ in the closing week of the presidential campaign and lasted only one month. Until the election was over, Bennett told the public, "politics will be the staple article of the Globe; but after that event I shall give it all that variety which makes a daily paper the welcome visitor of the tea table and the counting room." He predicted a daily circulation of five thousand within two years because "I shall give my readers the cream of foreign and domestic events. My sheet is moderate in size, but neat and manageable." He boasted of his editorial experience and told his readers that as editor he would be "an acquaintance – a friend – an intimate." Unfortunately, there seemed to be no market for a smaller and cheaper version of the commercial newspapers. An examination of the *Globe* of November 29, 1832, the last and only surviving issue of the paper, indicates that its contents were no different from, although shorter than, those of its contemporaries and that the writing was just as dull. The *Globe* was not different enough. Bennett announced the demise of the paper in that issue. His main purpose, the reelection of Jackson, had been served, and now he had "other views and other purposes."[39]

One of these was an opportunity to buy into Francis P. Blair's *Washington Globe,* the new national organ of the Jackson administration. The venture, buying one-half of the profitable paper, was suggested by Secretary of the Treasury Louis McLane, whose motives appear to have been irritation that the *Globe* had not pressed very hard for Van Buren's nomination for vice-president and anger at Blair's strident antibank editorials. Bennett discussed the proposition with Van Buren and Governor Marcy and sought aid from Nicholas Biddle. He also asked Secretary of the Navy Levi Woodbury to intercede. "I should like such a position remarkably well," Bennett wrote. "I think I could add a good deal of reputation and patronage to the Globe. . . . The approaching controversy with South Carolina will require every power of mind to manage it with success – argument, wit, good humor, courtesy, point, eloquence, all and everything manly and gentlemanly which give character to a newspaper." But the overture came to nothing. Blair was not ready to part with a piece of his profitable paper.[40]

Almost immediately another opportunity came to hand. In January 1833, Bennett began working for a Philadelphia Jacksonian daily, the *Pennsylvanian,* and on May 24 he became the editor. The *Pennsylvanian* was established in the summer of 1832, and it was a typical mercantile paper.

Over half of its twenty-eight columns were filled with advertisements, and most of its news was directed at local merchants. Under Bennett's direction it devoted more attention to crime and the police courts, and it took a strong anti-Negro and antiabolitionist position that was always characteristic of Bennett.[41]

The *Pennsylvanian* was most important for its position in the Jacksonian intraparty politics of the state. It was the leading Amalgamation newspaper. The Amalgamators were the original Jackson men who had supported the Old Hero since 1824 and were hostile to the Calhoun faction of Eleventh Hour Men who were latecomers to the Jacksonian standard. After 1832 the Amalgamators, with Bennett in the lead, supported Van Buren for the succession and called for a national convention. More immediately, they opposed the election of Samuel McKean, an Eleventh Hour Man, to the United States Senate.[42]

Bennett kept out-of-state Jacksonian leaders informed of the importance of his work in making Pennsylvania safe for Jackson and Van Buren and of the necessity of keeping McKean out of the Senate.[43] But he was unsuccessful in raising money from the Van Burenites to buy control of the *Pennsylvanian.* The failure caused a lasting bitterness between Bennett and Van Buren. The ingratitude of the vice-president, Bennett complained, was *"heartless in the extreme."*[44]

Part of the problem was Bennett's reluctance to accept party direction and discipline and his penchant for striking out on his own. An example was his premature announcement in the *Pennsylvanian* of Jackson's removal of the deposits from the bank. This led to a reprimand from Amos Kendall, who remarked that Jackson made his own decisions and had not yet decided on removal. "I was sorry to see the article," Kendall wrote.[45]

Bennett's role in keeping alive the intraparty feud in Pennsylvania bothered the administration more. The *Pennsylvanian* continued to assail McKean and his group as Calhounite nullifiers and to oppose McKean's election to the Senate. Blair's *Washington Globe* joined the fray, insisting that McKean was a regular and that the administration favored any Democrat who had the confidence of the party.[46]

Bennett then accused "Amos Kendall and certain confederates" of trying to silence the press and take over the administration from Jackson and his constitutional advisers. Bennett sent these charges directly to Jackson and to Levi Woodbury, and they were published in the anti-Jacksonian *Pennsylvania Inquirer.* He was astonished, he told a friend, that the *Globe* and the Kitchen Cabinet were siding with the nullifiers in Pennsylvania.[47]

Bennett realized that his days on the *Pennsylvanian* were numbered, and he again sought assistance from Nicholas Biddle. Administration officials in

Pennsylvania, he told the banker, were attacking "my conduct and my pe-cuniary resources. My friends must support me or they will break me up." He had a chance to buy the *New York Standard* but needed $50,000. "The K.C. [Kitchen Cabinet] must be disrupted or the B[ank] will—If I can get hold of the Standard I can do it easily—I can make it appear that the funds came from the Regency banks of N.Y. & Albany—Not a moment is to be lost." Biddle did not respond to this letter or to a personal visit.[48]

As expected, Bennett's connection with the *Pennsylvanian* was severed on November 30, 1833. He charged that "Amos Kendall and the irrespon-sible cabal stationed at Washington [were] the prime movers," and he threatened an exposure. A few days later, two columns of the *Inquirer's* editorial page were filled with Bennett's charges that Kendall and a group of corrupt stock manipulators dominated the administration, dictated its banking policies, and forced him out of the *Pennsylvanian.*[49]

Bennett never again was a party editor. This experience had taught him that he could not comply with party discipline, that he could not march to another man's beat. He returned to New York and for the next year and a half waited for an opportunity, supporting himself by free-lancing again, mostly for George P. Morris's *New York Mirror.* Perhaps Nicholas Biddle provided a subsidy; at any rate, Bennett kept Biddle informed of the New York political scene. The time was ripe, he told the banker, to work out a compromise on modified recharter. Regency leaders in Albany seemed willing.[50]

More important, Bennett made overtures to the *New York Sun* and the *New York Transcript* seeking employment. Both were new and successful penny newspapers, politically independent and aimed at a mass popular audience. He was not hired, but he watched them closely, studying their success. He talked to the printers who did the presswork for the *Sun* and *Transcript* and learned of the financing necessary to establish a penny pa-per. He tried unsuccessfully to interest printer Horace Greeley in a part-nership. By May 1835 he was ready for his own independent venture.[51]

He was a few months shy of forty years old, and his material assets were only $500 he had scraped together. But he did have other assets: a good formal education and a wealth of experience on the editorial side of newspapers, although none on the mechanical side. He had never set type or operated a press, which distinguished him from most of the printer-editors who established popular penny papers. He brought to his view of the world and his business the perspective of an educated professional, not that of a self-educated craftsman. Finally, he had a stubborn indepen-dence accentuated by his years of working for party newspapers. These assets would prove more important than material capital.

2

Sensationalism and the Newspaper Revolution

A convergence of technology and technique in the mid-1830s led to a newspaper revolution in New York City that resulted in cheap newspapers designed for a mass audience. Bennett did not start the revolution, but he quickly became its leader when he established the *New York Herald* on May 6, 1835.[1]

Cheap newspapers were not a new idea, nor were newspapers that tried to tap a wider readership beyond a narrow mercantile-political clientele. Seba Smith's *Portland* (Maine) *Daily Courier,* started in 1829, was much smaller than the Boston papers and sold for only four dollars a year, one-third the cost of the mercantile papers. It had no political connections and featured the humorous pieces of "Major Jack Downing." Smith's success led to three imitators in Boston in 1833: the *Morning Post,* a popular Jacksonian sheet; the nonpartisan *Transcript,* which gave most of its attention to literature and the theater; and the *Mercantile Journal.* All cost four dollars a year. That summer in Boston three entrepreneurs attempted to start penny dailies.[2]

Two New York journals had demonstrated that there was a market for gossip and sporting news. From 1826 to 1833 a weekly titled *Hawk and Buzzard* found enough readers to stay afloat by concentrating almost exclusively on gossip. Late in 1831 William T. Porter launched the *Spirit of the Times,* a weekly devoted to sporting news, which survived until 1856, covering the racing scene, the out-of-doors, and other frivolous topics.[3]

One of Porter's typesetters, Horace Greeley, undertook a different venture: a cheap newspaper sold by boys on the street for cash. On January 1, 1833, his two-cent *Morning Post* appeared, in the midst of a blizzard. It failed. Greeley had not learned enough from Porter; the tone of the *Post* was as ponderous as that of the six-cent mercantile papers. After two weeks Greeley reduced the price to a penny for a few more days, and then his *Morning Post* expired.[4]

19

The penny paper was inspired largely by the success of Charles Knight's *Penny Magazine,* published from 1832 for the Society for the Diffusion of Useful Knowledge, with the aim of educating and improving the poor in England. It eschewed politics and controversy and treated the working class with a benevolent and somewhat condescending attitude, but it did provide interesting and educational reading material at the cheapest rate possible. Much of the *Penny Magazine* was high-toned — biography, natural history, and scientific curiosity — but it attained a huge circulation for the time, twenty thousand by 1833. Many of these copies were sold in America, where the magazine was very popular.[5]

American printers and editors, Bennett included, were aware of the *Penny Magazine*'s success. One of them, Benjamin H. Day, was looking for new business for his job plant during the depression that coincided with the cholera epidemic of 1833. He decided to experiment with a penny paper that would advertise his printing plant. On September 3, 1833, Day launched his *New York Sun,* using a new circulation method, the London plan. Bundles of one hundred *Sun*s were sold for sixty-seven cents to carriers on regular routes who collected six cents from each customer every Saturday and to the unemployed who hawked it on the street. This cash-and-carry policy eliminated one of the persistent problems of the mercantile papers, unpaid subscriptions.

Day stated his aim in the *Sun*'s first issue: "To lay before the public at a price within the means of everyone, all the news of the day." Mercantile news and partisan politics were conspicuously absent. The readers for whom Day was looking cared for neither. Instead, the tiny four-page, ten-by-eleven-inch sheet concentrated on interesting and newsworthy tidbits, mostly local. An important feature was the small classified advertisement, sold by space rates for cash (instead of on an annual basis, which was the practice of the other papers), and especially the "Help Wanted" notices. This feature made it popular with the unemployed, but it also made it, like the mercantile sheets, more of an advertiser than a news medium. (Its appeal to low-income groups also exposed the *Sun* to the effects of the depression. Decline of circulation and advertising revenue after the Panic of 1837 led Day to sell his property in 1838 to paper manufacturer Moses Y. Beach for $40,000.)

The *Sun* was a runaway success at the start. Within four months its circulation of four thousand almost equaled that of the largest mercantile paper. By late 1834, with a new press capable of ten thousand impressions per hour, the *Sun*'s circulation exceeded ten thousand. A new steam press in 1835 increased its capacity to twenty-two thousand, and the paper was enlarged to fourteen by twenty inches in 1836.[6]

Inevitably the *Sun* had imitators. Most of them failed, in New York and elsewhere, but one other penny paper did take hold in New York, the *Daily Transcript*. Sold on the same penny cash-and-carry basis as the *Sun,* the *Transcript* also concentrated on local news and gossip, particularly crime stories, carrying the *Sun's* innovative police court reports a step further. The *Transcript's* circulation almost kept pace with the *Sun's*.[7]

New York's mercantile press disdained to notice the new penny papers, which were not rivals for their politically oriented mercantile audience. In 1835 half a dozen of these mercantile sheets competed for morning circulation and four appeared each evening. Besides Webb's *Courier and Enquirer* and David Hale and Gerald Hallock's *Journal of Commerce,* each morning saw the *Daily Advertiser,* the *Mercantile Advertiser,* the *Gazette and General Advertiser,* and the short-lived *Times.* At dusk the *Commercial Advertiser,* William Cullen Bryant's *Evening Post,* Charles King's *American,* and Noah's new *Evening Star* vied for patronage. The average circulation of these six-cent papers was seventeen hundred; Webb's with over four thousand was the largest. New York's population in 1835 was over a quarter of a million, but the total daily newspaper circulation was only about forty-five thousand.[8]

Bennett, watching the success of the *Sun* and the *Transcript,* believed that there was still a large audience of literate New Yorkers of the middle and working classes who liked the spice of the penny papers but wanted more substantial fare as well. They would buy a cheap newspaper that combined the zest and the local identification of the *Sun* and the *Transcript* with the news coverage of the mercantile press. They lacked much formal education and would be willing to spend a penny a day to enlighten and educate their households.[9]

On May 6, 1835, a Wednesday morning, Bennett was ready. From a basement office furnished with a few packing cases covered with planks he issued the first number of his *Herald,* priced at a penny a day or three dollars a year and sold on the London plan, like the *Sun* and the *Transcript.* About half the size of a mercantile paper, with four pages of four columns each, the *Herald* contained a statement of purpose by Bennett on page 2: "Our only guide shall be good, sound, practical common sense, applicable to the business and bosoms of men engaged in every day life. We shall support no party—be the organ of no faction or *coterie,* and care nothing for any election or candidate from president down to constable. We shall endeavor to record facts, on every public and proper subject, stripped of verbiage and coloring, with comments when suitable, just, independent, fearless, and good tempered." His political independence is understandable considering Bennett's unfortunate experiences as a party editor. He continued his inaugural statement with a discussion of the size and content of the *Herald*.

> If the *Herald* wants the mere expansion which many journals possess, we shall try to make it up in industry, good taste, brevity, variety, point, piquancy and cheapness. It is especially intended for the great masses of the community — the merchant, mechanic, working people — the private family as well as the public hotel — the journeyman and his employer — the clerk and his principal. There are in this city at least 150,000 persons who glance over one or more newspapers every day. Only 42,000 sheets are issued daily to supply them. We have plenty of room therefore, without jostling neighbors, rivals or friends, to pick up at least *twenty or thirty thousand* for the HERALD, and leave something for the others who come after us. . . . [The *Herald* will be the] equal of any of the high priced papers for intelligence, good taste, sagacity and industry, [so] there is not a person in the city, male or female, that may not be able to say — "well I have got a paper of my own which will tell me all about what's doing in the world — I'm busy now — but I'll put it in my pocket and read it at my leisure."

How well did the introductory issue of the *Herald* fulfill these specifications? Page 1 was filled with interesting miscellany. Most of it was devoted to a biographical sketch of the notorious fraud Mathias the Prophet. Three short pieces discussed books, the popularity of Shakespeare, and spring fashions.

Page 2 was the heart of the paper. Column 1, normally the editorial column, contained Bennett's statement about the debut, with a note that the next issue would not appear until Monday, May 11, after adequate distribution arrangements had been made. Most of a column, "LATE AND IMPORTANT FROM EUROPE," listed short items of foreign news: the defeat of the Peel ministry in England; the reported encounter between a Russian squadron and a British warship in the Dardanelles; the firm cotton market in Liverpool. A column, "Empire State," featured a glowing survey of the state's economic situation. Column 4 contained "Theatrical Chit-Chat" and a humorous story about a woman who imagined that she was a glass bottle.

Page 3 was the local page. Column 1 contained a long editorial piece, "The Mechanics," which affirmed the *Herald*'s friendship for the workingman and devotion to the gospel of hard work and laissez faire. These were the readers Bennett was trying to attract. A short article discussed the city's growing population; another announced the start of the Union Races. Column 2 had a long police court report, local political items, a short piece on a steamboat explosion, and another about a murder in Virginia. Column 3 listed marriages and deaths and contained some advertising, which filled all of column 4.

Page 4 had two columns of advertising and two of filler: two poems, a romantic story, a humorous Irish story, a poignant note about a dying infant, and another about a suffocation death. The advertisements were terse announcements for the job-printing plant that printed the *Herald,* for houses and rooms for rent, for Copenhagen porter, Badeau's Celebrated Strengthening Plaster, fancy silk cravats, *Le Revue Française,* the *Ladies' Companion Magazine,* and a steamboat line to Albany.[10]

Here was something for everyone: short, concise news summaries written with zest; local news emphasizing the humorous and tragic, especially in the police courts; entertaining and edifying features; and economic news. Unlike the *Sun* and the *Transcript,* the *Herald* tried from the beginning to cover world and national news and economic developments as fully as its limited space would allow.

As promised, the next issue appeared on Monday, May 11, and it is fairer to evaluate Bennett's initial success by examining this first regular number. Bennett was writing the entire *Herald* by himself after gathering the news and advertising. He then contracted with a job press to do the actual printing, as the *Sun* had done at first. In the May 11 *Herald* advertising space had doubled, from three columns to almost seven. The editorial commented on the success of the May 6 sample edition: "The broad relief which the lively *Herald* will afford to the dull business air of the large morning papers, will naturally induce every patron of the former to take in a copy of the latter, so as to diversify and exhilarate the breakfast table." Another editorial pressed the gospel of hard work on the mechanics. Two short pieces described murders.

There was almost a column of European news, several short items about national politics, a literary tidbit about James Fenimore Cooper, theatrical notes, a discussion of spoils in the city government, a review of the new issue of *Knickerbocker's Magazine,* commercial and marine intelligence, marriages and deaths, and several columns of miscellany, the longest of which discussed a chimney sweep who was trapped in a chimney. In a style that was to become routine, Bennett took two swipes at the rival *Sun,* one implying that the *Sun* was tasteless and would print anything, the other a warning to Day to be on his toes. "If they cannot do this by the time specified, then we shall incontinently extinguish the Sun and put out the light thereof, to the great gratification of all persons of taste, good sense and judgment in this city. So gentlemen of the Sun be up and at your task."

The most important addition to this second number was a "Money Market" column, irregular until June 13 when it became a daily feature. On May 14 the *Herald* published its first list of stock sales, which also became a daily event. The Money Market column tried to explain to the layman what was going on in Wall Street. Bennett's topic on May 11 was the shakiness caused by the stock speculations of a "secret conspiracy of our large capitalists." As he analyzed the manipulations on the money market which caused stock prices to rise and fall, with a warning to inexperienced merchants to be wary, he explained these complex factors as resulting from conspiracy, a concept his humblest readers could understand. Conspiracy was to become a standard explanation in the *Herald* for many complexities in the years ahead.

Bennett had a right to be proud of his handiwork. His promise to "give a correct picture of the world—in Wall Street—in the Exchange—in the Police office—at the Theatre—in the Opera—in short, wherever human nature and real life best display their freaks and vagaries" had been kept. [11]

The success of many newspapers was short-lived. Bennett's importance is that he was able to develop his cheap newspaper with its mass appeal into something more substantial, that he was able to place his *Herald* in the forefront of the "newspaper revolution."

The establishment of the penny press in New York City caused such fundamental changes in American newspapers that it can properly be termed revolutionary. The sudden and phenomenal popularity of the *Sun,* the *Transcript* (fleetingly), and the *Herald* with their cash-and-carry sales policy created the independent newspaper, free of political and mercantile patronage and dependent only on its own wide audience. The wide circulation attracted advertisers and led to financial independence; the revenue, in turn, financed the technological improvements necessary to produce papers for a large readership. There were, then, two interacting parts to the newspaper revolution. One was a change in style and technique to appease the tastes of the readers—sensationalism, in a word. The other was the improvement in technology and news-gathering, with an emphasis on news as a commodity—the substance of the newspaper revolution. Together they made the *Herald* the best and the most popular newspaper in America. [12]

Sensationalism involves both content and style. George Juergens in his study of Joseph Pulitzer has provided an extended definition that is useful here. He defines sensationalism as the "strategy of attracting a large audience by concentrating on stories of timeless appeal—sex, crime, tragedy." The goal, he continues, is to catch the interest, even to titillate, the vast body of men and women who for one reason or another are unconcerned with happenings in government, business, or the arts. . . . The first rule is that a different standard must apply in determining what articles will be printed. Sensational newspapers expanded the meaning of the human interest story to report what had hitherto been regarded as private, the gossip and scandals about individuals, and discovered a rich source of news in crime and everyday tragedy. A corollary of the same point, they began to pay as much attention to personalities as to local or national events. . . .

The second rule follows directly from the first. Sensational newspapers have their own idea of the relative importance of different stories. They can usually be counted upon to evict matters of statecraft from the front page if a provocative item of scandal is available to take its place. . . .

Finally, the form requires a unique prose style. The argument applies with different force to different papers, but in general the language in a sensational newspaper tends to be slangy, colloquial, personal. In such a way does the sensational journal express its identity with the masses of people who patronize it. [13]

Bennett did not invent sensationalism. The *Herald* merely expanded the successful formula of the *Sun* and *Transcript.* The *Sun*'s Benjamin H. Day described it well: "We newspaper people thrive best on the calamities of others. Give us one of your real Moscow fires, or your Waterloo battlefields; let a Napoleon be dashing with his legions throughout the world, overturning the thrones of a thousand years and deluging the world with blood and tears; and then we of the types are in our glory." [14] This recipe of "blood and tears" was present in the *Herald* from the start.

Bennett fed his readers a steady diet of violence, crime, murder, suicide, seduction, and rape both in news reporting and in gossip. In its first two weeks of publication the *Herald* had accounts of three suicides, three murders, a fire that killed five persons, an accident in which a man blew off his head, descriptions of a guillotine execution in France, a riot in Philadelphia, kangaroo hunting in Australia, and the execution of Major John André half a century earlier. [15]

If no immediate murder was at hand, a grisly one was revived from the past and described again. During the *Herald*'s first year there were stories of a wolf hunt, of the causes of infanticide among savages, of drownings and duels and more murders, of Vice-President Richard M. Johnson's relations with his mulatto mistress, of the veracity of Maria Monk's *Awful Disclosures,* of a juicy breach of promise suit, of the trial of an accused slave trader, and of the last hours and execution of a murderer. This was standard fare.[16]

The *Herald* was not merely salacious; Bennett also appealed to the self-interest of his readers. He took a booster attitude toward local developments and reforms, opposing corruption in city hall and the custom house and fighting for retrenchment. Bennett also shared the patriotic, nationalistic sentiments of his audience. The *Herald* supported the independence of Texas from mid-1835 and predicted the emigration of thousands of Americans "to aid their brethren against the rapacious and bloody Spaniards." During the difficulties over the French spoliation claims, Bennett backed Jackson's firmness and supported a war, if necessary, to force payment and safeguard American national honor.[17]

Bennett's most important continuing news story concerned his own importance and the meteoric rise of his *Herald*. He assumed that his readers would identify with the *Herald;* it was their paper and he was their spokesman. The rapid increase in its circulation was noted often, and at the age of two months it claimed to have passed the *Sun* and *Transcript*.[18] The claim was not true. After three months it was, Bennett said, the only New York paper operating on a cash basis, able to pay all its expenses out of its cash receipts. Burned out in a fire a few days later, the *Herald* bounced back "larger, livelier, better, prettier, saucier, and more important than ever." About once a month some new item of growth was noted: rising circulation, a doubling of advertising, a move into larger quarters.[19]

He gave himself all the credit. In October 1835, Bennett printed the first of many autobiographical pieces, boasting that he had started a "vast and important revolution" in journalism and predicting an ever-upward rise for the *Herald*. "I am no novice in the business, and I cannot make a mistake in public feeling."[20]

The *Herald* deprecated its rivals while puffing itself. No newspaper in the city escaped its barbs, and one day Bennett managed to attack in a single issue seven newspapers and their editors.[21] The *Sun* was his favorite target, but the mercantile press was also stung, especially Noah's *Evening Star*. The abuse was too much for Peter Townsend, one of the *Star*'s editors. He administered a public beating to Bennett in October, all duly reported in the *Herald* as a news story, as were later beatings by James Watson Webb and William Leggett.[22]

All of this was of a piece with the *Sun* and the *Transcript*. Bennett went further by devoting some attention to society news. He appreciated the interest of the common people in the doings of the rich, and he made a marketable commodity out of what had been back fence gossip. For example, the *Herald* during its first year carried long accounts of masked balls in New Orleans, the social season at Saratoga Springs, and President Jackson's Christmas ball in Washington.[23]

There were other innovations. Bennett tried to move the news from the inside of the paper to page 1, where it appeared for several months until he abandoned the experiment and in April 1836 returned to conventional practice.[24] Illustrations were first used in December 1835 to enhance the *Herald*'s coverage of New York's great fire.[25]

The most amusing new departure was the parodies Bennett wrote of Jackson's messages. The first one appeared on December 9, 1835, purporting to be an original of Jackson's annual message, smuggled out by a secret connection in the Kitchen Cabinet. The early paragraphs surveyed the state of the Union:

> In performing my duty at the opening of another session [Bennett had Jackson begin] I have great pleasure in stating to you that the country is going ahead as fast as ever, and much faster than any country ever did under heaven. For this we ought to thank God Almighty and the democratic party — not forgetting the little aid I have given in helping to keep things in the right trim.
>
> The country is in flourishing condition. Cotton fetches a good price — corn is abundant — beef and pork plenty — the dews of heaven fall as richly as ever — gold and silver overflows the land — the United States Bank is down and I have got my foot on the monster's neck.
>
> Our foreign relations wear the most favorable and peaceful aspect imaginable. You all know how fond I am of peace, love, union, and harmony. Through my long life it has been my invariable practice to try mild measures before picking up pistols or shouldering the rifle. This peaceful disposition has invariably been successful with the solitary exception of two or three wars and about forty or fifty rows. The Honorable Senator from Missouri can tell you how calm and considerate I talked to him on the streets of Nashville about twenty years ago before I cocked my pistols and let fly. That gentleman has long since regretted his conduct on that occasion, and in consideration of his helping me to put down the monster, I have ordered him a plate of pork steaks at the Kitchen Table.
>
> I have merely alluded to these glorious days of my past life as a illustration of my course toward Louis Phillippe [sic] and the French nation.

And so on, at length, until the conclusion, where Jackson was used to puff the *Herald:*

I cannot leave you, however, without one word more. For some time past, I have been receiving a little neat penny paper from New York called the HERALD. — It is uncommonly smart, and tells its whole mind on every subject. This is exactly what I have always done myself. It is the only honest method of getting through the world. The editor, I believe, is some fellow by the name of Bennett, who once wrote me a letter blowing up Amos Kendall. I could not attend to him on that time, but on further inquiry, I find that he was once Editor of the New York Enquirer, when it first came out for me, and generally wrote two-thirds of that paper, for which Noah claimed and got an office. Bennett never came to Washington seeking an office, for which my Kitchen Cabinet called him "a d——d fool." I recommend every member of Congress to order the Herald during the season. They will be pleased with it — for it has, daily, a world of information on politics, stock, fashion, police, accidents, news, markets, and every thing in every line.

Trusting that you will attend, one and all, to the hints I have hereby given you, I subscribe myself

ANDREW JACKSON.[26]

In the next few months there were three more parodies of Jackson's messages and one of Governor Marcy's. They are all similar in their plays on Jackson's plain talk and idiosyncrasies, and they are very funny.[27]

The Robinson-Jewett murder case confirmed the sensational trend already apparent in the *Herald*. Early on Sunday morning, April 10, 1836, someone murdered a beautiful young prostitute, Ellen Jewett, with a hatchet, and then set fire to her body and bed at Rosina Townsend's luxurious brothel. Richard P. Robinson, a wealthy and handsome young man about town and a frequent visitor of Ellen's, was arrested for the crime on circumstantial evidence. The *Herald* and the penny press seized upon the case and created an excitement not known before in American journalism.

On April 11 the lead editorial in the *Herald* was headed: "Most Atrocious Murder." All of the ingredients were present for a human interest story of rare dimensions. The *Herald*'s account was a column and a half long and presented every detail then known, even the most trivial. Bennett, like almost everyone else, initially assumed that Robinson was guilty.

Bennett had visited the scene of the crime, and he described it vividly for his readers. He entered Ellen's room.

What a sight burst upon me! There stood an elegant double mahogany bed all covered with burnt pieces of linen, blankets, pillows black as cinders. I looked around for the object of my curiosity. On the carpet I saw a piece of linen covering something as if carelessly flung over it.

"Here," said the Police Officer, "here is the poor creature." He half uncovered the ghastly corpse. I could scarcely look at it for a second or two. Slowly I began to discover the lineaments of the corpse as one would the beauties of a statue of marble. It was the most remarkable sight I ever beheld. I never have and never expect to see such another. "My god," I exclaimed. "How like a statue! I can scarcely conceive that form to be a corpse." Not a vein was to be seen. The body looked as white, as full, as polished as the purest Parisian marble. The perfect figure, the exquisite limbs, the fine face, the full arms, the beautiful bust, all, all surpassed in every respect the Venus de Medici.

The editor went on to describe the room in detail—Ellen's clothes, her desk, her books and magazines, the decorations on the wall.[28]

Bennett's role was that of a gossip, telling as much of the story behind the news as possible. As Helen Hughes said: "He was just the person his readers would have loved to have a long talk with—one who had seen everything and was ready to tell all about it."[29]

The next day the *Herald* carried a mass of detail and speculation about Ellen's background and the circumstantial evidence responsible for Robinson's arrest. There was moralizing: the reasons that Ellen had lost her virtue, the men responsible, her passion for Byron's *Don Juan,* which "has no doubt produced more wretchedness in the world, than all the other moral writers of the age can check." Other news, such as the revolution in Texas, was shunted aside to satisfy the public craving for information about the murder case.[30]

Bennett gave his readers further details on April 13. He returned to Ellen's room and again described its contents, along with the letters, scrapbooks, and miscellany confiscated by the police. The article concluded by raising doubts about Robinson's guilt. These questions were repeated the next day and each day thereafter. "How could a young man perpetrate so brutal an act? Is it not more likely the work of a woman? Are not the whole chain of circumstances within the ingenuity of a female, abandoned and desperate?" One of the paintings in the Townsend house was of a beautiful woman on her knees about to be scalped by two Indians (probably a copy of John Vanderlyn's *The Murder of Jane McCrea.* "What a remarkable type—or hint—or foregone conclusion of the awful tragedy perpetrated upstairs." Why were none of the other girls held for further questioning? Why did the police believe Madam Townsend rather than Robinson?

Obviously the case had more appeal if there was an element of mystery, if there was some doubt of the murderer's identity. The *Herald* the next day suggested a conspiracy at the Townsend house involving the police and the suppression of evidence. It retained this position until Robinson's trial.[31]

On April 16 Bennett reported an interview with Rosina Townsend in verbatim dialogue, the first formal interview published in an American newspaper. The madam discussed her recollections of the night of the murder and of Robinson's visits to her house, with Bennett interjecting questions.[32]

The *Herald*'s circulation leaped markedly with the intense interest in the case, as did that of the *Sun* and the *Transcript*. Bennett boasted daily of the rise to fifteen thousand copies, which he predicted would reach thirty thousand before long. The editor's defense of Robinson embroiled him in a controversy with the *Sun* and the *Transcript*, which he had accused of conspiring with the police to cover up the true story.[33] Other papers attacked Bennett for devoting so much space to the case, but he was able to justify his coverage: "Instead of relating the recent awful tragedy of Ellen Jewett as a dull police report, we made it the starting point to open up a full view upon the morals of society — the hinge of a course of mental action calculated to benefit the age — the opening scene of a great domestic drama that will, if properly conducted, bring about a reformation — a revolution — a total revolution in the present diseased state of society and morals."[34]

As interest in the case sagged while Robinson was awaiting trial, Bennett revived it with a long analysis of how and when Ellen lost her virtue. Other stories of similar crimes capitalized on the craze. One, "Another Awful Consequence of Seduction," told of how a New Jersey girl of seemingly good character had strangled her illegitimate infant and then taken poison.[35]

The trial itself received exhaustive coverage in the *Herald*. On a typical day, June 7, almost all of the front page was devoted to the trial transcript and the lead editorial analyzed crucial testimony. Bennett was delighted when the jury agreed with him and acquitted Robinson. The mystery was never solved, and he continued to intimate a conspiracy and police collusion. He moralized again:

> The evidence in this trial and the remarkable disclosures of the manners and morals of New York is one of those events that must make philosophy pause, religion stand aghast, morals weep in the dust, and female virtue droop her head in sorrow. A number of young men, clerks in fashionable stores, are dragged up to the witness stand, but where

are the married men, where the rich merchants, where the devoted
church members who were caught in their shirts and drawers on that
awful night? The publication and perusal of the evidence in this trial
will kindle up fires that nothing can quench.[36]

The case was not dropped, finally, until mid-July, and Bennett continued to speculate about the murderer's identity. Journalism would never
be the same again. The sensational press, Hughes observes, "by focusing
general interest on a topic to which the demos was, it seemed, spontane-
ously responsive, brought it about that murder trials became occasions of
great popular excitement, just as hangings were in Tyburn and Newgate."[37]

By his coverage of the Robinson-Jewett case Bennett made his *Herald*
the best-known newspaper in New York. In fairness it must be said that
the other cheaps, the *Sun* and the *Transcript,* gave the case almost as much
attention as the *Herald* did, and of a similar kind. But neither was as in-
ventive as the *Herald* in manufacturing human interest stories about the
peripheral aspects of the case, and both tended to drop the story after a
week until the trial to concentrate on other news, which the *Herald* would
not do. When the trial began, all three papers provided analysis of the
testimony, vivid descriptions of the trial, and speculation about the verdict. And the *Sun,* like the *Herald,* refused to drop the case. Convinced
of Robinson's guilt, it decried the miscarriage of justice for another
month.[38] In contrast, the mercantile press treated the murder case as a traditional news item or neglected it completely. Most of these sheets printed
a news item about the murder on April 11 and then nothing until the trial.
They did present a complete trial transcript, but few did more except for
a moralizing editorial on the day of Robinson's acquittal.[39]

Bennett learned much about popular taste from his treatment of the
case. For the remainder of its first decade the *Herald* became more sensational, continuing along lines it had already marked out and adding new
touches. The same gossipy, probing treatment was given to other murders,
suicides, seductions, and accidental deaths. In at least eight other murder
cases in the next eight years the *Herald* provided coverage as extensive as
that of the Robinson-Jewett case, or more so, and usually included an engraving of the victim, the accused, or the scene of the crime.[40]

Other human interest stories were also featured. When one prizefighter
bludgeoned another to death, there was a long moralizing account. Fires
were always news, as were shipwrecks, and transatlantic steamboat races
were exciting. The death of Aaron Burr, an interesting and tragic person-
ality, was the occasion for a serial sketch. Nationally important stories such

as the *L'Amistad* affair, the arrest and trial of Alexander McLeod, and the *Somers* mutiny were treated in all of their human interest aspects as sensational items.[41]

Bennett had an unerring sense of what would appeal to his readers. Not only violence and gore but Joseph Smith and his Mormons, the capture of a strange-looking giraffe, the discovery of the ruins of Maya civilization in Central America, and Millerite camp meetings covered by the *Herald*'s own correspondent all were treated at length in the *Herald*.[42]

Something of merit could be found even in a dull week. In March 1837, one summary of the week's news conceded, "It is not of very much importance. Yet the most insignificant events can be swelled to matters of great moment, if they are traced up eternity to their causes, or down eternity to their consequences." But "the superficial blockheads who conduct newspapers" suppose them to be "of trifling moment. And so it is to them. To the philosopher who digs deeply into things, it is different."[43]

Bennett continued to cater to the preconceptions of his audience. He boosted New York City and supported a variety of reforms in the police, the custom house, the quarantine laws, and the debtors' prison. He was always on the side of the average citizen against the speculators and a "landlord conspiracy."[44]

He was patriotic and nationalistic to the point of chauvinism. A staunch expansionist, Bennett began to preach Manifest Destiny as early as 1842, and in 1843 he could write that "the Anglo Saxon race is intended by an over-ruling Providence to carry the principles of liberty, the refinements of civilization, and the advances of the mechanic arts through every land, even those now barbarous. . . . Mexico, too, must submit to the O'erpowering influence of the Anglo Saxon."[45] By 1844 Bennett was a bellicose advocate of Texas annexation, as jingoistic an expansionist as anyone: "It is now assumed as being the destiny of this republic, that her power will be incomplete and her civilization restricted, until her institutions of all kinds be spread from the Isthmus of Panama at the South to Hudson Bay at the North, and from the shores of the Pacific to the shores of the Atlantic—thus embracing the whole of North America. . . . This is believed to be the ultimate destiny of this republic." He was aware, as Frederick Merk has observed, that "nothing was more sensational or exhilarating than the soul-stirring doctrine of Manifest Destiny."[46]

Bennett's own genius and the success of his *Herald* continued to be his most important news story. He regularly detailed its circulation increases and its general prosperity. In 1836 its price was raised to two cents and he began weekly and evening editions.[47] Bennett boasted that his genius was solely responsible. He called himself "the NAPOLEON of the newspaper press" and compared himself to Zoroaster, Confucius, Charlemagne, Homer, Herodotus, Alexander the Great, Caesar, Luther, and Byron. "Accompanied with talent, independence, genius, and success, my vanity and egotism will in two years be deemed and taken for inspiration and virtue."[48] After presenting his readers with "Sketches of My Own Life" he commented: "What Shakespeare did for the drama—what Milton did for religion—what Scott did for the novel, such shall I do for the daily newspaper press." With such colossal egotism, Bennett regarded himself as one of the most newsworthy figures of the time, and he kept his name constantly before his readers.[49]

Abuse of his less talented rivals continued. The mercantile press was denounced regularly for concentrating on "the fashionable vices and profligacy of London and Paris" and for "catering to speculators, hypocrites, stock-jobbers, bankers, brokers, and political and moral rascals of all kinds." The *Sun,* he said in 1838, was "entirely in the abolition interest" and declining so rapidly as a result of the *Herald*'s competition that it resembled a real newspaper only as much "as a respectable nigger generally gets to an Anglo Saxon."[50] When Horace Greeley's *Tribune* was established in 1841, Bennett immediately saw the potential competition and shifted his attacks to it. Greeley's eccentricities, especially his vegetarianism, made him an easy target. "Horace Greeley, BA and ASS," went a typical *Herald* jibe, "is probably the most unmitigated blockhead concerned with the newspaper press. Galvanize a large New England squash, and it would make as capable an editor as Horace."[51]

After the first year the *Herald* expanded its coverage of society. Bennett's trips to Europe, Washington, Saratoga Springs, and Niagara Falls and the dispatches of the *Herald*'s Washington correspondents gave regular and detailed reports of the vacation resorts and galleries, of anything that was interesting in the way of fashion and taste. Bennett justified this reporting of the social life of the elite: "No one has ever attempted till now to bring out the graces, the polish, the elegancies, the bright and airy attributes of social life. . . . Our purpose has been, and is, to give the highest society of New York a life, a variety, a piquancy, a brilliance, an originality that will entirely out-strip the worn out races of Europe, who have been degenerating for the last twenty generations."[52]

By 1840 the *Herald* was sending a reporter and an artist to the most prominent society balls in New York, providing its readers with long descriptions, and usually an illustration, of the ball and the fashions. During the hard times of 1840, for example, Bennett devoted his entire front page to a ball at the Brevoort mansion, a sumptuous affair which the *Herald* proclaimed "a greater sensation in the fashionable world than anything of the kind since the creation of the world, or the fall of beauteous woman, or the frolic of old Noah, after he left the ark and took to wine and drinking."[53]

Illustrations were commonplace in the *Herald* by this time. Bennett started slowly because of the great expense of woodcut engravings. In 1838 six of them appeared; in 1839 they were used more frequently; and by 1840 the month was rare in which there was not an illustration or map or both — of murderers and their victims and the scenes of the crimes, fires, President William Henry Harrison's inauguration and funeral, Fourth of July celebrations, fashionable balls and distinguished foreign visitors, camp meetings, a giraffe, a mermaid, and, perhaps inevitably, "Dancing Girls of Egypt." The maps depicted every newsworthy location. The *Herald* was printing about twenty illustrations a year by the 1840s, all of them either educational or titillating.[54]

The message parodies were dropped after a short time. A bogus "original" of Jackson's last annual message appeared in December 1836, and Bennett tried his hand at Van Buren's Inaugural Address. This was the last of the parodies, Bennett explained: "General Jackson's character was an excellent subject for such *jeux d'esprit*. It had some strong, original, excellent points about it, mixed up, cunningly enough, with some absurdity and folly. Mr. Van Buren is a tame, insipid creature, and does not deserve to go down in future ages in any original message of mine. His real message will, no doubt, be sufficiently absurd, without any attempt to make it absurder. . . . The present state of the country is too serious a thing to make a jest of."[55]

There had been frequent complaints of Bennett's bad taste and of the space the *Herald* gave to patent medicine ads and the announcements of medical quacks which no other paper would accept. Benjamin Brandreth, the "king of the patent medicines" with his Vegetable Universal Pills, was an early and lavish advertiser in the *Herald,* and he may have advanced Bennett $1,000 to start up again after the fire of 1835. In 1837 Bennett "expunged" Brandreth's ads from the paper on the grounds that he was a quack. Brandreth responded that he had withdrawn his advertising because of the paper's price increase to two cents. In any event, the *Herald* advertised nostrums just as bad as the Vegetable Universal Pills, and by 1840 Brandreth's ads were back, bigger than ever.[56] Worse, the *Herald* regularly carried announcements for New York's abortionists, especially the notorious Madame Restell.[57]

Of all the controversies in which Bennett was involved, none brought him more trouble than his attempt to treat religious developments in the same manner as other news. His light and frivolous coverage of religion was an important cause of the "Moral War" of 1840.

In May 1840, Bennett greatly overstepped the bounds of propriety with an assault on editor Park Benjamin of the *Evening Signal* (whom he had accused of plagiarism) as "half Jew, half infidel, with a touch of the monster," who was crippled because of a "curse of the Almighty."[58]

At the same time Bennett criticized the annual meetings of various religious and charitable societies that were being held in New York, as they were each May. "The Moral and Religious Anniversaries," he wrote on May 14, "are getting surrounded on all sides." The editor then lashed out at his own Roman Catholic church:

> As a Catholic, we call upon the Catholic Bishop and clergy of New York to come forth from the darkness, folly, and superstition of the tenth century. . . . But though we want a thorough reform, we do not wish them to discard their greatest absurdities at the first breath. . . . We have no objection to the doctrine of Transubstantiation being tolerated for a few years to come. We may for awhile indulge ourselves in the delicious luxury of creating and eating our divinity. A peculiar taste of this kind, like smoking tobacco or drinking whiskey, cannot be given up all at once. The ancient Egyptians, for many years after they had lost every trace of the intellectual character of their religion, yet worshiped and adored the ox, the bull, and the crocodile. They had not discovered the art, as we Catholics have done, of making a God out of bread, and of adoring and eating him at one and the same moment. This latter piece of sublimity and religious cookery . . . was reserved for the educated and talented clergy from the tenth up to the nineteenth century. . . .
>
> There must be a thorough reformation and revolution in the American Catholic Church. . . . If we must have a Pope, let us have a Pope of our own, — an American Pope, an intellectual, intelligent, and moral Pope, — not such a decrepit, licentious, stupid Italian blockhead as the College of Cardinals at Rome condescends to give the Christian world of Europe.[59]

This intolerant and insensitive criticism of Catholicism, reminiscent of Tom Paine's *Age of Reason,* threw anti-Catholic nativist papers in alliance with the Roman Catholic church against the infidel Bennett. Four groups in New York denounced the *Herald:* the clergy, the stockbrokers because of Bennett's financial articles, the editors of rival papers, and "the politicians of the Van Buren machine, who were eager to punish Bennett for his bitter opposition to Van Buren's re-election."[60] Webb's *Courier and Enquirer* led the Moral War, whose forces included almost every newspaper in the city (even the sensational *Sun*) and many out-of-town papers. The purpose was to ruin Bennett by persuading respectable New Yorkers to boycott the *Herald* and ostracize its editor. A committee of editors, politicians, clergymen, businessmen, and social leaders directed the campaign. Advertisers were asked to withdraw their patronage from the *Herald* under threat of a boycott and hotel owners to bar from their premises anyone carrying the *Herald*.

The most bitter attacks came from Bennett's old employer Webb, who described Bennett as a moral "pestilence," a "worthless vagabond," a "disgusting obscenity," who should be ousted from Manhattan because his paper was afflicted with "moral leprosy." Prostitutes, Webb continued, regarded the *Herald* as "their special organ." Indeed, a gentleman would as soon choose a wife in a brothel as marry a woman who read the *Herald*. The solution was to fight the *Herald* as though it was a pestilence. "The creed of *all* should be — *purchase* not, *read* not, *touch* not."[61]

As the Moral War moved into full gear, Bennett added to the outrage of his enemies by announcing his engagement and coming marriage in his usual egocentric manner. On June 1, 1840, the following notice appeared in the *Herald:*

TO READERS OF THE HERALD
DECLARATION OF LOVE — CAUGHT AT LAST — GOING TO BE MARRIED —
NEW MOVEMENT IN CIVILIZATION

I am going to be married in a few days . . . to one of the most splendid women in intellect, in heart, in soul, in property, in person, in manners, that I have yet seen in my interesting pilgrimage through life.

I cannot stop in my career. I must fulfil the awful destiny which the Almighty Father has written in broad letters of my life against the wall of Heaven. I must give the world a pattern of happy wedded life.

A week later, the *Herald* was more terse:

MARRIED

On Saturday afternoon, the sixth instant, by the Reverent Doctor Power, at St. Peter's Catholic Church, in Barclay Street, James Gordon Bennett, the proprietor and editor of the New York *Herald,* to Henrietta Agnes Crean. What may be the effect of this event on the great newspaper contest now waging in New York, time alone can tell.

His bride, Henrietta Crean, was a music teacher the editor had met at a party, a migrant to the United States from Ireland in 1838, who in addition to her musical ability had a flair for languages. She was immediately thrown into the caldron of the Moral War with her husband. Pressure was brought on the Astor House, New York's finest hotel, to deny the bridal suite to the newlyweds. But Charles Stetson, the proprietor, refused to yield to the pressure.[62]

Bennett, his wife now at his side for support, could easily reply in kind to the abuse he got from Webb. He charged that jealousy over the *Herald*'s success — its combined daily and weekly circulation was 51,000 as compared to the combined circulation of all the "Holy Allies" of only 36,550 — and its influence in boosting Harrison for president were the causes of the Moral War. The attacks had only enhanced the *Herald*'s popularity. Every genius had his detractors, and Bennett likened himself to Socrates and Galileo. "When did any master spirit of the day rise up that the dull dunces of the day did not conspire to put him down?" He denounced "Field Marshall [sic] Webb" of the "New Moral Reform Society" and predicted that Webb would soon be taking holy orders. The "combination of blockheads" had not killed Bennett, although they had murdered the English language. The *Herald* was as lively and as prosperous as ever.[63]

After less than a month, the Moral War slackened. Bennett claimed that the public supported him. The mercantile papers shifted their tactics in July, pressuring Congress to prohibit the bulk shipment of newspapers through the mails, but the measure was "too hostile to the first principles of civilization, and the diffusion of knowledge, ever to pass an enlightened Congress." Bennett trumpeted his alleged victory by enlarging the *Herald* by about a third, to six columns per page, in September and installing a new press capable of five thousand impressions an hour. By late October Bennett claimed that the *Herald*'s daily circulation had increased by 2,600 and its weekly issue by 2,400 in the past month.[64]

Certainly the Moral War failed to destroy the *Herald*. Perhaps Bennett's boasts should be discounted, and there was a slight but temporary drop in circulation. The tone of the *Herald* did improve. Its religious news was less frivolous, although Bennett continued to treat religion like any other news topic. Each May the meetings of the religious and moral reform societies in New York City received fuller coverage in the *Herald* than in any other paper. And starting in 1844, each Tuesday the *Herald* summarized the leading sermons preached in the city on Sunday.[65]

The *Herald*'s sensationalism should not be treated in a vacuum. What was the rest of the New York press doing? How did other papers treat events that appeared in the *Herald* as sensational stories? Several random examples suggest an answer. In 1836 the New Orleans papers reported a gruesome murder. All the New York papers except the *Evening Post* picked up the item and gave a short summary of the crime, about the same length as the *Herald*'s. But except for the *American,* which copied its account from the *Herald,* they all appeared two to five days later than the *Herald*'s.[66]

Another example was the "Shocking Suicide — Supposed Murder — Imputed Adultery" that occurred on Long Island in 1843 and received two full columns in the *Herald* on July 13. The next day there was a two-inch summary in the *Courier and Enquirer.* None of the other papers mentioned the story, although it had all the ingredients to make it popular reading.[67]

The Long Island racing season of 1837 provides a different example. The *Herald* published regular reports written by "Old Turfman" and on June 21 carried a three-column lead editorial on the famous racehorse Mingo. The other papers published advertisements for the racetracks and terse race results, but none of them treated horse racing as a news story as Bennett did.[68]

One of the *Herald*'s most complete society stories was the account of the lavish ball on the yacht of J. C. Stevens in 1840. The *Herald*'s story on October 17 was long and detailed and included a three-column-wide woodcut of some of the ladies in attendance. None of the other New York papers covered the fete except the *Courier and Enquirer,* which merely mentioned it.[69]

Was the reverse true? Did the other New York papers publish human interest stories that the *Herald* missed? A random search did not uncover any. Bennett's energy and enterprise were such that if a story escaped his attention it was likely to be dull or unimportant.

The sensationalist course that Bennett charted for the *Herald* continued through his lifetime. As the technical proficiency of the press increased, the maps and illustrations in the *Herald* became more numerous, almost routine. Maps were included not only to illustrate the most obvious news stories — the Mexican and Crimean wars, filibusters in the Caribbean, Fort Sumter and the defenses of Charleston harbor — but of the approaches to New York harbor, the Arctic explorations of Elisha Kane and Sir John Franklin, and the gold district in Colorado.[70] The same was true of the engravings: the *Herald* included not only the obvious murderers and murder scenes, fires, presidential inaugurations, "The Grand Funeral Procession in Memory of Andrew Jackson" in 1845 (the first full-page illustration in an American newspaper), but also the "monster" steamer *Great Britain* and a new revenue cutter of the navy (both with elaborate section charts), racehorses, and the cable ship *Niagara* and its equipment to lay the transatlantic cable.[71]

Sporting news continued to be prominent. Yachting regattas were news to the *Herald,* as was horse racing. In 1845 the *Herald* treated the challenge between the southern horse Peytona and the northern Fashion as a sectional clash. Bennett consistently supported horse racing as a method of improving and testing the breeds, and he urged an expansion of racing facilities in the New York area. Nor was prizefighting neglected. The great fight between Yankee Sullivan and Tom Hyer in Baltimore in 1849 featured complete *Herald* telegraphic descriptions from there, with no bloody detail overlooked. (Hyer won; Sullivan was almost beaten to death.) The Morrisey-Heenan contest in Buffalo was also given a full and graphic account, along with a continuing discussion of why prizefighters became successful New York City politicians. The "fight of the century" — the first of many — between American John Heenan and Englishman Tom Sayers was featured a year in advance in the *Herald,* at the time of the challenge, and in the spring of 1860, when Heenan whipped his British opponent, the fight was given as much space as the coming presidential nominating conventions.[72]

Disasters such as fires, a steamboat lost in a hurricane, and train wrecks remained staple fare. Suicide had a morbid interest for Bennett, which he indulged with several speculations on its causes.[73] Murders remained a specialty, particularly killings that had a twist of the unusual or grotesque or had a moral to point. The same complete treatment that Bennett gave to the Robinson-Jewett case he devoted to the Boston trial of Professor John W. Webster for the murder of Dr. George Parkman in 1850, using telegraphic dispatches of every detail of the trial and a grisly description of Webster's execution.[74] A local murder in 1857 received more space in the *Herald* than any news story that year, with diagrams, illustrations, complete trial transcripts, and much editorial speculation.[75] Full treatment was also given to the "unwritten law" killing by Congressman Daniel Sickles of his wife's lover, Philip Barton Key, with the *Herald* editorially supporting Sickles.[76]

Bennett's genius and the success of his paper continued to be trumpeted as news. Attacks on rivals were less frequent but did occur. When Bennett was sued for libel by the manager of the local opera, he provided verbatim coverage of the trial as crucial to freedom of the press. He noticed a laudatory front-page story about himself in the *Democratic Review* in 1853 and Isaac C. Pray's eulogistic *Memoirs of James Gordon Bennett* published in 1855. These were news, as was a testimonial dinner and silver service given to him in 1855 by New York merchants in recognition of his support of the Constitution and American interests. Even the education of his son James Gordon Bennett, Jr., was featured in a news story, with a prediction that the Bennett dynasty in New York would be as important as the Bonaparte dynasty in France.[77]

He contrasted the press of the 1850s with that of 1835 and took most of the credit for the improvement. Bennett marked the *Herald*'s twentieth anniversary in 1855 by noting the commanding position of his paper, "proof that it has kept pace with the most marked of the progressive improvements of the age." He claimed to be solely responsible for the newspaper revolution that replaced the party press with an independent press. In 1859 he listed a series of innovations for which he took credit. These firsts included financial articles about Wall Street, a corps of reporters covering the debates in Congress, verbatim reports of political meetings, verbatim trial reports, complete reports of the annual meetings of the religious and moral reform societies, expresses from Boston with European news, Mexican War expresses to New York, pictures and maps, and enlarged double, triple, and quadruple sheets. Indeed, he remarked in 1860, his paper occupied the same ascendant position in America that the London *Times* had in England.[78]

The *Herald*'s broad conception of human interest led to an expansion of its coverage of cultural affairs as interesting news. Despite a long-standing feud with promoter P. T. Barnum, Bennett trumpeted the tour of Jenny Lind, "the Swedish nightingale, the soul of song," that Barnum arranged in 1850. The singer was the "woman of the century — one of the wonders of an age."[79] Art exhibitions were regularly described; there were summaries of the papers read at the American Association for the Advancement of Science meetings; and the annual state fair at Syracuse, covered by the *Herald*'s own reporter, occasioned a discussion of agricultural progress.[80]

But its cultural news could be flawed, as two examples illustrate. One of the most important such story was on the Great Exhibition of 1851 held at the Crystal Palace in London. When the plans for American participation in the international fair were announced, the *Herald* believed that the United States, "as yet unknown in the market of Europe except as producers of raw material," could show the world "that we can work them up into manufactures often equally, but sometimes surpassing the oldest nations in a perfection and with a facility unknown to them." It continued optimistic that American mechanics would "take their due share of the premiums; . . . the more we are tested the more we triumph. The human mind in the United States being as free and untrammelled as it can possibly be, takes everything within its grasp." England, with "corruption pervading every fibre and muscle of the body politic," would be unable to compete "with a young, vigorous, athletic, powerful republic." But when Congress declined to appropriate money to advance the American showing, and when fewer exhibits than expected were sent from New York to London, the *Herald* lost its optimism. It began attacking the exhibition for bringing about the prospect of a revolution in England; socialists from around the world (not the least of them, Horace Greeley of the *Tribune*) were gathering in London for the fair. As for the fair itself, it "will be a humbug." The exhibition at the Crystal Palace, as a result, received no coverage in the *Herald* except to call Greeley's reports in the *Tribune* "silly" and to remark that the "meagreness" of the American showing was not surprising. The *Herald*'s readers were poorly served by their paper, and Bennett's judgment proved defective. The Americans did very well in both industrial and agricultural tests, but because of Bennett's spite, none of this appeared in the *Herald*.[81]

Bennett turned the pages of the *Herald* into a one-man vendetta against the American Art-Union and brought about its demise. From 1839 to 1851 the Art-Union had placed American art patronage on a democratic basis by maintaining a permanent free gallery of American paintings and by distributing nationally thousands of original American works of art and hundreds of thousands of engravings based on them through a public drawing. A committee of the Art-Union decided which original works to hang and distribute. Thomas W. Whitely, an Ohio artist, was disappointed by the committee's less than enthusiastic reception of his entries, and he decided to retaliate.

Whitely had no luck in dealing directly with the Art-Union, but he had worked as an occasional correspondent for the *Herald,* commenting on artistic and theatrical matters. He persuaded Bennett that the Art-Union's annual distribution was an illegal lottery. Late in 1851, just before the distribution, the *Herald* questioned its legality and brought about a postponement of the prizes. Then the *Herald* charged that the Art-Union was controlled by "an abolition clique" that had diverted its funds to establish "a daily abolition journal." The reference was to Henry J. Raymond's newly established *New York Times;* Raymond was one of the directors of the Art-Union. The Art-Union retaliated by suing Bennett for libel, but an indictment was quashed. Bennett joined the Art-Union and then sought an injunction to restrain its distribution of art works. The lottery issue, in turn, was pushed by the district attorney, who was under intense political pressure, and in June 1852 the state supreme court declared the Art-Union's distribution system to be an illegal lottery.

Thus ended this useful institution of mass culture and democratic patronage of art. What is strange is that this was a nonaristocratic, non-foreign cultural body such as Bennett usually championed. There are no mitigating circumstances in this blow to native American artists which the Bennett-Whitely vendetta caused.[82]

But the *Herald* continued to treat the human interest dimensions of important national news stories. Some examples are the persecution and migration of the Mormons from Illinois to Utah, the court-martial of John C. Frémont, the American visit of the Prince of Wales in 1860, and the Japanese embassy that visited earlier that year.[83] Even a routine story of an overdue steamship could be built into a suspenseful account in the *Herald*. Bennett was also adept at slanting the news to a wonderful degree by use of ridicule, as his coverage of reforms such as the women's rights movement illustrates.[84]

Finally, Bennett continued to treat religion as news; the Moral War had not intimidated him. The Episcopal trial of Bishop Benjamin Onderdonk in 1845, the theology of Unitarianism, the new doctrine of the Immaculate Conception of the Virgin, conflicts over the ownership of Roman Catholic church property, and the effect of the depression of 1857 in stimulating religious revivals all were prominent news stories to the *Herald*.[85]

Although Bennett did not invent sensationalism, he carried it as far as it would go to make the *Herald* the most interesting, entertaining, and popular newspaper in America. What is remarkable is that he made the *Herald* the most newsworthy, complete, and innovative newspaper as well. He was able to harness the new technology of the "printing revolution" and outdo the mercantile press in its own area of specialization.

3

Technology and the News

For a mass circulation newspaper to survive, a large number of copies had to be printed quickly so that all customers would receive the paper at about the same time, when the news was still fresh, and the news had to be gathered early enough to make this possible. Improved technology, then, was essential to the newspaper revolution.

When the *Herald* was established, it and most other New York papers used a single-cylinder Napier press built by Hoe and Company, capable of about two thousand impressions per hour. It would take a press run of ten hours to supply a circulation of twenty thousand, or five hours with two presses (which would double the labor of the compositors, who would have to set everything into type twice.) For the paper to be ready for its subscribers in the early morning, printing would have to start in the evening, omitting the latest news because the southern mail with news from Washington did not arrive in New York until midnight.

The first major improvement was the *Sun*'s use of steam power. In 1835 Day installed a steam-powered press that was capable of five thousand impressions an hour. But a truly adequate press for a mass circulation newspaper was not introduced until 1846, when Arunah S. Abell bought the Hoe "lightning press" for his *Philadelphia Public Ledger.* The lightning press was rotary and was fed by four impression cylinders, quadrupling the rate of the old flatbed Napiers. Later the number of impression cylinders was increased to six, then eight, then ten, giving the press a capacity of twenty thousand sheets per hour and permitting the paper to go to press much later with news that was fresher. These presses were expensive, and the larger presses and the steam engines to power them would often necessitate a larger building in which to house them.[1]

Bennett kept his *Herald* in the forefront of these technological improvements. In the spring of 1836 the *Herald* moved to a new building on the corner of Nassau and Beekman streets, where a new steam press was installed. Six months later he paid Hoe $3,200 for a new double-cylinder press, which enabled him to enlarge the *Herald* and meet a projected daily circulation of thirty thousand. Another new press was added in 1839, which made possible another enlargement by about a third, and in 1840 a set of double-cylinder presses from Hoe led to another enlargement.[2]

In May 1842 Bennett moved into a new granite building on the corner of Fulton and Nassau streets. He spent about $15,000 on two new double- and two single-cylinder presses, with an improved steam engine to drive them. He was proposing to publish about eight magazines (a hope that never materialized) in addition to the *Herald* and job printing so that he would be able to keep all the presses busy and serve all his customers with all the news by six in the morning. (The southern mail now arrived in mid-afternoon rather than midnight.)[3]

The *Herald* started using a lightning press on July 3, 1848. It could produce ten thousand impressions an hour, and Bennett hoped to be able to publish an hour earlier and handle a circulation as large as eighty thousand. Further expansion was necessary, and in 1850 Bennett bought the three adjoining buildings and spread into them. In 1852 he spent about $40,000 on two more six-cylinder presses and new steam engines and boilers. When in 1857 the *Herald* installed two new ten-cylinder presses and two forty-horsepower steam engines, 150,000 copies could be produced in a few hours. To accommodate the new machinery, the *Herald* building had to be remodeled, and the total cost of the machines and renovations was about $90,000. But Bennett gloated that the London *Times* did not begin using ten-cylinder presses until two years later.[4]

Supplying these machines with paper could be a problem. Before the establishment of the *Herald*, the Fourdrinier papermaking machine had been introduced, and new bleaching processes made it possible to manufacture paper from colored rags. Before that, one sheet of paper cost about one cent. Now papermaking became a concentrated industry, and imports of rags from Europe soared. Further improvements in papermaking dropped the price to between eight and fourteen cents a pound, a third to a half of the pre-1830 price.[5]

Bennett bought his paper from the firm of Perese and Brooks, which had a paper mill at Windsor Locks, Connecticut. He paid cash at each Saturday's delivery. He estimated in 1852 that he spent about $130,000 a year for paper out of an annual income of $400,000. Then in 1854 the price of paper rose sharply because of increasing demand and restrictions on European exports of rags.[6]

The editor had two other major fixed costs: labor and news-gathering. The latter was directly affected by technology. In 1823 Bennett had witnessed the news-gathering innovations of Aaron Willington in Charleston, and he had participated in the newsboat-express rivalry between the *Courier and Enquirer* and the *Journal of Commerce*. As soon as it was financially feasible, the *Herald* entered the news-gathering race. In December 1835 its horse express beat the regular expresses of the *Courier* and the *Journal* by almost three hours in bringing Jackson's annual message to New York.[7]

But not until 1837 was Bennett able to organize a newsboat fleet to rival that of the mercantile press. Starting in March with a single newsboat, he had added two more by December that were large enough to go 150 miles to sea from Sandy Hook. He boasted that his newsboats made the *Herald*'s shipping and foreign news the earliest and most complete and that this resulted in the sale of hundreds of extras. In 1840 he considered adding a small steamer to his fleet.[8]

Dissatisfaction with late mail deliveries from Washington and the South led Bennett to establish his own express to the capital in 1840, using several connecting railroads and usually beating the regular mails by half a day. This news appeared in a special column headed "BY EXPRESS. in Advance of the Mails." On special occasions, such as important speeches, the *Herald* would run a special express to the scene. To meet British mail steamers that stopped in Boston before they anchored in New York, Bennett started a regular express in 1844, a combination of railroads and a steamer across Long Island Sound, that usually beat the mails by a day. Early in 1845, to bring news of the cotton market as well as the tense conditions along the Texas border, the *Herald* started an exclusive daily express from New Orleans, by way of Mobile, Augusta, and Charleston, which beat the mails by from one to four days and was continued until the telegraph reached New Orleans.[9]

The telegraph did more to transform news-gathering in the nineteenth century than any other invention.[10] In mid-1844 Bennett waxed eloquent over the potential of the new device:

> Once this extraordinary invention shall have been fully applied all over the country, the wonderful spectacle will be presented, of a vast continent, as consolidated and united, and possessed as much, nay, in greater degree, of the means of rapid communication as the city of New York. It will tend to bind together with electric forces the whole Republic, and by its single agency do more to guard against disunion, and blend into one homogeneous mass, the whole population of the Republic, than all that the most experienced, the most sagacious, and the most patriotic government, could accomplish.

He expected in late 1845 that the telegraph connecting New York with Washington, Boston, and Buffalo would be of such great value to news transmission that the post office would be obsolete. Unfortunately, private telegraph companies were charging extortionate rates. "And we do not believe it to be at all possible that individuals or associations will be able to conduct these lines with satisfaction and full justice to the public. It must be a public affair — belong to the general government, and controlled by the people through their representatives. The sooner the subject is taken up by the next Congress, the better for the whole country." In anticipation of the completion of the line to Washington, Bennett made arrangements with the Magnetic Telegraph Company to supply reports from the capital during the 1846 session of Congress and with the Boston and New York Magnetic Telegraph Company to send reports from Boston when transatlantic steamers arrived there.[11]

The Mexican War made completion of the telegraph line to New Orleans all the more urgent. The *Herald*'s coverage of the war was extensive — twenty-seven extra editions and seven supplements, with several maps during one three-week period in May 1846 — using expresses from New Orleans, the center for gathering the war news, to the closest telegraph point. When the lines reached New Orleans, each paper leased a wire for its own exclusive use. Bennett paid these costs willingly. He had a "sense of urgency and an open-fisted entrepreneur's desire to beat the opposition with the freshest battlefield reports, casualty lists, or campaign dispatches from the armies of Scott and Taylor. If it meant hiring two dozen express riders and four dozen fast horses to bring the news . . . to a southern telegraph point, Bennett gladly paid the price."[12]

When the telegraph company limited each paper to fifteen minutes of transmission, the more prosperous New York dailies decided to band together, as some of them had done in the harbor newsboat association years earlier. The *Herald* had been sharing the costs of common telegraphic dispatches from Washington and Boston with other New York papers from as early as May 1846. The city dailies probably planned the cooperative news-gathering venture some months before the articles of partnership adopted in 1849, perhaps in May 1848, at a meeting in the *Sun*'s office, the date traditionally cited as the origin of the Associated Press. In early 1849 the *Herald, Sun, Tribune, Courier and Enquirer, Journal of Commerce,* and *Express* organized a partnership, the New York Associated Press, to lease a telegraph line for their own exclusive use and to charter a steamer from Halifax, where transatlantic ships stopped before proceeding to Boston and New York. The same news would be delivered to the six member papers at the same time, and they would divide the costs equally. Bennett's managing editor, Frederic Hudson, and Webb's managing editor, Henry J. Raymond, were to oversee the operation. To cut costs, news would be sold to out-of-city papers.[13]

Telegraphic news transmission was expensive. The *Herald* estimated that its share of the Associated Press expenses for the first half of 1852 was $3,800. In addition, the *Herald* was maintaining its own newsboats in the harbor at a weekly cost of $150 and transmitting telegraphic dispatches exclusive of the Associated Press at over $300 weekly. By 1860 telegraphic costs had risen to over $1,000.[14]

The telegraph supplemented rather than replaced the traditional methods of news-gathering by exchanges with other papers and correspondence sent through the mail. The telegraphic dispatches were usually short summaries, terse, with the inverted-pyramid flow of the story line. Longer commentary would follow by mail several days later, and only a small proportion of the news came by telegraph.[15]

The announcement of the success of the transatlantic cable in 1858 made Bennett even more ecstatic than the telegraph had done. "We look forward to the time when the Herald will contain, besides its local and city intelligence and advertisements, nothing but a mass of faithful telegraphic reports of the events in the whole world on the previous day, with our editorial comments thereon. This is the electric power of journalism that we mean to open." The caustic New Yorker George Templeton Strong thought Bennett was too effusive. He wrote in his diary:

> Newspapers vie with each other in gas and grandiloquence. Yesterday's *Herald* said that the cable . . . is undoubtedly the Angel in the Book of Revelation with one foot on land, proclaiming that time shall be no longer. Moderate people merely say that this is the greatest human achievement in history. . . . The diverse races of man certainly seem tending towards development into a living organic unit with railroads and steam-packets for a circulating system, telegraph wires for nerves, and the London *Times* and New York *Herald* for a brain.

Not all editors were enthusiastic. Some feared that the expense of the cable, which they would be forced to pay to compete, would be prohibitive.[16]

The *Herald* was lavish in its coverage of the cable-laying operations, with illustrations of the machinery and the ship *Niagara* that laid the line. But Bennett's enthusiasm was wasted because the completed cable did not work properly, and it was of no use in news transmission until after the Civil War.[17]

To gather the news, Bennett organized the most extensive network of reporters and correspondents of any newspaper in the nation. During 1835 and 1836 he had a regular correspondent in Washington and an occasional correspondent in Albany, both of whose articles were unsigned. During the congressional session of 1836–37, "Al Raschid" sent daily dispatches, witty but too partisan to suit Bennett. By late 1837 two correspondents filed from Washington and one from Albany, and others occasionally were located in London, Canada, Boston, Philadelphia, Key West, and Jamaica. Even when Congress was not in session "Horace" sent regular reports from the capital. When some local event had special news value, Bennett would send his own reporter, even if the occasion was only an exclusive political dinner.[18]

When the first transatlantic steamers dropped anchor in New York on April 23, 1838, Bennett recognized their importance in speeding European news. When the *Sirius* returned to Europe on May 1, Bennett was on board, promising to set up a "vast corps" of foreign correspondents in Europe. The first letter from one of them, from London, appeared in the *Herald* on July 17.[19]

The regular reporters changed frequently. In 1839 "The Eye in Albany" covered the state capital and "Horace" the Washington scene. During the 1839–40 session "Tobias Trott" and "Terence" did the Washington reporting with regular correspondents in Albany, New Orleans, and Harrisburg and special reporters for a trial in Philadelphia and the *L'Amistad* trial in Hartford. For the 1840–41 congressional season Bennett used three specialized reporters, one for the House, one for the Senate, and one for society and the White House.[20]

When John Tyler became president after Harrison's death and called a special session of Congress, the *Herald*, which had supported Harrison and Tyler, reorganized its reporters in Washington into a news bureau headed by Robert Sutton. Bennett was almost foiled because the president pro tem of the Senate, in a surprise move, decided to admit only representatives of the Washington papers to the Senate press gallery. Bennett exploded against this "short-sighted illiberality" and enlisted Henry Clay's aid to get the ruling reversed. In contrast to the weak and subsidized capital papers, Bennett argued, "*we propose, and will give, a daily report and circulation of these debates, better and more comprehensive, without asking a cent of the public treasury.*" After a Senate committee investigated the situation, the *Herald* reporter was admitted. Sutton's news bureau worked well, and he managed it again during the 1841–42 regular session.[21]

Special events such as a speech by Daniel Webster were usually covered by a *Herald* stenographic reporter, and the paper developed a reputation for accuracy of which it was proud. Indeed, Bennett suggested that the government rely on the *Herald*'s accurate stenographic reports of the debates in Congress and stop subsidizing their publication by a Washington sheet; the *Herald*'s reports were more accurate, he claimed, than those in the semiofficial *Washington Globe*. One of these stenographic reporters, William H. Attree, took over the *Herald*'s Washington bureau in 1842.[22]

After Bennett went to Europe on one of his regular visits in 1847, the *Herald*'s foreign correspondence was reorganized and expanded. On a typical day the *Herald* would print accounts from London, Dublin, Rome, Madrid, Paris, Berne, and Constantinople. Bennett was among the first in New York to hear of the California gold strike in 1848 because he employed the consul at Monterey, Thomas Larkin, as a correspondent there. Skeptical at first, Bennett had Larkin's gold dust sample assayed before he printed the dispatches. Then he made special arrangements for the transmission of California news across Mexico and the Isthmus of Panama.[23]

The best example of the *Herald*'s reporting enterprise is the beat scored by Washington correspondent John Nugent in 1848 when he procured a copy of the Treaty of Guadalupe Hidalgo while the Senate was still shrouding the treaty in secrecy. Nugent had been writing from Washington for Bennett since 1846 as "Galviensis." He usually took a position favorable to the presidential aspirations of Secretary of State James Buchanan and critical of those of Lewis Cass and President James K. Polk. As a result, he was a frequent and welcome visitor at the State Department.[24]

The Senate received the treaty from Polk on February 22, 1848, and after a secret debate it was ratified, with slight amendments, on March 10. The secrecy was not lifted because Mexico had yet to ratify. But on February 22 the *Herald* carried an accurate summary of the treaty's provisions; on February 25 it provided a detailed summary of each article of the treaty; and on March 11 it printed a series of telegraphic dispatches about the March 10 ratification, including the names of some of those voting for and against the treaty. Then on March 13 Bennett announced that the *Herald* had had the text of the treaty in its possession for over two months but had not published it out of concern for the public interest. Now that the Senate had ratified, the complete text was presented to the *Herald*'s readers. Some of Polk's confidential correspondence that had been submitted to the Senate with the treaty followed a few days later.[25]

The Polk administration was as disturbed as the Senate. How had Nugent gotten a draft of the treaty? The Senate launched an inquiry and appointed a select committee to examine Nugent, who admitted that he had obtained the treaty copy but refused to reveal his source. Nugent was confined by the sergeant-at-arms from March 27 until April 28. Bennett was furious and editorialized on the issue of freedom of the press, although the Senate insisted that it had a right to determine whether one of its members or employees had given away its secrets. Bennett called the Senate action "an insolent and ludicrous attempt . . . to establish in this land some of the discarded principles of Louis Philippe, and to fetter the independence of the press here, in this free land, as that worthy did in Paris." Cass was blamed for the Senate inquiry, which Bennett likened to the Alien and Sedition Acts. Through April Bennett kept up the fire in a series "Galviensis and the Senate," abusing Polk and praising Buchanan. Finally, at the end of April, Nugent was released without having disclosed his source.[26]

Bennett did not drop the matter until May 3, when he had the last word by publishing a table of "leaks," listing a dozen newspapers, their Washington correspondents, and the "Leaky Senators" who supplied them with information, with Cass given three times as a leaker. All of this, Bennett argued, was well known to the administration because "some of the democratic Senators were the most accurate leakers."[27]

By the mid-1850s Bennett had an extensive network of regular and special correspondents, usually two or three in Washington and one in Albany, London, Paris, Vienna, Havana, and Mexico City. During one four-day period letters were published in the *Herald* from the above places and China, Hawaii, Peru, Uruguay, Nicaragua, New Granada, California, Kansas, the Washington Territory, Arkansas, Kentucky, Florida, New Jersey, Virginia, Pennsylvania, Massachusetts, Connecticut, New Hampshire, Rhode Island, many localities in New York, and about forty vacation resorts.[28] During the sectional crisis of 1860 the *Herald* published reports on the tensions from special correspondents around the country. After Abraham Lincoln's election Bennett hired Henry Villard of the *Cincinnati Commercial,* who knew Lincoln from his coverage of the debates with Stephen A. Douglas in 1858, to go to Springfield and remain until the inauguration.[29] Bennett was always searching for talented correspondents, and he would meet their terms when necessary. Francis J. Grund, for example, the capital correspondent of the *Baltimore Sun* and *Philadelphia Public Ledger,* the most celebrated Washington reporter of the 1840s and 1850s, contributed occasional pieces to the *Herald.*[30] Above all, Bennett prided himself on his coverage of Latin America, the most complete of any northeastern newspaper, as befit the *Herald*, which ardently supported expansion southward.[31]

Bennett remained his own most important correspondent. His reportorial experience was extensive, and before he could afford to hire a large staff he combined business trips and vacations with reporting for the *Herald*, in Albany, Washington, Philadelphia, Saratoga Springs, and Niagara

Falls.[32] He made at least four extended trips to Europe and sent back regular, almost daily, reports on conditions there. In 1838 he left on May 1 and was gone until October 10 setting up a network of foreign correspondents. His major themes in dozens of letters to the *Herald* were financial and economic conditions and the stability of Louis Philippe's regime in France. As always, his writing combined wit, enlightenment, and entertainment. He made a shorter trip to England and France in 1843 and sent back several letters on the Irish situation.[33]

Then he returned to Europe for almost a year from the summer of 1846 through the summer of 1847. (His wife and son were now spending almost all of their time in France.) This time his dozens of letters had the flavor of a travelogue and dealt with society and fashions more than politics and finance. Mrs. Bennett contributed several pieces. During the trip he reorganized his European correspondents with new central offices — news bureaus — in Liverpool, Paris, Antwerp, and Bremen, and with regular correspondents in London, Brussels, Vienna, Munich, Trieste, Berne, Rome, Madrid, Naples, Constantinople, Alexandria, and Bombay. He arranged to participate in an overland express to India to get later news from India and China than could be obtained through the regular channels in London. In 1851 he returned to Europe for a few months but filed no reports. And in the winter of 1850–51 he visited Cuba to see firsthand the island that he so ardently hoped would be annexed to the United States.[34]

What did his network of reporters and correspondents cost Bennett? Although he started as a one-man staff, Bennett soon enlarged his venture. By 1839 he employed four editors and reporters, two of them at $20 weekly; by 1840 there were six, plus a dozen foreign correspondents, and by 1841, ten, plus occasional correspondents. The staff remained stable for about a decade. During the 1850s there were about fifteen editors and reporters in the New York office, each averaging about $20 weekly.[35]

A much larger group of employees set the type, operated the presses, kept the books, and circulated the paper. Bennett was using eight compositors as early as 1836, and by 1842 he employed about fifty in the composing room, pressroom, and business office. By the 1850s about two hundred people worked for Bennett, including his correspondents and news agents. They were not paid well despite a union in the print shop. Bennett was antagonistic to union demands, and the wage scale remained low. In the 1830s the New York Typographical Union had recommended a weekly wage of $12 for compositors and $9 for pressmen. A questionnaire submitted to union members in 1850 revealed that compositors were averaging only $12.50 weekly on the best-paying papers, with pressmen getting $9 and both working sixteen-hour days.[36]

Bennett could have afforded to treat his workers better. Profits on the

Herald rose steadily, partly as a result of advertising innovations. The mercantile papers charged advertisers $32 a year and allowed them almost unlimited space, a practice they did not abandon until soaring paper costs forced a change in 1853. But the *Sun* from the beginning had run onetime ads of two or three lines for fifty cents, and this "want" column was one of the reasons for the *Sun*'s popularity. Bennett followed this example and charged fifty cents for a sixteen-line square, later reduced to squares of twelve and eight lines at fifty-two cents daily for the larger. Payment was to be by cash in advance.[37]

The *Herald* carried a plethora of patent medicine advertisements for which it was criticized. Bennett responded that he would publish any ad that was paid in advance. In 1836 the *Herald* carried the first two-column ad with a two-column illustration, a scene of the great fire of December 1835 for Harrington's New Grand Moving Diorama. By 1840 he was using illustrations in ads for pianos, cooking stoves, and shaving cream. One advertising tradition Bennett refused to change: advertisements could appear only in tiny agate type. Resourceful advertisers then made designs out of the type, and the ingenious Robert Bonner of the popular literary weekly the *New York Ledger* in 1856 would repeat the same short two-line ad for an entire column with similar ads for the remaining columns to fill an entire page, making an acrostic that spelled *Ledger* across the page. But the agate rule remained.[38]

The *Herald*'s advertising formula was successful. By the summer of 1837 it was claiming more cash ads than any other New York paper, and by 1839 the volume of advertising was causing a space problem. Bennett cautioned his customers to "be short and pithy in your advertisements. They will be more read and better remembered." He had to issue an eight-page number of the *Herald* on June 6, 1839, the first of many double sheets, because of the volume of advertising. By 1840 he was carrying theater ads from Philadelphia, where the *Herald* had a daily circulation of over a thousand, and was rejecting government advertising because the rates were too low. Advertisers were often reminded that because of the *Herald*'s circulation lead, it gave them more for their advertising dollar.[39]

Because fresh ads attracted readers, in 1847 Bennett began to limit ads to two days in the hope that they would be changed each day. The advertising columns were headed "Advertisements Renewed Every Day." The volume continued to rise, and by 1849 double sheets were a regular Tuesday feature.[40] Bennett continued to plead for freshness and brevity in his ads, and he claimed that his advertising columns were news, that they gave a panoramic view of life in New York City, expressing the wants, hopes, and anticipations of its people, some grave and severe, some gay and lively.

It has been argued that this form of advertising was democratic; that it addressed the newspaper reader as a human with mortal needs (patent medicines and want ads); and that it made advertising a strictly economic exchange, with a laissez-faire policy of allowing anyone to advertise who could pay the price, excluding no one.[41]

This laissez-faire advertising policy extended even to abortionists. One of the *Herald*'s best advertisers was Anna Trow, better known as Madame Restell, who was married to Charles Lohman, a *Herald* printer. In 1837 she began selling abortifacients and advertised them in both the *Herald* and the *Sun*. Under the guise of medicine the products were euphemistically said to promote monthly regularity and to remove obstructions and stoppages from the female tract. Madame Restell had vigorous competition, especially from a "Madam Costello," who advertised herself in the *Sun* as a "FEMALE PHYSICIAN" and provoked Madame Restell to counteradvertising in the *Herald*. In 1845 a new periodical, the *National Police Gazette*, began a crusade against New York's abortionists, but neither the *Herald* nor the *Sun* noticed it. Madame Restell spent a year in prison in 1847–48 but on her release resumed her advertising and her business, becoming so successful that she was able to buy a Fifth Avenue mansion.

From 1845 to 1850 her printer husband, Charles Lohman, advertised an abortion handbook that went through twelve editions by 1852, *The Married Woman's Private Medical Companion* by "Dr. Mauriceau, Professor of Diseases of Women." His advertisements in the *Herald* promised to "correct all irregularities of the female system." The most careful student of the subject calls the abortion advertising in the *Herald* and *Sun* "frequent and highly competetive. . . . Madame Restell helped build her business through advertising. She also may have been buying protection, as there was an absence of editorial criticism of abortion in both the *Herald* and the *Sun*." The laissez-faire attitude of carrying any ad that was paid for in cash made it easy for the *Herald*, which still carried abortion ads in the 1870s, also to advertise the services of prostitutes with a similar use of euphemisms and without a twinge of concern about morals or ethics.[42]

The *Herald*'s advertising and circulation receipts made Bennett a wealthy man. When the *Herald* was a year old, he boasted of a net revenue of $30,000, sufficient to finance many improvements, with a daily circulation of 10,080 and at least 50,000 regular readers. The reasons for his success were clear: "I have entered the hearts of the people—I have shewn [sic] them their own sentiments—I have put down their own living feelings on paper—I have created a passion for reading the Herald among all classes." This passion was national so Bennett started a weekly edition at $3 annually in December 1836 and an evening edition (at first called the *Chron-*

icle) in May 1837. His net profits by the end of that depression year were an impressive $20,000. He claimed an aggregate daily circulation of 20,000 by 1839 and almost 30,000 by 1842 with annual receipts of over $125,000.[43]

Bennett had by this time made arrangements for the *Herald* to be delivered regularly to Philadelphia, New Haven, Providence, Boston, Albany, Newark, Paterson, Troy, and Poughkeepsie, and he soon added Washington, Baltimore, Hartford, and Harrisburg. To do this he published two morning editions, one at midnight for the out-of-towners, the other in the early morning with fresher news for local readers. He started a Sunday edition, which led in New York City Sunday circulation in less than a year, and a weekly journal of medicine, *Lancet,* both in 1842. The sixteen-page octavo magazine cost $3 a year and combined popular quackery with valuable medical news and information. But it was short-lived because a court order prohibited Bennett from publishing reports of lectures in the New York University Medical School.[44]

By 1848 the *Herald* claimed an aggregate daily circulation of 47,000 and was given the post office contract to advertise letters not called for, proof of its circulation leadership in New York. Within five years it boasted of a daily circulation of 52,000 and a combined daily and weekly circulation of 103,000, an astonishing growth that was checked, Bennett claimed, only by the physical limitations of his presses. His *Herald*, with its average daily circulation of 57,000, had a larger weekly bill for paper than the London *Times,* he asserted in 1855. Circulation exceeded 60,000 in 1856 and neared 70,000 in 1857, he claimed. By the end of the decade he boasted of weekly advertising income of over $4,000, aggregate annual receipts of almost $1 million, and so large a volume of advertising as to necessitate regular triple sheets.[45] The *Herald* was the most emulated newspaper in America, and he predicted that its style would soon spread to England. He believed that the repeal of the newspaper tax there would result in a popular and independent press like the *Herald.*[46]

Circulation claims were notoriously unreliable, but even if the regular daily circulation of the *Herald* in 1860 is scaled down to 60,000, as one authority puts it,[47] there is no question of Bennett's material success. He was able to finance new presses and buildings, an extensive staff, a lavish home in Washington Heights, an extended stay in Europe for his wife and family, frequent trips abroad for himself, and a large yacht for his son.

He worked hard for his success. The *Herald* was his life, to the exclusion of almost anything else, and he had a right to be proud of it. The popular press had triumphed over the mercantile press by the 1840s, and if imitation was flattery Bennett should have been flattered indeed. In New York the *Sun,* the *Tribune,* and Henry J. Raymond's *Times* (established in 1851), all cheap and popular papers, trailed the *Herald* but led the mercantile press in circulation and influence. In other cities the *Herald*'s formula was repeated by such successful new cheap popular papers as the *Herald* in Boston, the *Sun* in Baltimore, the *Public Ledger* in Philadelphia, the *Picayune* in New Orleans, and the *Dispatch* in Richmond.

Moreoever, the mercantile press had begun to change, adopting many of the attributes of the cheaps in a counterrevolution of both style and substance. It ultimately failed because the popular press had taken over its specialized functions. By the 1850s there was more mercantile, commercial, financial, and maritime news in the *Herald, Tribune,* and *Times* than in the mercantile *Courier and Enquirer* or *Journal of Commerce.* Why should a reader pay six cents when the same news, and more besides, could be had for half that price?[48]

New York newspapers had reached a state of equilibrium by the late 1850s. Metropolitan papers had followed the *Herald* in adopting the new technology so they were all *news*papers. They paid a price in conformity, as content analyses of newspapers in all parts of the country from 1820 to 1860 have demonstrated.[49] The news-gathering rivalry of the Civil War strengthened this conformity. The equilibrium was not seriously disturbed until the adoption of pulp paper a decade later.[50]

But there was another facet of Bennett's creation that should not have made him proud. Though complete, the *Herald*'s news coverage was slanted. Bennett's paper was interesting reading in part because of its idiosyncratic editorial policy and the emotional, vituperative language in which the editorials were couched.

4

Editorial Jingoism

Bennett had a reputation for being politically erratic and inconsistent in his editorial columns, being, as James Parton said, "the best journalist and worst editorialist this continent has ever known." Bennett claimed to be a political independent. Usually he was on the Democratic side, and his editorial policy was coherent and consistent in that regard. In domestic policy he was prosouthern and proslavery, favored the laissez-faire economic policies of the Democratic party, and was a booster of New York City and its improvement. In foreign policy he was an uncompromising advocate of territorial expansion and a rabid Anglophobe.[1]

His view of America's place in the world followed from his republicanism, which he embraced with all the zeal of a convert. Bennett's adopted country was the best in the world and deserving of recognition as a leader in the family of nations. Territorial expansion was one way to gain this recognition and to bring the American system of republicanism to less favored peoples. But Bennett did not merely support an expansionist foreign policy; he was its most ardent champion in the American press. The jingoism of the *Herald* was related to its prosouthernism because Dixie was more united in favor of Manifest Destiny than was the North. It was also related to the *Herald*'s sensationalism. Bennett knew, as Frederick Merk observed, that "for general news, nothing was more sensational or exhilarating than the soul-stirring doctrine of Manifest Destiny."[2]

Bennett's strident nationalism was more significant than the rantings of an eccentric editor. The *Herald* was the best-known American newspaper in Europe, especially in England, where the *Herald* and the American newspaper press were synonymous and what Bennett said was American editorial opinion. The *Herald*'s European edition circulated two thousand copies in 1856. He was the only American editor recognizable by name and sight in England, savagely caricatured in cartoons in *Vanity Fair* magazine and the regular target of editorial blasts in J. T. Delane's

London *Times.* Abroad the *Herald*'s views about foreign policy were taken to be the views of the entire American press.[3]

During its first few years the *Herald* concentrated on racy local news and depression-related issues, only occasionally raising its yet small voice in support of an expansive foreign policy. In its early months in 1835 Bennett's paper expressed sympathy for its Texas "brethren . . . against the rapacious and bloody Spaniard" in Mexico and predicted a revolt of the Texans against Santa Anna. The editor was delighted when Texas won its independence at San Jacinto, and he saw a glorious future for the Texas Republic, which would probably absorb the rest of Mexico. Bennett believed that President Van Buren was wise in 1837 when he refused to consider the annexation of Texas to the United States.[4]

Anglophobia was another attitude the *Herald* manifested early. It was natural enough considering Bennett's Scotch Catholic ancestry, his committed republicanism, and his growing audience of Irish immigrant readers. Bennett sincerely believed that England was the most powerful enemy of republicanism in the world and that it was committed to denying the United States its rightful place in the family of nations. When Canadians rebelled in 1838, Bennett argued that American sympathies were strongly with the rebels. Also in 1838 the *Herald* asserted American claims to the whole of the Oregon country. And when the British authorities in Bermuda liberated the rebel slaves of the American slaver *Creole,* Bennett denounced the action as a flagrant violation of international law.[5]

The simmering Texas annexation question was the issue that most stirred Bennett's jingoism. In late 1841 he still considered annexation "a measure of very questionable expediency," and he seldom raised the issue for the next year and a half. Then in the summer of 1843 he announced in the *Herald* that in the event of a settlement between Texas and Mexico, the outcome was predetermined:

> The Anglo Saxon race is intended by an overruling Providence to carry the principles of liberty, the refinements of civilization, and the advantages of the mechanic arts through every land, even those now barbarous. — The prostrate savage and the benighted heathen, shall yet be imbued with Anglo Saxon intelligence and culture, and be blessed with the institutions, both civil and religious, which are now our inheritance. Mexico, too, must submit to the o'erpowering influence of the Anglo Saxon.

Bennett wrote these words while in England that summer.[6] In London he visited Duff Green, a former editor now a special agent of the Tyler administration negotiating a tariff reduction, and Green won Bennett to the administration's annexation policy and the rationale behind it by promises of influence and inside information. On his return to New York, Bennett published a letter by Green that stressed the threat of a conspiracy between abolition societies in England and America to abolish slavery throughout the world. A month later the *Herald* predicted that Tyler would recommend the annexation of Texas because of England's intrigues to abolish slavery there and to raise that republic as an economic counterweight to the United States.[7]

Annexation negotiations between Texas and Secretary of State Abel P. Upshur proceeded in secrecy for the next few months. Then, early in 1844, Upshur was killed in an accident. To replace him, Bennett suggested John C. Calhoun.[8] Tyler reached the same conclusion and appointed Calhoun Secretary of State in early March. The *Herald* became more strident for Texas annexation. If this meant war with Mexico, "we look at it with the indifference and contempt that power witnesses the ravings of imbecility and weakness." A March 19 editorial exulted:

> It is now assumed as being the destiny of this republic, that her power will be incomplete and civilization restricted, until her institutions of all kinds be spread from the Isthmus of Panama at the South to Hudson Bay at the North, and from the shores of the Pacific to the shores of the Atlantic — thus embracing the whole of North America and forming the North American Republic, comprehending within its wide-extended arms the British Possessions in the North and all of the Texian [sic] and Mexican territories in the South, as far as the Isthmus. This is believed to be the ultimate destiny of this republic.

This was Manifest Destiny with a vengeance, although the phrase itself was not used until John L. O'Sullivan's *Democratic Review* coined it the following summer. Bennett used the word *destiny* twice in the piece. The difference between *ultimate destiny* and *manifest destiny* is surely a semantic one, and the concept was full-blown in the *Herald*.[9]

"It is our firm conviction," Bennett wrote, "that, sooner or later, not only Texas, but Mexico, Canada, and Oregon, and all, will be absorbed in the mighty bosom of the North American Republic. It is destiny."[10] Samuel F. B. Morse's new magnetic telegraph made expansion inevitable. The telegraph "will tend to bind together with electric forces the whole Republic. . . . The extension of the republic to the uttermost extremities of this vast division of the earth, must now be seen as natural, justifiable and safe as the extension of New York to the Harlem River." The defeat of the annexation treaty by the Senate in June would not stem the tide of expansion.[11]

Annexation became a leading issue in the 1844 presidential campaign, with the *Herald* backing annexationist James K. Polk, the Democrat. Opposition to annexation was an attempt to gain abolitionist votes. Polk's victory was a mandate for annexation by the joint resolution of Congress.[12] British intrigue in Texas was again cited as a major reason for annexation, but Bennett rejected the notion that England would resist annexation with war; the cotton trade would guarantee peaceful relations. The passage of the joint resolution in March 1845 ended the exciting question and continued "the mighty work of extending systems of free government throughout this great division of the earth."[13]

The *Herald* believed that if Texas accepted the invitation to join the Union as a state, war with Mexico was almost certain. Mexican opposition to Texas annexation was the result of the activities of British and French secret agents there. England, especially, was determined to arrest the spread of republican institutions over the continent. Texas rejected the British overtures and entered the Union on July 4, 1845. Bennett expected that soon California, Canada, and all of Oregon would follow into the North American republic.[14]

Mexico now had no alternative to war, Bennett reiterated; she knew that California would be the next plum to fall. The United States had an obligation to defend Texas, and a special session of Congress should empower Polk to spend up to $10 million of the surplus revenue for that purpose. Indeed, by September 1845 the *Herald* featured news from the Rio Grande area under such captions as "The War" or "The Seat of War" as if war had already begun.[15]

The *Herald* repeatedly invoked the Monroe Doctrine as a justification for war with Mexico. England and France must not be allowed to regulate Mexican affairs; that was the "prescriptive right" of the United States. The European powers had no right to extend their "balance of power" ideas to America.

> That these governments . . . are itching to meddle with us; ever longing to plant their foot upon our continent, and interfere with our affairs and government, or with those of other people of the American continent, no one, who has considered passing events of late years can for a moment hesitate to believe. Texas, Buenos Ayres, Tahiti, California, Oregon, Mexico, all prove the disposition of Europe to interfere with us, and to attempt to control, or at least to impede our policy and our progress on our own continent. They, in a word, must crush republi-

canism or become republicans themselves. The question of the unwar-
ranted interference of the powers of Europe with the peoples of this
continent . . . is destined to be the absorbing question in the politics
of the age. [16]

The *Herald* had often predicted the acquisition of "the whole hemisphere, from the icy wilderness of the North to the most prolific regions
of the smiling and prolific South," and it had great interest in California.
That area's attractions were celebrated, and the paper's columns were filled
with letters from and about it. Soon California would follow the example
of Texas, throw off the Mexican yoke, and request annexation. [17]

The war the *Herald* had been forecasting for almost a year came in May
1846, following months of political instability in Mexico, the fruitless mission of John Slidell, and the advance of General Zachary Taylor's army
to positions along the Rio Grande. Unfortunately, Bennett complained,
Polk had not given Taylor enough men. But "We are now at war!" the *Herald*
screamed on May 12, and Polk's war message was carried in full in several
extras that day. [18]

Bennett returned to his old theme in accounting for the Mexican aggression: "There is no doubt that European intrigue is at the bottom of
the action of the Mexican government." The United States was united behind the war except for the "sheer niggerism" of the abolitionists. The war
aims were clear: "payment for her lawless spoliations of the past, security
for the future, and also a new boundary line between the two republics."
As a practical measure, the United States should seize California immediately as an indemnity; this would give us Pacific ports, guarantee a major
share of the China trade, and lessen the need to acquire all of Oregon. [19]

Soon the *Herald* was demanding more: New Mexico and the parts of
Sonora, Chihuahua, and Baja California that lay north of thirty degrees.
This acquisition would square off the southern boundary and provide temporary security. Northern objections to expanding the area open to slavery were ridiculed; slavery would become less important in the Old South
by diffusion into the Southwest. Ultimately, all of Mexico would fall to
the United States: "Their fate will be similar to that of the Indians of this
country — the race, before a century rolls over us, will become extinct." But
for the present, the cession of Mexico north of the thirtieth parallel would
suffice. [20]

The *Herald* had been pressuring the Polk administration for some time
to win a victory when, on April 20, 1847, the paper scored a beat with
the news of the appointment of Nicholas P. Trist to negotiate a settlement.
The mission was supposed to be a closely guarded secret; the administration took unusual precautions; but the story was leaked to the *Herald* by

someone in the State Department. Polk was "outraged" by the *Herald*'s accurate report of Trist's departure for Vera Cruz, but he was unable to discover the source of the leak.[21]

As prospects for a peace settlement increased, Bennett became erratic and inconsistent on the question of whether all of Mexico should be annexed. He stressed the American mission of regenerating Mexico. But mission or not, on the question of absorbing all of Mexico the *Herald* was, in Frederick Merk's description, "almost flighty in its frequency and suddenness of change. It seemed to wish to titillate, rather than to educate or persuade, its readers."[22]

On September 22, 1847, the *Herald* opposed the annexation of all of Mexico: "Her absorption would at present injure us, and scarcely ameliorate her condition. She must eventually be absorbed, but the longer that event is delayed the better." By October 8 Mexican absorption would be beneficial to Mexico: "Like the Sabine virgins, she will soon learn to love her ravisher." But by October 19 Bennett shifted again: "When the bride is reluctant, the marriage is generally ill-starred and unhappy." A week later he was urging a war of complete subjugation: "We must ride over them rough-shod; grind them to the dust; place the most onerous burdens upon them in the shape of taxes; crush them in every way; and we shall soon obtain whatever we may ask." Reluctantly Bennett concluded that the Mexican refusal to make peace imposed on the United States "the absolute necessity of subjugating and annexing her whole territory."[23]

The *Herald* was also flighty in its response to the Treaty of Guadalupe-Hidalgo. Before definite terms were clear, Bennett cautioned that Trist had disregarded his instructions so that the treaty was hardly worth the paper on which it was written. All of Mexico must be retained; the treaty was an "abomination." Three days later the *Herald* found the treaty "satisfactory" and considered it "a sublime spectacle of national magnanimity in not keeping possession of all of Mexico." But after another week, Bennett doubted that Mexico could survive the withdrawal of the American army. When this happened, England, France, and Spain would set up a monarchy in Mexico as a check on further United States expansion. The peace would last only until Mexico spent the $15 million she received in the treaty. Then "we may be ready for new purposes and new projects."[24]

The annexation of all of Mexico continued to be desirable and inevitable, and it would probably be the leading issue in the 1848 presidential campaign. Planning should start at once: "We may as well prepare for our destiny; and that destiny really seems to be, the annexation and final absorption of all Mexico. Possibly Canada, Cuba, and the other West Indies may follow; but one is enough at a time."[25]

The *Herald* supported expansion northward into the Oregon country with less zeal than it pressed for southward expansion. There was the same vacillation between a hard and a soft line as on the Mexican question, and when Bennett took an uncompromising hard line on Oregon it was part of his more general Anglophobia.

In 1842 the *Herald* hoped the Oregon question would be postponed; "it is not worth quarreling about." As late as 1844, when Calhoun took over the State Department, Bennett wanted him to compromise the Oregon question with England. But when Polk was elected on a platform calling for all of Oregon, Bennett approved to the point of writing a personal letter to him lauding the Oregon hard line in the Inaugural Address, especially our "clear & Unquestionable" title to all of the Oregon country.[26]

For the remainder of 1845 the *Herald* stood firm against any compromise: "We go for Oregon at all hazards. If war is to come, let it come." The next day the *Herald* repeated: "We are extremely sorry that we are likely to be driven to give Great Britain a sound drubbing. It is a sad, sad thing, to be obliged to whip one's own flesh and blood. But we can't help it."[27] In May, when war with Mexico loomed, the *Herald* beat a brief retreat to support of a compromise boundary, but by July "every inch of Oregon is ours and must be preserved." The need was not for the land but to force England to respect American rights: "The British government have not a particle of right to an inch of ground on this continent. Every foot of the continent is ours by prescriptive right."[28]

Bennett became a compromiser in early 1846, by then anticipating a war with Mexico and southward acquisitions: "The giving up now of a small portion of the Oregon territory, for the sake of having peace a few years longer, will not deprive the United States of the certainty of having all hereafter, together with all Canada, in due course of time." An offer from England of a boundary at forty-nine degrees should be accepted; an Oregon settlement was a necessary prelude to a commercial agreement with England. The compromise Oregon treaty that was negotiated and ratified had the *Herald*'s warm support.[29] Bennett, like the southern Democracy whose position he so often reflected, was willing to yield territory for northern free state expansion, but he was rigid on southwestern slave state expansion.

Once the Mexican cession and Oregon were secured, Bennett turned his attention to the acquisition of Cuba, and until the Civil War he pressed for the annexation of that island. It was only a matter of time before Spain would sell Cuba to the United States. "The Spanish race, on this continent, are destined to be displaced by the Anglo-Saxon."[30]

Repeating Polk's successful tactics that joined Texas and Oregon to attract both northern and southern support, Bennett now coupled Cuba and

Canada. Most Americans were continentalists in favor of annexing contiguous territory, he argued. "Poor imbecile" Spain could not hold Cuba in her "palsied grasp." Manifest Destiny was broadened to include "the gradual and complete subjugation of the whole continent and the adjacent islands."[31]

The *Herald* scored another diplomatic beat on the Cuba issue: Romulus M. Saunders, the American minister to Spain, had in September 1848 begun secret negotiations for the purchase of Cuba. Bennett's correspondent in Madrid had picked up rumors of these negotiations, and his report was published in the *Herald* on October 20. It caused a stir in London, Madrid, and Washington, but coming late in the presidential campaign in which Bennett was supporting Whig Zachary Taylor, most observers regarded the story as untrustworthy or denounced it as a politically motivated fraud. But corroborating evidence emerged when the secretary of the legation in Madrid returned home and aired the story of the purchase offer.[32]

Once again Bennett warned of British designs on Cuba, and he was critical of the Taylor administration's attempts to suppress filibustering expeditions to the island. By 1850 the filibusters that were being organized in the South seemed likely to succeed. "No Spanish Minister . . . nor a Secretary of State . . . can check the progress of certain movements which have begun in the Southern States, having for their object, at the proper time, a revolution in Cuba, and the annexation of that country." The farcical failure of Narciso Lopez's filibuster did not matter.[33]

Bennett decided to take a firsthand look at the Cuban situation. On November 25, 1850, he and his wife left for Havana on the steamer *Ohio,* and he sent back to the *Herald* his own detailed reports and Cuban newspapers. Despite efforts of Cuban officialdom to keep the Bennetts out of polite Cuban society, they did circulate and he described a gala social season.[34]

In late 1851 the editor was predicting that the annexation of Cuba would be the major plank in the Democratic party platform, with the Whigs certain of defeat because of the irresistible annexationist impulse. But the Cubans must throw off the Spanish yoke themselves; filibustering attempts would not succeed. Cuba would be acquired by sale, not by seizure, and the victory of Democrat Franklin Pierce in the 1852 election made it simply a matter of time. Cuba was growing "too hot [for Spain] to hold"; its acquisition would make enforcement of the Monroe Doctrine practical; it would end the African slave trade, chiefly centered in Cuba, and transplant the humane southern slave system to the island.[35]

Initially the *Herald* was warm in its support of the Pierce administration. Bennett was unhappy with the appointment of fellow New Yorker William L. Marcy as secretary of state but delighted with James Buchanan's selection as minister to England and "enthusiastically vociferous" about the appointment of expansionist Pierre Soulé as minister to Spain. Bennett warned Marcy of the danger of British abolitionist-inspired intervention in Cuba and the need to instruct Buchanan and Soulé to counter it.[36]

Then Bennett broke with the Pierce administration. The reason is clear. He asked Pierce to appoint him minister to France, where in Paris his wife and family lived most of the time and where the *Herald*'s main European bureau was located. If appointed, he promised to resign within a year because he could not leave the *Herald* for longer than that. He was wealthy and did not need the patronage. Rather, he needed the personal vindication of such an honor. "For more than twenty years," he told the president-elect, "bitter calumnies have been poured not only on my name and reputation but also over that of my family, my friends and my all. . . . [An] act of confidence extended by your administration towards me personally, such as I have indicated, might perhaps put the cap on the pyramid—the keystone in the arch, and place my calumniators where yours now are and where all such ought to be placed." Pierce delayed making an appointment to France until October 1853, when he gave it to Senator John Y. Mason of Virginia. From this point the *Herald* became a relentless critic of Pierce and his policies, domestic and foreign.[37]

Soulé was now portrayed in the *Herald* as a bull in a china shop. Bennett was getting accurate information about Cuban developments from his London correspondent George Sanders, a "Young America" expansionist who was the consul at London.[38] He learned that Spanish officials in Cuba had rashly forced a showdown when they seized an American steamer, *Black Warrior*, on a technicality. The *Herald* talked of war; "we have had enough of diplomatic messages to Spain." The navy should seize Havana until Spain made reparations. Meanwhile, the influx of American capital, merchants, newspapers, and spirit would double the value of the island. War with Spain was only a slight possibility, but it was preferable to an internal war over slavery in Cuba which might result in a free Negro state only a few miles from Florida.[39] Soulé should be recalled from Madrid: "We wanted an ambassador there, and we have sent a matador."[40]

Buchanan and Soulé had conferred secretly at Ostend with several other American diplomats. The most careful historian of the Ostend conference, Amos A. Ettinger, credits the *Herald* with "penetrat[ing] to the core of the matter. Hesitant at first as to its actual occurrence," he writes, "Bennett's newspaper was now replete with reference to the conference. In rapid succession, the *Herald* passed from rumor to fact, from fact to mild judgements, from mild judgements to stinging indictments of American diplomats." The source of the *Herald*'s reports was probably Sanders in London. An October 31 story accurately described the substance of the conference's report, the Ostend Manifesto: "What we must have is security for the future. This is to be found only in our possession of the island of Cuba. We tender to you twice the amount of its actual value. If you do not accept our proposal we must take the island."[41]

Before the Ostend business faded, in the spring of 1855, the *Herald* carried more information about it than any other newspaper. "Among the first in exposing the activities of the Ostend conference," says Ettinger, "it was the first journal to ascertain and print that gathering's conclusions, and the first to ask [for] a Congressional investigation, and publication of the documents."[42]

Bennett's attacks on the administration's inept Cuban policy did not mean that he had abandoned Cuban annexation. But he had little hope that Pierce would achieve it. "Had England been in our place, she would have tapped Cuba long ago, and the London *Times* would prove in a trenchant leader, that all men disapproving of the rape were enemies to civilization and blots on human nature. We can wait until Heaven sends us a President with nerve and backbone." If only Pierce would emulate Andrew Jackson's approach to the French spoliation claims: call a special session of Congress, detail what Spain owed the United States, and authorize reprisals on Spanish property, including Cuba. A bold, decisive, "dashing" policy was needed.[43]

The *Herald* continued to stress the twin dangers of abolition and "Africanization" in Cuba and British intrigue there. Convinced by England that abolition in Cuba would make the island unattractive to the United States, Spain would turn Cuba into a free black "desert" like Jamaica, or into another Haiti, and perhaps even part of a Negro confederation in the West Indies under the protection of the European powers. These prospects made Pierce's weakness the more deplorable. England and France were preoccupied in eastern Europe and would not act if the United States took a strong position in defense of its treaty rights and the rights of American citizens in Cuba.[44]

Bennett was hopeful that James Buchanan's election in 1856 would revive an effective Cuban policy. He stressed the advantages to the North of Cuban annexation: Cuban markets would be a boon to the northern economy, and the African slave trade, which was centered in Cuba, could be suppressed.[45] Buchanan should ask Congress for an appropriation to buy Cuba, and if convinced that the entire American nation supported annexation, Spain would be pressed by the European powers to sell. This is exactly what the president recommended to Congress in late 1858, and the *Herald* praised him and his supporters and chided the Republicans for their opposition. Cuba, like Texas in 1844, might prove to be the salvation of the Democratic party. But the Democracy did not rally around Cuba, and the Republican victory in 1860 relegated the island to a minor concern.[46]

Through the 1850s the *Herald* had pressed for the acquisition of more of Mexico with only a little less zeal than it pushed for Cuba. Plans were afoot in Baja California and Sonora to follow the example of Texas and declare their independence, and they would eventually be annexed. The Mexican republic was crumbling, unable to maintain order or execute treaty obligations, an open invitation to European intervention. "Of the final destiny of these Northern provinces, and indeed of all the provinces of Mexico, there can be little doubt. . . . Surely must the *debris* of the Mexican republic, as it tumbles to pieces, be absorbed by the Union."[47]

The situation was deteriorating rapidly, and the Gadsden Purchase had only delayed the inevitable. "In any event, the crisis is fast approaching when the issue must be between a European protectorate, or the absorption of our sister republic by the United States." The maintenance of the Monroe Doctrine and of the balance of power in the Caribbean required the annexation of Mexico. The Mexicans were incapable of self-government; only the "advent of Anglo-Saxonism" could provide Mexico with the statesmanship she needed.[48]

By 1855 the *Herald* was less concerned with Mexico. Now, next to Cuba, its major interest in the Caribbean was Nicaragua, where William Walker, the "grey-eyed man of destiny" and the most successful of the filibusters, had established himself. Bennett thoroughly approved of Walker's activities and gave them front-page coverage. Central America was plagued with decay and anarchy, and it was only a matter of time before it went the way of Texas. (The *Herald* compared Walker favorably with Sam Houston.) It was in the interest of the United States to support good government in Central America, and the Pierce administration should recognize Walker, who was in de facto control of the country.[49]

Walker's Nicaragua was soon at war with neighboring Costa Rica, but with El Salvador supporting Walker it was "highly probable that within a short period, under force of arms, the American movement will become a permanent power in the Isthmus States, which being consolidated, the left flank of Mexico will have been turned, and that republic placed literally in the hands of Anglo-Americans." Bennett continued his criticism of Pierce's refusal to recognize the Walker regime, which had more popular support there than Pierce did in the United States. "The Nicaragua movement is wholly Anglo-American in character, orderly in administration, just in principle, and beneficial in results."[50]

Through the spring of 1856 the *Herald* gave the war in Central America lavish coverage in both news and editorial columns. It continued to berate Pierce for nonrecognition; it lamented that many American citizens were being killed fighting with Walker; and it emphasized the strategic importance of Nicaragua for a direct route to the Pacific. There was no question that England was behind the Costa Rican effort — the bogey of John Bull's machinations again — and that Costa Rica was determined to annihilate the Anglo-Saxons in Central America. Despite the lack of support from Pierce, Walker won a decisive victory over Costa Rica by mid-1856, and the *Herald* was jubilant for its new hero.[51]

Then in the fall of 1856 Bennett retreated. He was supporting Republican John C. Frémont for president against the Democratic expansionist James Buchanan, and now he became critical of Walker. The *Herald* warned that Walker's decree legalizing slavery in Nicaragua was of a piece with Pierce's pushing slavery into Kansas. The slave-driving Democracy wanted Cuba and Central America as outlets for the surplus slaves of the upper South. Walker had promised law and order; instead, his regime was one of bloodshed. But his overthrow was unlikely because he was supported by the southern slavocracy, even though his Wall Street backers were divided and feuding.[52]

With Frémont defeated and Buchanan elected, Bennett quickly became reconciled to the new administration. He shifted his support back to Walker, now involved in a critical civil war. The *Herald* asked pro-Walker forces to unite to give Walker the victory that would be so beneficial to Nicaragua, hoping that he would then annex the rest of Central America to form "a great Anglo-American Confederacy in the tropics." The transit route was vital and was the source of the unrest. The *Herald* suggested that the United States intervene to occupy the transit route and guarantee it to all nations, but the Clayton-Bulwer Treaty prevented such action. The decay of the mixed-breed Central Americans was proceeding so rapidly, making Anglo-American domination and pacification there inevitable, that the administration should immediately abrogate the treaty.[53]

After Walker was defeated, Nicaragua dropped from the *Herald*'s attention for almost two years. In 1860 Walker led another filibuster to Nicaragua, and this time he was captured and executed. The *Herald* covered the event with sympathy, compared Walker to Garibaldi, printed in full Walker's last speech before his execution, and wrote finis on the filibustering era in America.[54]

Bennett was never so engrossed in expansionism that he missed an opportunity to criticize John Bull — for aggression against Brazil to enforce the ban on the African slave trade, for activities in Central America in violation of the Clayton-Bulwer Treaty, and for intervention in Santo Domingo in violation of the Monroe Doctrine.[55] French interventions in Santo Domingo, Sonora, and the Sandwich Islands were also scored, but more gently.[56] Bennett's chest-beating bellicosity disgusted at least one New Yorker, George Templeton Strong.

> I'm very sick and weary of the perpetually recurring newspaper announcements under the telegraphic head or in the truculent editorials of the New York *Herald* that the President and Cabinet have at length "concluded to take a decided stand" or to "forbid all further French or English intervention or interference in Central America." As if either France or England couldn't silence our brag at any moment by sending half a dozen of their spare war steamers to the Gulf, and drive us out with the naval tail between the national legs. Were I an Englishman or Frenchman I should long to give this braggart republic a wholesome lesson, a good vigorous pounding, without the gloves, that should teach it humility and decorum.[57]

One wonders how many other readers of the *Herald* had the same feeling. Frederick Merk, in his study of the jingo press of the period, especially the *Herald* and the *Sun,* argues that readers bought these papers for their freshness and news coverage and sensationalism "and not at all because their editorial views had deep-seated popular support." He doubts whether the papers stirred up much popular support for expansionism.[58]

All that can be said with certainty is that the *Herald*'s editorial support for expansionism did not alienate enough readers to make them stop buying the paper. Whatever its editorial policy, the *Herald* carried in its news columns complete and informed coverage of foreign policy. On occasion, the *Herald* did open its news columns to planted stories, as when Francis J. Grund placed a story, actually written by Buchanan himself, defending Buchanan's upholding of the Monroe Doctrine, which the *Herald* had criticized.[59] But in general the *Herald* was enterprising in its news of foreign affairs, as its many beats indicate. They reveal both inside sources of information and perceptive foreign correspondents. The *Herald*'s expansionist views were expressions of its prosouthern and proslavery attitudes, but this did not inhibit its coverage of diplomacy in the news columns.

5

National Issues

t is amazing to see the greed with which the *Herald* is snatched up and devoured on its earliest arrival here," a northern editor wrote to his newspaper from Washington in 1859, "and, what is worse, to see the simplicity of these Southern fellows who seem to pin their whole faith upon it. Where Northern men look at it only for amusement . . . Southern swallow it gravely with a sign and a knowing shake of the head."[1] Samuel Bowles was correct in his appraisal. The *Herald* was the North's most prosouthern newspaper. The antislavery movement coined a word, *doughface*, to malign northerners who were prosouthern. To them, Bennett was the most notorious of the doughface editors.

The *Herald* gave its readers extensive and impartial news coverage of the South, relatively free of editorial bias. Issues and stories concerning the South were usually given thorough treatment in the *Herald*, and a random sample indicates that items of southern news and opinion appeared almost every day.[2]

Bennett claimed that the *Herald* was independent in politics, and for the presidency he supported Democrats Jackson, Polk, and Pierce, Whigs Harrison and Taylor, and Republican Frémont. He criticized all of New York's state and local parties at one time or another with a blistering impartiality. Usually, however, he sided with the Hunker Democrats, the prosouthern faction. He was consistent in defending the rights of the South and its institution of slavery, in his belief in Negro inferiority, and in his view that the antislavery movement was the major threat to the Union.

Slavery was not an abstract institution to Bennett. He had seen it at first hand as a young man when he worked on the *Charleston Courier.* Not only had he made friends with slaveowning Carolinians, but he was in the city in the immediate paranoid aftermath of the Denmark Vesey conspiracy. From the time that he established the *Herald* in 1835 he warned against agitating the slavery question because it "is more calculated to shake

the pillars of this Union than any other ever introduced into Congress."
To avoid the danger, the North must agree that the South was right and
just in its approach to race relations. A recommendation by the governor
of South Carolina a few months later that abolitionists should be punished by death was "splendid and unanswerable."[3]

Bennett's views about slavery and abolition remained the same for the
next three decades, with several recurring themes. His basic premise was
white racial superiority and black inferiority. "The destiny of the Cauca-
sian or Anglo-Saxon race is to occupy the whole earth," he wrote in 1845.
"The African and Indian will gradually go out of existence in the process
of ages." The physical and mental inferiority of Negroes was clear (although the word *Negro* was seldom used in the *Herald; nigger* was the word
of choice). Blacks occupied the political and social position they did
"simply because the great Creator has made them an inferior race. In the
same community with the white man, the black, enslaved or emancipated,
must forever occupy a degraded position. In a community purely African,
even the civilized black relapses again to African indolence and barbarism."[4]

Comparisons of slaves with the free blacks of the North and the West
Indies were instructive. Bennett never tired of pointing to the fate of the
emancipated slaves of Haiti and Jamaica as proof "that the African race
is unfit for self-government in any civilized form." Based on the West Indian experience, what would be the result of emancipation in the South?
Most freedmen would never work or acquire property; the South would
no longer produce its great staples; thieves and beggars would multiply;
the plunder of southern granaries would lead to murder and famine; over
a million blacks would migrate to the North; northern whites would use
violence to prevent being overwhelmed by the black hordes; and the blacks
would be massacred in the end.[5]

The condition of free Negroes in the North showed that whenever free,
Negroes were reduced to a terrible state of degradation. Indeed, the mor-
tality rate of free blacks in New York City was so high that Bennett concluded that the race was dying out. In 1859 he suggested that northerners
come to their senses and reenslave the free blacks because Negroes could
survive in the United States only under slavery.[6]

Another recurrent theme was that "a more comfortable or happier race
does not exist in any portion of the world, among a laboring population
of that color, than will be found in the Southern States." Slaves were well
fed, well clothed, well housed, and had only light labor to perform; wit-
ness how rapidly they multiplied. "In truth, the negro race are loved by
the whites of the South, and the best proof of it is that they are taken
good care of."[7]

Bennett agreed with William J. Grayson that slaves were well off compared to white factory workers in the North and in England. Slaves had security and were provided with food, clothing, and shelter that ensured comfort and happiness. Sambo in his snug cabin did not suffer during the depression of 1857 as northern paupers did. The rash of strikes and violence in New England shoe factories proved how badly off those workers were. Bennett compared the holiday merriment of southern slaves with the desolation of oppressed white wage slaves of northern industry, employees of the likes of Henry Wilson, who used his sweated profits to support abolitionism. The irrepressible conflict was between northern capital and northern labor.[8]

Bennett repeated another staple of the proslavery argument, that slavery was beneficial to the northern economy. The South was thriving, exporting more than twice as much as the northern states although it had a much smaller population. This line was especially prominent during the crisis of 1860–61, when the *Herald* predicted economic ruin for the North if cut off from southern raw materials and markets. The North would then realize that its profits were based on southern staples.[9]

The *Herald*'s editor also argued, needlessly if slavery was so beneficent, that slavery had been introduced to the South by outsiders, Englishmen and Yankees, and that the slave trade had continued because of the greed of the New Englanders. Most shocking was the discovery that the free black republic of Liberia was engaging in the slave trade "and sold its fellow niggers, just the same as if it were a colony of white men." Bennett opposed the slave trade and any attempt to reopen it because it would depress the value of slaves in the upper South. Since the bulk of the illegal trade was with Cuba, the surest way to end the traffic was to annex the island.[10]

The *Herald* also championed the argument made by many moderate southerners that slavery had reached the natural limits of its expansion and would die out in the upper South. Within fifteen years Delaware, Maryland, Virginia, and Missouri would be free states for purely economic reasons. "These . . . are the agencies that are destined to settle the slavery question," Bennett said, "soil, climate, the pressure of population and immigration, and the solid argument of dollars and cents." Instead of exacerbating sectional conflict by insisting on expanding slavery into Kansas and New Mexico, southerners would do better to look to the tropics, where slavery would thrive.[11]

Bennett's opinion of abolitionism followed directly from his beneficent view of slavery. The *Herald* began attacking the abolitionists in its early issues in 1835, and it never relented. Eventually Bennett included the Free

Soilers, Seward Whigs, and Republicans in his assault. At bottom, they were all abolitionists. These impractical hypocrites, exciting the lazy and discontented blacks, had "a species of monomania." The most dangerous aspect of their fanaticism was that it contained "the germs of disaster and ruin to the American republic, the seeds of civil war, anarchy and insurrection."[12]

The abolitionists, Bennett believed, were part of an international conspiracy, centered in England, whose goal was to destroy America. Bennett was fond of conspiratorial explanations for this and other issues. "This is no fancied picture," he wrote in 1838. "We are on the brink of danger. . . . The abolitionists of England are operating here. *We know the fact.* Between now and the [state] election we shall develop a conspiracy that will astonish the whole union." The abolitionists were bringing free blacks to New York and arming them in preparation for a race war.[13] Yet Bennett would not condone violence against the abolitionists because such attacks made martyrs and only strengthened them. Antiabolition riots in northern cities were counterproductive.[14]

Consistent with his belief in Negro inferiority, Bennett opposed extension of the franchise to blacks and integrated education in the North. In New York in 1846 and again in 1860 the *Herald* opposed constitutional amendments to remove the property qualification for Negro voting. Bennett doubted, in 1860, "whether a sufficient number of white men can be found in this state willing to consummate the act of self-degradation which will bring them down to the level of blacks, to the same political status as the niggers of the Five Points. We cannot believe it." Attempts to integrate the common schools of Massachusetts were "the ultra abolition doctrine of amalgamation."[15]

There is little doubt that Bennett's white working-class readers shared his racial prejudice. They had little to be thankful for, but their white skin did give them status in society. The *Herald* also reflected their resentment at philanthropy to blacks, when no one was helping them. The same antislavery politicians who would help the Negro, Bennett argued, were trying to curtail the liberties of whites, most notably by their campaign to enforce Sunday blue laws.

The most compelling reason for Bennett's prosouthern and proslavery position and his hatred of antislavery agitation was his firm Unionism, his belief that attacks on the constitutional guarantees granted to the South by the Founding Fathers would lead to secession and the breakup of the Union. This fear would account for his tendency to champion moderates regardless of party and his concern to maintain a political and sectional balance. He was very fearful of the sectional conflict that developed in the 1850s. Bennett was a fire-eater in print but not in the real world.

Bennett and the *Herald* took a southern view on all prominent national questions, especially southward expansion. He was an advocate of independence for Texas, the annexation of Texas, war with Mexico, the seizure of California, the acquisition of all of Mexico, and annexation of Cuba.

Bennett's estrangement from Martin Van Buren led him to remain neutral in the 1840 campaign, and "the *Herald* became the first newspaper in journalistic history to give equal prominence to both candidates." By election day he endorsed William Henry Harrison as the lesser evil. Bennett was more enthusiastic about Harrison's successor after a month, John Tyler. The accidental president was a Virginian, and the *Herald* became an important part of the "corporal's guard" of his supporters. Tyler's crusade for Texas annexation endeared him to Bennett, and the *Herald*'s support of Tyler's opposition to Whig domestic policies resulted in its acquiring direct access to news sources in the White House. But Tyler was unable to form a party around his administration and had no chance of nomination in 1844 so Bennett supported James K. Polk and his expansionist program. [16]

The editor took a southern position on other issues that arose after the Mexican War. The *Herald* had backed James K. Polk in 1844, but despite Polk's support of the war and his opposition to the Wilmot Proviso, Bennett's support of the president was always lukewarm. By 1848 the *Herald* favored the Whig nominee, Zachary Taylor, a plain man uncorrupted by politics, an independent rather than a party man, whose election Bennett hailed as a great popular revolution against the party system. [17]

An important reason for the *Herald*'s support of Taylor was its belief that a politically independent southerner (Taylor was from Louisiana) could best settle the vexing question of slavery in the Mexican cession. But after mild initial backing of Taylor's plan to do nothing except admit California and New Mexico as states when they were ready, Bennett soon disavowed the plan as a "purgatory" and called for a compromise that would "be based on the same equality of representation among the slave States and the free States which now exists in the Senate." When Henry Clay introduced his own compromise plan on January 29, 1850, the *Herald* praised Clay's proposals as "sufficient . . . to calm and quiet all those intelligent minds who have the courage to meet the question openly, and endeavor to settle it on the principles of equality, of compromise, of good sense, and practical discretion." [18]

Bennett was unflagging in his support of the Compromise of 1850. Northern extremists opposed its passage, and he warned them that the "South are in earnest and the South are right" in opposing the Wilmot Proviso, which would exclude slavery from the entire Mexican cession. It would be unfair to shut southerners out of the new territories which they had done so much to win. The *Herald* took seriously the pressures from the southern rights convention at Nashville. After a study of one hundred southern newspapers, Bennett concluded that the vast majority of southerners supported the convention for the purpose of reflection and consultation rather than action; it was a Unionist body "resolved upon the maintenance of the constitution, while they preserve the rights of the South and the integrity of the Union." He continued to blame fanatics for opposition to the compromise, and he was delighted in September when the individual measures of the package passed Congress, putting "a *quietus* . . to the ultras and fanatics."[19]

Disillusioned with the Whigs, who were the captives of northern ultras such as William H. Seward, Bennett supported Franklin Pierce in 1852 with some enthusiasm, and he viewed Pierce's sweeping victory as a rejection of disunionism. He was soon disappointed. Bennett broke with the administration in the fall of 1853, charging that it had abandoned the compromise and had appointed free-soil extremists from the North and disunion extremists from the South to all patronage positions. The real cause was Bennett's failure to receive the French mission.[20]

The break with Pierce did not alter Bennett's enthusiasm for the policies of the southern Democrats. He implored the North to obey the new Fugitive Slave Law. He pressed for locating a Pacific railway along the extreme southern route. He opposed homestead legislation as a "bribe" that was "iniquitous, dangerous, corrupting and destructive in its tendencies."[21]

Most important, Bennett backed the Kansas-Nebraska Act under which popular sovereignty would supersede the Missouri Compromise prohibition of slavery in the new territories of Kansas and Nebraska. He praised Stephen A. Douglas's proposal because the issue was clear: "Shall the citizens of new territories enjoy the same rights on entering the Union as the old States enjoyed?" It was a new compromise, providing the Nebraska Territory for the North and the Kansas Territory for the South, entirely consistent with the Compromise of 1850. Bennett emphasized that the measure would settle the slavery question permanently and silence the agitators, and he was exultant when the bill passed.[22]

He did not foresee the events to come in "bleeding Kansas." Bennett took a prosouthern position on Kansas until the summer of 1856. He deprecated stories of violence there as abolitionist propaganda; he believed that a majority of the settlers were southerners; and he predicted that Kansas would become a slave state. Justice to the South required that new states be admitted in pairs to maintain the balance in the Senate, and the *Herald* backed Robert Toombs's bill for the immediate admission of Kansas as a slave state. The North could afford to sacrifice Kansas in return for sectional peace.[23]

When violence spread to the Senate floor and Senator Charles Sumner was struck down by Congressman Preston Brooks of South Carolina, the *Herald* blamed the assault on Sumner's offensive "Crime against Kansas" speech. But like the antiabolition riots, the assault only made a martyr of Sumner, a victim of "the intense and revolting evil of party niggerism."[24]

By this time the Kansas issue had become enmeshed in presidential politics and Bennett was promoting Republican John C. Frémont. Now the *Herald* saw Pierce's Kansas policies as border ruffianism and the Democratic nominee James Buchanan pledged to perpetuate them. The solution was to elect Frémont and give him a free hand on Kansas. Congress should supersede the spurious territorial legislature and its bogus laws, but the Democrats were determined to make Kansas a slave state. "Fremont's election is the only remedy for this democratic ruffian despotism which now reigns supreme over Kansas and over the Southern States."[25]

His support of Frémont in 1856 was the most curious of Bennett's political aberrations. Parties were in a state of flux following the Kansas-Nebraska excitement, and Bennett regarded the political reorganization as wholesome. During 1855 he had hoped that the Know-Nothing party might answer the need for a new conservative national party. At the same time, the *Herald* attacked the new Republican party as an antislavery coalition intent on destroying the slavery compromises in the Constitution and pitting North against South. Bennett could see no difference between a Republican, usually called a "nigger worshipper" in the *Herald,* and an abolitionist.[26]

By early 1856 Bennett began to despair of any of the parties doing anything constructive. The Know-Nothings were divided and impotent, the Democrats were controlled by "Southern niggerism," and the coming election appeared to be between northern Republican "nigger worshippers" and southern Democratic "nigger drivers." The Democratic nomination of Buchanan confirmed Bennett's feelings. He had conferred with Buchanan on one of his European visits and had been assured by the Pennsylvanian that he was not a candidate for president. Bennett felt betrayed when he announced for the office. More important, Bennett despised Philadelphia editor John Forney, who was leading the Buchanan campaign and would become his editorial spokesman if he were elected.[27]

The solution was an independent candidate who, like Taylor in 1848, would be uncontaminated by partyism. John C. Frémont was Bennett's choice. He suggested Frémont to the Republican convention (which the *Herald* was calling the "fusion convention") as "a fresh man . . . a man of fine education and fine talents, who has no personal or party grudges to reconcile, no old speeches or resolutions to cripple him. . . . Opposed to the extension of slavery, he is not a nigger worshipper."[28]

Bennett championed the young explorer after his nomination, not feeling at all strange with his new Republican bedfellows. Frémont represented sectional peace and prosperity and the admission of Kansas as a free state, which a majority of its settlers favored. He was a new candidate, uncontaminated by the old party corruptions or by sectionalism; he was detested by Seward and the antislavery ultras; and he had considerable support in the upper South, making him less sectional than Buchanan, who had little northern support. In other words, Frémont was the most Unionist and the least party-bound of the candidates. But Frémont, who was never referred to as a Republican in the *Herald,* was the only Republican on the ticket Bennett endorsed.[29]

In describing southern ultraism as "niggerism" and southern Democrats as "nigger drivers," words that seem out of character with his racism, the editor was concerned with preventing sectional strife, not abandoning his southern position. But as the election neared, Bennett became pessimistic about Frémont's chances, and he began hedging. If Buchanan selected a conservative cabinet and adopted a national, conciliatory policy, his administration would have the *Herald*'s cordial support.[30]

Having cleared the way, Bennett gave the Buchanan administration his support; his earlier abuse of Buchanan was forgotten as the sectional crisis intensified. Bennett was enthusiastic about the Dred Scott decision, "wise, just and right," which settled the territorial question forever and destroyed the revolutionary program of his recent allies, the Republicans.[31]

Kansas remained a critical problem, and Bennett's position was circuitous. At first he reiterated the inevitability of Kansas becoming a free state because of its soil and climate, the clear majority of northern settlers, and Buchanan's wise determination not to interfere. The appointment of Robert J. Walker as territorial governor was proof of the administration's determination to do justice in Kansas. The editor was certain that both Buchanan and Congress would require popular ratification of a Kansas constitution. Slavery was of no practical consequence there, and the free state party's victory in the 1857 territorial elections closed the question. But the Lecompton constitutional convention in a "Sweeping Coup d'Etat" tried to force a slave state constitution on Kansas by the devious strategy of submitting only the question of slavery or no slavery to the Kansans, a meaningless choice because the body of the constitution protected slavery. With a decided three-to-one free state majority in Kansas, support of the Lecompton Constitution would be "the political death warrant of every responsible Northern man."[32]

Then Bennett changed his position. The submission of the slavery or no slavery question rather than the entire constitution was not important. Even if Kansas was admitted as a slave state, it could promptly amend its constitution and become a free state. When Buchanan adopted this position, Bennett backed it as the most certain way to quiet the agitation over Kansas. The continuing trouble was caused by the meddling of Douglas and Walker, who were linked in a conspiracy to ruin the administration by keeping the issue alive.[33]

By 1858 the South's insistence that Kansas be admitted as a slave state seemed a simple act of justice to Bennett. The admission of several new free states was imminent, and the real question was the balance of power in the Senate. Admission of Kansas as a slave state would restore southern confidence in the Union and remove any danger of southern secession. Once again, Unionism and the need to preserve the sectional balance instituted by the Founding Fathers seemed to determine Bennett's position. What had the North to lose? The acceptance of the Lecompton Constitution left the people of Kansas free to to as they pleased. What was important was to end the imbroglio by admitting Kansas. When the English bill passed Congress, a compromise requiring the resubmission of the Lecompton Constitution to the Kansas voters, the *Herald* accepted it. No matter what Kansas decided, the agitation was ended.[34]

By 1859 Bennett had become almost hysterical over the deepening sectional crisis and the widening rift in the Democratic party. He interpreted Hinton R. Helper's *Impending Crisis,* for example, as advocating forcible abolition, and he was shocked when leading Republicans endorsed the book.[35] Then John Brown struck at Harpers Ferry. Bennett described the foray as a well-organized Negro insurrection, and he believed that leading abolitionists and Republicans participated in the conspiracy. The final responsibility was Seward's: "The brigand epoch of the 'irrepressible conflict' has been inaugurated." Bennett stressed, however, that not a single slave had come forward to join Brown voluntarily, proof of the beneficence of the slave system. Bennett had come a long way since his association with the Republicans in 1856. Now he viewed them as traitors, revolutionaries who would leave the South no choice but secession in the event of Republican victory in 1860.[36]

Bennett did not go to the other extreme. He opposed southern ultras and extremist proposals by such fire-eating sheets as the *New Orleans Delta* and the *Charleston Mercury.* The *Herald* also criticized the annual southern commercial conventions as impractical gatherings of extremists for the purpose of agitation. "The South needs industry, agriculture, and rational mercantile and industrial enterprise; it does not need speeches or buncombe, or trash about disunion . . . or fraternal embraces between political pickpockets." Bennett deprecated southern disunion talk in general and specifically proposals by the ultras such as reopening the African slave trade. He was convinced that a majority of southerners were moderate and that they remained strongly attached to the Union.[37]

The election of a Republican president would alter this situation abruptly. As early as February 1857, Bennett predicted that "we shall have, in 1860, the most terrible sectional contest that the confederacy has ever endured." Occasionally in the months before the 1860 election, the *Herald* hoped for a Democratic split and two opposition parties, making it a four-way "scrub race" to be decided in the House, where a Republican could not be elected. Or perhaps a new national conservative party would be formed of moderates of both sections and nominate someone like Sam Houston or Winfield Scott.[38]

Sometimes Bennett indulged in the wishful thinking that the Democrats would rally behind the conservative Unionist program of Buchanan or even draft Old Buck for another term, but usually the editor believed that southern extremists controlled the party and would control the Charleston convention. This was lamentable but understandable; "thirty years of anti-slavery agitation at the North has at last culminated in a crisis which has driven the South to the wall and compels it to stand at bay." As the Charleston convention approached, Bennett rested all his hopes on it. "Let us now use the dirty materials of which the democratic party is composed, and when we whip the Republicans with it, and put down revolution, then let us turn our attention to the purification of the Democracy."[39]

The Democrats did not take Bennett's advice. The Charleston convention broke up and failed to reunite when it reconvened in Baltimore, resulting in two Democratic tickets, all because of the meaningless abstraction of slavery extension that was pressed by Douglas and his free-soil wing. The nomination of Abraham Lincoln by the Republicans deepened Bennett's gloom. The rail-splitter was "a third rate Western lawyer . . . a fourth rate lecturer, who cannot speak good grammar . . . [and] in his anti-slavery opinions . . . the most ultra and revolutionary of all the candidates" at the Republican convention, "an extreme abolitionist."[40]

The *Herald* initially backed John C. Breckinridge as the best hope to defeat Lincoln, but in August it shifted to John Bell as the only truly national candidate, the only man around whom all anti-Republicans could rally. Fusion was the only way to defeat Lincoln, but even hysterical predictions, ultimately accurate, that Lincoln's election meant certain southern secession did not bring the divergent forces together into a fusion ticket in most places.[41]

After Lincoln's election, Bennett counseled against rashness: "Secession is revolution, and what the South is now considering is the policy of using the sacred right of revolution in self-defense." The South must be reassured that it was not in danger by a conservative statement from Lincoln and by an outpouring of support for a constitutional convention to suggest amendments that would protect the rights of the southern minority. Coercion of the South was impossible, even after South Carolina seceded in December and seized federal property within the state. Nine-tenths of the northern population opposed coercion and loathed the prospect of civil war. When the war came in April 1861, Bennett blamed it on abolitionist "nigger worship" and on Lincoln's aggressive coercion of South Carolina.[42]

Then there was a breeze of optimism in the *Herald*. Perhaps the loss of the South would result in a new northern confederation with Canada. At least the war would be short and salutary. After a few battles both sides would return to their senses, and the end result would be the purification of the corrupt party system.[43]

What is the significance of Bennett's doughface stance? The *Herald* had the largest circulation of any paper in the nation by 1860 so its views were widely disseminated. Because of its prosouthern stance it is understandable that the *Herald* was the favorite northern exchange paper reprinted in southern newspapers. It was also one of the new northern journals that circulated freely in the South after early 1860, when an embargo interdicted many northern newspapers. Southerners learned what northerners were thinking from the newspaper exchanges, and they must have gleaned a strange picture of northern attitudes from the *Herald*.[44]

Moreover, because Bennett's bite was so sharp, politicians were concerned about what he said. Buchanan, for example, was distressed by Bennett's attacks during the 1856 campaign and so delighted with the *Herald*'s shift after the election that he took the risk of inviting Bennett and his wife to dinner and to his last White House reception.[45] Lincoln was also concerned about Bennett's opinion; if he had time to read a newspaper, "it was likely to be the New York *Herald*," which in 1860 he tried to neutralize because Bennett "is powerful for mischief. He can do us much harm if hostile."[46]

Bennett's prosouthernism made him normally a Hunker Democrat in local, state, and national politics. Although he veered from this line occasionally in local and state politics and he did not support Democratic presidential candidates in 1840, 1848, or 1856, he was usually in the party of Andrew Jackson, which was also the party of southern slaveholders. He was earnest in his doughface position and consistent in his support of the Union as it was, with full recognition and protection of slavery and with a sectional balance in the Senate.

But the tone of his prosouthernism need not have been so shrill. This tone was part of his sensationalism. His coverage of the "nigger worshippers," of Cuffee and Sambo and Uncle Tom, and of the black insurrectionists in the West Indies was aimed at arousing his readers' interest in the same way an account of a bloody murder or prizefight would. These readers undoubtedly shared his racist attitudes and liked the *Herald*'s strident tone. Bennett did not misjudge his audience; it was as doughfaced as he was.

Another constant in the *Herald*'s attitudes toward national affairs was its encouragement of economic development without government interference, of a laissez-faire policy the Jacksonians had advocated. As on other issues, Bennett had a tendency to explain economic happenings by a theory of conspiracy.

Bennett always believed that economic analysis was his special forte, and from the beginning he made his *Herald* a pioneer in economic news and analysis, especially of the financial scene, through his Wall Street column and soon through a regular financial page. He explained the purpose of his Wall Street column: "The spirit, pith, and philosophy of commercial affairs is what men of business want. Dull records of facts, without condensation, analysis, or deduction, are utterly useless. The philosophy of commerce is what we aim at, combined with accuracy, brevity, and spirit."[47]

His economic position was no doubt a result of his education in Adam Smith and the economic philosophers of the Scottish Enlightenment, his own success in the *Herald* with a cash-and-carry, no-credit policy, and his sympathy with the strict construction, anti–American System views of the southern Democrats. In his analysis he made the distinction noted by Marvin Meyers in his study of the Jacksonians between the "real people" who relied on hard currency and the cash system, and the "money power" of paper, credit, and speculation.[48]

Before he began the *Herald,* Bennett had been a regular contributor on finance and banking news to the *Courier and Enquirer* and the *Pennsylvanian,* and he had sent Nicholas Biddle a great deal of advice. In general, he had taken a pro-Jackson and antibank position, although he had often been devious in his attempts to obtain a loan from Biddle. With the Bank of the United States winding up its affairs in preparation for its demise at the time the *Herald* was established in 1835, it was natural that Bennett should devote some attention to the banking situation.

As early as August 31, 1835, the *Herald* warned that trouble was on the way and that the process of liquidation of the branches of the Bank of the United States was putting great pressure on New York City banks and stockbrokers. He noted on his daily rounds on Wall Street that "the crowd is increasing—business is increasing—everything is increasing but specie and real money." The prospects were not good: "What a flourishing year we might have, if the government and U.S. Bank—General Jackson and Mr. Biddle would shake hands and be friends! The very thing now that mars the prospect is the winding up of the Bank." There was a noticeable increase in stockjobbing and gambling after the central banking restraints of the bank were eliminated.[49]

When the expiring Bank of the United States was given a state charter by Pennsylvania early in 1836, the situation changed. Now the administration would be forced to establish a new national bank, headquartered in New York City and capitalized at $50 million. "This country is earnestly a banking country. We live by banks—we breathe by banks—we sleep by banks—we fatten by banks—we are ruined by banks—and we are resuscitated by banks." The current crisis had been triggered by an increasing surplus revenue in the national treasury, which was causing the speculation that would lead to a collapse of the banking system. The destruction of the national bank had hastened the crisis; the creation of another national bank might delay it.[50]

But the distribution of the surplus revenue to the states in 1836 was an "act of wickedness and corruption," and Bennett was critical of Jackson for not vetoing the distribution bill. The best way to reduce the surplus was to reduce the tariff. Bennett denied that he was probank because he called for another bank.

> The great principle on which this Journal was established is directly the antagonist of all banks—the very antipodes of the very principle of banking. The New York Herald is entirely conducted on the *cash system*. We never had, and never will have the slightest favor from any bank. We despise incorporated banks and bankers. The business of banking should be free to all. Incorporating only makes them a purse-proud, contemptible, ignorant, empty race of men. . . .
>
> The chartered banking system has woven this country in a web of credit. It has destroyed the liberty of the press and checked the very thoughts of men.

A few days later Bennett attacked the banking system again for stimulating speculation. After this warning he returned to his original diagnosis, that the surplus revenue was the major cause of the speculation and the deranged currency.[51]

The most dangerous speculation was the overtrading in land. "Real estate is the monomania of 1836-7. Real estate has swelled the surplus —made the western merchants mad—increased the interest of money— doubled the exchanges—and shaken the whole fabric of commerce in this country and in Europe—Farmers have become speculators instead of tillers of the soil." A crisis in real estate was approaching. But happily, a tariff cut that would sharply reduce the revenue seemed likely. "This is the wisest movement we have yet seen attempted in Congress. . . . We hail it as the first glimmer of day."[52]

The tariff reduction did not materialize, and Bennett became gloomy again. About two thousand bank directors controlled the "whole legislation of the Union" and both political parties, he wrote. As a result, the great mass of people were suffering: "The banks furnish with means the speculator in houses—the speculator in flour—the speculator in beeves and cattle. The banks, after stealing away, in the name of democracy, the privileges of the people for a season, then turn round, aid and support the leeches who prey on these very people."[53]

By late March 1837, a major panic had begun. The *Herald* urged the new president, Martin Van Buren, to call a special session of Congress immediately to lower the tariff and repeal the distribution law. The problem began, Bennett reiterated, with the surplus revenue that was first created by high tariffs and then magnified by distribution. Meanwhile, the state legislature could help by chartering a bank in New York City to deal in foreign and domestic exchanges. The nation was looking to New York for leadership in the crisis.[54]

On May 3 Bennett dealt at length with the causes of the panic. "One thing alone has produced it, and that is *underploughing*. . . . Millions of acres have been bought—but it was not purchased to plough, only to sell again, and make a quick dash, and cut a figure on." The mania started in 1829 with Martin Van Buren's safety fund banking system in New York, the first "union of politics and banking—politics and speculation in this state." Van Buren was also to blame for the destruction of the Bank of the United States and the "wild, unregulated banking" it stimulated. "The Democrats opposed all banking in Congress but carried it to all lengths in the states." Bennett concluded his analysis on a moralistic note, calling for a return to "tilling the earth instead of selling it—to ploughing the soil instead of lithographing it—to dwelling in the country instead of starving and agitating in the large cities—to living a moral, pious, and quiet life instead of indulging in all sorts of licentiousness and immorality."[55]

In May all the banks in New York suspended specie payments, refusing to redeem their notes for specie as the law required. Bennett charged that this step was "legalized and chartered swindling, without a parallel in the annals of crime and imposture." The enormity of the crime was increased because the banks had over $40 million in specie in their vaults. Perhaps the creation of another national bank would force the resumption of specie payments. Bennett was willing to try this solution in the face of the rottenness of the state banking and paper currency system. At least Congress should create a central agency, whatever it was named, to control the currency and public finance. But Van Buren, who should have been pressing Congress to pass a general free banking law, a bankruptcy law, a reorganization of the Treasury Department, the issuance of treasury notes to assist commerce, and a reduction of the tariff, was doing nothing. He was stirring up popular feeling against the banks and paper money while indulging in the same paper money manipulation he was denouncing. It was a "species of the sublimest machiavellism without a parallel in history."[56]

By August the *Herald* saw no excuse for the banks' refusal to resume specie payments. They had been wrong in suspending in a body, and only resumption could restore public confidence in them. Again Bennett argued that another national bank in New York City could force a resumption. But Van Buren's message to the special session of Congress was disappointing. It was "cunningly devised," but it would throw the mercantile community "entirely on its own resources. This will cause a new crisis — a further depression of stocks — more failures — and continued conflict among the banks." Politics had been reduced to the question of banks or no banks.[57]

Then a month later, in a turnabout, Bennett supported "Separation of Bank from State" in a lead editorial endorsing Van Buren's proposed independent treasury system. "Let them be separated forever. Let the government go on its own hook — and so let the banks do. Destroy all surplus revenue. Give the government the power to collect taxes equivalent to its expenses, and no more."[58]

Bennett's endorsement of a hard-money, antibank position was an aberration. After his vigorous support of the independent treasury plan, a month later Bennett concluded that Van Buren's only hope politically was to abandon the hard-money Democrats and recommend establishment of another national bank. Such a bank would be an effective manager of the money power of the nation, but the independent treasury system would not.[59]

Bennett did concede that Van Buren made an able and forceful argument in support of the independent treasury in his December 1838 annual message, but the editor also printed a letter from Nicholas Biddle with a very different prescription for the current financial woes which the *Herald* praised as a calm and philosophic analysis. "Hereafter Mr. Biddle will occupy his natural position—the first financier—and first statesman in this country. If we could get such a man for President of the U.S., what a treasure it would be!" Biddle was praised again for his speculation in southwestern cotton in an attempt to bolster cotton prices, "putting in motion the clogged wheels of trade and benefitting the whole country." This was in "contrast to the narrowminded and selfish policy of those Wall Street institutions, who took the financial affairs of the country upon their shoulders, under the pet bank system, and whose loud vauntings ended in failure."[60] Bennett's praise for Biddle is difficult to explain. The *Herald* was prospering, and Bennett did not need a loan from the banker. Perhaps he simply admired the way Biddle earlier had restrained the overexpansion of bank credit to finance speculation. In any event, the praise did not last very long.

Recovery had been well under way and the banks had resumed specie payments when another suspension occurred in October 1839, started by all the banks in Philadelphia, including Biddle's. There was no excuse for the "disgrace and dishonor" of these institutions, led by the "gross and wicked mismanagement" of Biddle. They had destroyed American credit in Europe. Bennett hoped that New York's banks would refuse to go along with the suspension and would assert their financial leadership in the new crisis.[61]

Bennett believed the economic crisis could be resolved by a Whig victory in the 1840 national elections: "This country will never be free from financial disorder till a national bank be established, and every event is rapidly tending to produce this result in the public mind. An anti-commercial, anti-banking, anti-social, anti-Christian government never can be permanent in this land." Disorder in the credit system would continue until Harrison was elected.[62]

The hopes that accompanied Harrison's victory were short-lived because of the president's death in April 1841. Bennett immediately attached himself to the new president, John Tyler, and became part of the "corporal's guard" of consistent Tyler supporters against Henry Clay and the Whigs in Congress. The conflict between the two groups centered on economic policy: Clay wanted another national bank, a protective tariff, and a distribution bill, and Tyler opposed these measures. Harrison's victory in 1840 had been a personal mandate, Bennett explained, not a mandate for Whig party measures. The editor had shifted ground again in opposing a national bank, but consistency did not concern him. "And as to a uniform currency, the experience of New England shows conclusively that well-regulated, healthy, local institutions, are abundantly capable of supplying a circulating medium."[63]

Indeed, Clay's proposals for a national bank, distribution, and repeal of the independent treasury system, which he introduced in a special session of Congress, "tend to one vast result — *an entire revolution in the present commercial system of the country, and a forced change of nearly $200,000,000 out of capital from one series of channels to another.*" Clay's plan was "a continuation of the experiments in the currency which have agitated the country for the last ten years, and precipitated thousands and thousands into utter ruin." The Whigs were becoming divided with Tyler, Secretary of State Daniel Webster, and Secretary of the Treasury Thomas Ewing on one side and Clay and the congressional Whigs on the other. Clay was leading Congress like Napoleon marching on Moscow. But Tyler was certain to veto a national bank, and this veto was the "only obstacle to the entire success of the speculator's plan, of a great bank for purposes of plunder."[64]

Bennett's advice was that Congress pass neither Clay's bank bill nor Ewing's plan for a government "fiscal agent" but simply repeal the independent treasury system and pass a general bankruptcy law. The country would be on a sound financial basis as soon as the banks began paying specie. The vultures were flocking to Washington because Clay's plan would make the rich richer and the powerful more so. When a watered-down version of Clay's bank bill passed Congress, Bennett predicted a Tyler veto of the "miserable hermaphrodite," which would cause most of the cabinet to resign. "The reign of party shackles and party delusion is at a close. John Tyler kills the monster — and the country is free." Clay's program was "one of the finest pieces of machinery *for taxing the poor for the benefit of the rich — for taking away the property of the real owners and giving it to the speculator — that ever was devised.*"[65]

The cabinet, except for Webster, resigned after Tyler vetoed a bank bill in September, as Bennett had predicted. The *Herald* praised the veto: Tyler had broken the stranglehold of the financiers and speculators on the people. Bennett gloated that several Whig papers were blaming the *Herald*'s influence with the president for the veto. In contrast to the Wall Street papers, which were agents of the stockjobbing conspiracy, Bennett pointed out, his *Herald* "has invariably taken the high American, the purely republican, the strictly honest side of the question. It has been against paper money — against stock-jobbing *cliques* — against public debts — because such a policy would destroy American liberty, and place this glorious republic at the foot of the brokers of monarchy in Europe."[66]

Bennett also supported Tyler on other matters at issue with the congressional Whigs. The editor favored a continuation of the general bankruptcy law (which was repealed in March 1843); he organized public meetings in New York City in behalf of the unfortunate bankrupts. In addition, he backed Tyler's issuance of $15 million in treasury notes to relieve the currency shortage.[67]

The other questions, distribution and the tariff, were closely connected. The final cuts in the 1833 compromise tariff that were due to take effect in 1842 would reduce government revenue, and in response the Whigs pressed for a large increase in the tariff duties. They also proposed that the proceeds of land sales be distributed to the states, which would require increased tariff duties. Bennett supported the president's opposition to this package. There was no need for protective tariffs; manufacturing had never been so prosperous. "The only danger is to be apprehended from the influence of the foreign stockjobbing interest, who would like very much to have a high tariff, yielding a surplus revenue to be divided among the states, in order to benefit their mad speculations in state stocks."[68]

When Tyler proposed a modest tariff increase without distribution, the *Herald* called it a "great, open, noble, and important step." The president's veto of a high tariff bill that was tied to distribution delighted the mass of honest people. Bennett likened the courage and practicality of the veto message to "the iron nerves of 'Old Hickory.'"[69]

Bennett and the *Herald* remained in the anti-Whig camp on economic questions for the rest of the antebellum period. He had supported Polk in 1844 and backed his plans to lower the tariff and reestablish the independent treasury system which the Whigs had abolished in 1841. On the latter issue, the subtreasury, Bennett was only mildly supportive. The most important need was for the treasury to operate on a specie basis and accept and pay out only gold and silver. But the subtreasury proposal was better than the existing system and would provide a check on currency expansion. Its passage in 1846 ended the evil and corrupting influence of banks over public finance.[70]

There was no need for high tariffs, Bennett argued; they led to a surplus revenue that was removed from the active capital of the nation. Industry was so strong that it did not need protection. The *Herald* endorsed efforts of Polk and the Democratic Congress to reduce the high Whig duties of 1842. The resulting Walker Tariff of 1846 was a move in the direction of free trade and an important victory.[71] Bennett's views on the tariff, of course, were those of the southern Democrats.

In 1855 the Democrats tried unsuccessfully to make further tariff reductions, and Bennett supported the move as an encouragement to foreign trade. It was a fallacy that industry needed protection; past experience demonstrated that high tariffs brought distress, not prosperity. Another attempt at reduction the following year also won the *Herald*'s support, and a moderate reduction was legislated in 1857. The volume of foreign trade would continue to increase as a result.[72]

The multifaceted internal improvements issue was also important to Bennett. In general, he favored improvements in transportation, especially more rapid transit to the Pacific, but by the late 1850s his political antagonism to Stephen A. Douglas led him to oppose a Pacific railway when it was proposed by the Illinois senator. Bennett's position on internal improvements, as on most questions, echoed the southern view.

Bennett was distressed at American failure to establish transatlantic steamship lines, with the result that Atlantic steamers were a virtual British monopoly. Therefore, he favored a subsidy to the American Collins Steamship Company, the only possible rival of the British Cunard line. The *Herald* criticized Pierce's shortsightedness in vetoing aid to the Collins line. When the subsidy was ended by Congress in 1858, Bennett feared that the line would be abandoned. The false economy of the United States was in marked contrast to the British support of Cunard. England and France would now monopolize both transatlantic tariff and the transatlantic mails.[73]

The cheapest and most practical way to connect the Atlantic and the Pacific, Bennett argued, was to construct a railroad or canal across either the Isthmus of Tehuantepec or the Isthmus of Panama. Bennett also believed that a railroad to the Pacific was feasible. Cost should be no obstacle, nor should constitutional interpretation. A Pacific railway would secure the trade of Asia and make the United States commercially preponderant in the Far East.[74]

Bennett supported a Pacific railway until 1854, when the measure became connected with both Douglas and the Pierce administration. The editor had earlier recommended a way around constitutional objections to federal financing by a land grant to railroad companies, which would then build the road as a private undertaking. Then in 1854 Bennett set himself firmly against such proposals. They were mere speculation, he argued; such a railroad across the desert and the Rockies would not be needed for another fifty years. The scheme was a gigantic swindle by the corrupt railroads in league with the corrupt Pierce administration to rob the nation of its public domain.[75]

Congressional appropriations for wagon roads and military posts on the route to California and a plentiful supply of camels were all that was necessary for another half-century. Bennett repeated that the railroad scheme was a conspiracy, which included Douglas and his land speculators and Seward and his Albany ring. Congress should recover the public domain from the railroads rather than despoil more of it. A Pacific railway would not recover the construction costs. Most important, railroad overbuilding and corruption were threatening a general economic collapse, which came in 1857.[76]

But if Congress did authorize a Pacific railway, it should be constructed by a southern route, which topographically was the only practical one. A railroad across Texas and Arizona would be the shortest and cheapest. The federal government could build that portion of it that ran through the territories, and the states could construct the remainder.[77]

On another facet of the internal improvements issue, Bennett was apprehensive that New York State would bankrupt itself by lavish expenditures for canals. Supportive of canals generally, he nonetheless believed that New York had overextended itself in enlarging its canal system and that further enlargement should be financed out of canal revenues or by a direct tax. Failing that, the state should sell the system.[78]

Free homesteads on the public domain was another economic question of the 1850s that concerned the *Herald.* In 1850 Bennett favored a plan to give free homesteads to settlers as a means of easing the urban congestion caused by immigration. But within two years he saw the plan as a western scheme to squander the public domain, which the government needed for the revenue from the sale of land. Homestead legislation was a Seward and Greeley humbug, "iniquitous, dangerous, corrupting and destructive in its tendencies; . . . it offers a bounty to idleness and vagabondism, while to the industrious and prudent it turns a cold shoulder."[79]

When homestead legislation was endorsed by the Republican party in 1856, it seemed even more dangerous to Bennett. The public domain was a great source of fraud and corruption; it had a potential for evil even greater than the Bank of the United States. Homestead legislation was a delusion that would help the land monopolists but not the poor. The Homestead Bill, passed by Congress but vetoed by Buchanan, would have crippled the treasury. The poor lacked the capital to establish farms in the West even if the land was free. The whole business smacked of Republican demagoguery.[80]

Bennett had been wary of extravagant internal improvements and lax bank management for some time. From early 1855 he began to warn the *Herald*'s readers to be prudent, that hard times were coming. Several factors led him to predict the Panic of 1857 two years before it struck: enormous speculation in railroad stock; hostility between New York banks and western banks; the Crimean War, which would force England and France to liquidate their American holdings for specie; a grain surplus that would bring falling farm prices; bad weather in the South; and a shortage of agricultural laborers in the North because so many young men were migrating to California.[81]

By midsummer of 1856 the news from Europe became ominous, with reports of wild speculative schemes, grain shortages, and a massive specie drain caused by the Crimean War. And by late 1856 Bennett became anxious about fraud, speculation, and mismanagement on Wall Street, especially in railroad securities. Railroad and patent renewal lobbyists had never been so active. The speculative bubble was bound to burst, the *Herald* warned in December, with a probable repetition of the crash of 1837.[82]

The commercial prospects for 1857 were not bright. The balance-of-trade deficit was too large and European investors were becoming shy. The credit system had gotten out of hand and Americans would have to pay the penalty for extravagant living. A storm was coming. The symptoms were the same as in 1836–37 but on a grander scale. Speculation was rampant.[83]

"What can be the end of all of this," Bennett asked,

> but another general collapse like that of 1837, only upon a much grander scale? The same premonitory symptoms that prevailed in 1835–36 prevail in 1857 in tenfold degree. Government spoliations, public defaulters, paper bubbles of all descriptions, a general scramble for western lands and town and city sites, millions of dollars made or borrowed, expended in fine houses and gaudy furniture; hundreds of thousands in the silly rivalries of fashionable parvenues, in silks, laces, diamonds and every variety of costly frippery are only a few among the many crying evils of the day. The worst of all these evils is the moral pestilence of luxurious exemption from honest labor, which is infecting all classes of society. The country merchant is becoming the city stockjobber, and the honest country farmer has gone off among the gamblers in western land. Thus, as this general scramble among all classes to be rich at once, and by the shortest possible cut, extends and increases, our rogues, defaulters and forgers are multiplied. The epidemic and its attending evils must run their course.[84]

Although earlier Bennett had argued that the Crimean War and the gold production of California were important factors in the economic crisis, now he concentrated on the evils of speculation. Banks were investing too much in railroads. Then in August 1857, Leonard Jerome, an enterprising *Herald* financial reporter, examined old railroad reports and discovered that the Michigan and Southern Railroad had printed and pledged several hundred thousand shares of stock for a bank loan, trusting to future profits to retire the stock with no one the wiser. The news caused a sensation on Wall Street.[85]

The collapse of the Ohio Life Insurance and Trust Company in August triggered the Panic of 1857. Bennett tended to gloat; he had been predicting this crash for over a year, warning against overinvestment and speculation, but his warnings had been ignored. Now the banks that had invested their depositors' money in railroad stocks would be "wrecked and ruined in fortune."[86]

The responsibility for the panic was the speculators', and they would be the victims of their own foolishness. The economy was fundamentally sound, and the depression would benefit the poor by ending inflation and bringing down consumer prices. The country had learned a valuable lesson about the dangers of speculation, and the panic demonstrated the need for closer regulation of financial affairs. Bennett also made a political point: it was easy to see the connection between the defaulters and Seward's Republican cronies.[87]

Several banks in New York suspended specie payments on September 1, which taught another lesson: "Banks are excellent institutions, when properly managed; but when they become the mere instruments of grasping monopolies, and the support of speculators . . . they are a nuisance, and the sooner they break the better."[88]

Only the Wall Street gamblers were in real trouble. Thanks to the *Herald*'s warnings and its teachings for two decades of the perils of honest traders and bankers becoming involved with speculators, the depression would be less severe than that of 1837. To bring about recovery there must be a rigid retrenchment, a strict reliance on the cash system, and a general bankruptcy law. The New York delegation in Congress should take the lead in proposing federal regulation of the banking and currency system. But the retrenchment should not be pressed too hard; the public works in progress should be finished, and there was enough hard cash in the treasury to finance their completion. Bennett gloated again that most New York City newspapers were feeling the pinch and had to cut their size, yet the *Herald* was as large and solvent as ever, operating on a strict cash basis.[89]

The panic had political overtones. It proved, Bennett asserted, that the slave system was beneficial. Hunger and unemployment seemed confined to the North; the South had no need for soup kitchens. The economic issues raised by the panic would overshadow "bleeding Kansas" and the "nigger question." The Republican party was in disarray, and the parties would soon be reorganized around economic issues. The money question would be foremost. Then the acquisition of Cuba and the establishment of a protectorate over Mexico would bring about an unprecedented prosperity and redound to the benefit of the Democrats.[90]

By November the panic was abating, and New York banks were resuming specie payments. The financial convulsions occurring at the same time in England would mean that banking and commercial supremacy would pass to the United States. Revival was well under way by the end of 1858, with bountiful crops, ample specie, and fewer speculators, although the troubles continued in Europe.[91]

The symptoms of recovery were evident everywhere in 1858. Confidence was restored on the stock market, trade was expanding, specie supplies were up, the demand for luxuries had fallen off, and credit had eased. By the close of the year the *Herald* marveled at the vitality of the American economy. Recovery was complete, and this would be of great benefit to the Democrats in the 1860 elections.[92]

In the national election campaign, Bennett used an economic argument against the Republicans. A proposed economic boycott of northern goods by the South would certainly result from a Republican victory, the *Herald* pointed out, and it would mean economic disaster for New York City. By summer Bennett was predicting southern secession if Lincoln won. The end was in sight, he warned: New Yorkers should sell their southern securities and collect what debts they could from southerners.[93] In October he predicted a financial panic brought on by the political uncertainty. When a New York City bank suspended, the *Herald* screamed: "The premonitory symptoms of a financial revulsion are upon us. . . . They are visible everywhere. . . . Nor can we comprehend how we can possibly escape a general financial earthquake in the event of Lincoln's election." Banks and businesses would fail, factories would close, and shipping would rot at the wharves. The Panic of 1860 was at hand.[94]

Bennett's economic news and analysis were unusually complete but seldom objective. He habitually resorted to simplistic explanations of conspiracy which his readers could grasp—the Wall Street stockjobbers were usually at the root of a problem—and he was often inconsistent. He identified himself, in Marvin Meyers's paradigm, with the "real people," the productive members of society, against the "money power." He used economic analysis to make a political point, and that point was usually in the interests of the southern Democrats.

6

Monitor of New York

The great majority of the *Herald*'s readers were New Yorkers, and Bennett provided them with extensive coverage of city and state affairs. He recognized their interest in the complex world around them. Metropolitan newspapers like the *Herald,* writes Gunther Barth, "pioneered journalistic practices that satisfied the people's need for information about the bewildering world they found themselves in, the other inhabitants, and themselves. It spoke of their hope and despair, honesty and corruption, success and failure, and virtue and sin, in a world that let a few dreams come true by shattering many. It captured the greatest news story of the nineteenth century—modern city life."[1]

Bennett demonstrated his interest in the concerns of his local readers, even the most humble and poor, who were so often the innocent victims of New York City's spectacular growth in the middle third of the nineteenth century. He thus took a reformist position that was usually independent of local partisan politics. But the problems he saw in New York City did not inhibit his consistent boosterism of Manhattan.

New York's greatness and growth were continually chronicled in the *Herald*. In an early issue Bennett predicted that "New York is just beginning a new era." A few months later the great fire of December 1835 failed to dampen his optimism. Even though the *Herald*'s office was destroyed, he stressed the bright side; one result of the fire was to make spring bargains available in New York to out-of-town merchants.[2]

New York's choice location and transportation advantages made the city's growth predictable. From 1836 Bennett pressed for New York to become the American terminus of a transatlantic steamship line, and he always championed the superiority of New York port over its rivals. He also urged a railroad connecting New York to Albany to provide access between the two cities when the Hudson River was frozen, and by 1859 he predicted that New York City would become the hub of the nation's growing railroad network. Indeed, "in the course of another half century New York will be the richest and most populous city on the globe."[3]

The *Herald* also praised New York's cultural facilities, but its news coverage of the theater, the opera, and other cultural events was tinged with an antiaristocratic bias that proceeded from Bennett's republicanism. When New York University was reorganized in 1837, Bennett promised "to take it under our particular patronage" and recommended an elective system whereby no one would be forced to study subjects for which he had no talent or interest. "Our seminaries of learning have been conducted upon the most absurd principles of mental philosophy. They have studied out a beau ideal of human excellence, and then tried to bring every mind to their standard, instead of taking it as it is, and improving its own natural powers, and taking advantage of its peculiar predispositions."[4]

Aristocracy was a subject of concern to Americans of the mid-nineteenth century, as was documented at length by Alexis de Tocqueville, by James Fenimore Cooper in *An American Democrat,* and by Francis J. Grund in *Aristocracy in America.* Bennett was ambivalent toward aristocracy, inconsistent on this as on so many other matters. He was an elitist who disdained exclusivity, especially what he saw as Whig exclusivity. He was rich and proud of his material success, but too *nouveau* to feel comfortable around old established wealth. The social ostracism he and his family experienced made him feel like an outsider in society. He championed the masses while they were suffering, but he became terrified as soon as they were aroused to action, as they were during the antirent movement. He befriended the immigrants as long as they were an inert political mass but turned on them when they tried to organized their own political group.

Bennett refused to believe that high culture existed only for the elite, and his criticism of cultural events sponsored by the local Whig aristocracy helped to provoke the Astor Place riots of 1849. The trouble developed out of a feud between the two most celebrated actors of the time, the Englishman William C. Macready and the American Edwin Forrest, when both were in New York to perform Shakespeare at rival theaters. (The *Herald* had told its readers many times that the Astor Place Theatre, where Macready was playing, was the city's aristocratic theater.) Forrest's partisans blamed Macready for severe criticisms of the American actor that appeared in the English press during a recent tour. After threatening for several days to disrupt Macready's performance, a mob attacked the Astor Place Theatre on May 10, and before order was restored several persons were killed. Throughout, the *Herald* called for order and denied that Macready had been responsible for the English criticisms of Forrest. When several of the rioters were convicted in September, Bennett praised the verdict as a vindication of law and order.[5]

The same antiaristocratic spirit led Bennett to oppose the organization of an Italian opera company on a subscription basis. Seats should be available to everyone. "Nothing but a popular system can succeed in this or any other kind of amusement, in such a city as New York." In 1855 the "codfish aristocracy" tried again to organize an Italian opera company. It was doomed to fail, Bennett warned, because such high culture was too expensive. After the company reorganized in May, the *Herald* conceded that after eight unsuccessful years the Italian opera might at last have a foothold in New York.[6]

Bennett's denunciations of the "codfish aristocracy" reflected a consistent antipathy to New England. He had been unable to make his fortune in Boston as a young man, and he had been refused a teaching position in Connecticut because of his Catholic background. New England was the hub of abolitionism, which he detested, and of puritanism and its attempts to regulate morals, which he also found distasteful. New York had established commercial leadership over Boston in the Northeast, but its influence still lagged behind New England in national politics, and Bennett found this difficult to accept.[7]

Another target of Bennett's dislike of aristocracy, which reflected another constant, his dislike of monopoly, was the enormous aggregation of wealth and privilege of Trinity Episcopal Church. The privileges granted to Trinity Church in its colonial charter were inconsistent with republican institutions, and in addition the church was mismanaging its huge trust funds, spending them for high church purposes instead of for benevolence. The legislature should revoke these special privileges. "Let us weed out from our system these rotten relics of the bastard unity of Church and State."[8]

Bennett's republican dislike of monopoly was one of the major themes underscoring the *Herald*'s championship of the poor, the workingmen, and the immigrants. These groups were, of course, an important part of its readership. During the depression following the Panic of 1837, Bennett charged that a conspiracy of landlords was raising rents in New York, and he urged tenants to conduct a rent strike. Mass meetings against the Clinton Hall Association of landlords were reported with sympathy. Housing was not scarce, and there was no justification for the high rents. "Of all the crying evils" with which New Yorkers were cursed, "extortionate" rents were "the greatest."[9]

Twenty years later housing was still a major concern. In the summer of 1855 the *Herald* did an exposé of housing in three long articles, which examined the city census figures showing a 24 percent increase in the population since 1850. There were 123,899 more New Yorkers than five years earlier. As a result, in some wards twenty persons lived in a single apartment, and in others as many as twenty families lived in one unsanitary tenement. The following spring Bennett praised the report of a legislative committee on tenements. If they could not be eradicated, landlords should be forced to use their ample profits to make them safe and sanitary. But the problem persisted. [10]

The *Herald* also carried exposés of conditions in other institutions that affected the poor of New York. It assailed the debtors' prison: "In a land of freedom and equal rights, that such a thing should be tolerated but for an instant, is monstrous — wicked — blasphemous." The New York City Lunatic Asylum was as deplorable; more financing from the state was needed. The same was true of the almshouse, into which seven thousand persons were crowded in 1856. Bennett's suggested solution to pauperism meant abandoning his laissez-faire tenets; the city should establish a massive public works program to provide jobs. [11]

Chartered monopolies were an important cause of the distress of the poor. Bennett was a friend of labor but not of labor unions, which he considered a form of monopoly. His attitude was expressed during the turbulent summer of 1836. "The mechanic who attends quietly to his business — is industrious and attentive — belongs to no club — never visits the porter-house — is always at work or with his family — such a man gradually rises in society and becomes an honor to himself, his friends, and to human nature. On the contrary, look at the Trade Unionist — the pot-house agitator — the stirrer-up of sedition — the clamorer for higher wages. After a short time, he ends his career in the Pen or State Prison." [12] But Bennett conceded that there were legitimate grievances behind much of the labor violence of the period. A landlord monopoly, a gas monopoly, a beef monopoly, and a provision monopoly were responsible for the distress of the poor workingman. [13] Conspicuously absent from the list were the employers who set the low wage rates.

Another group of monopolies threatened the lives of New Yorkers. These were the ferries and railroads that failed to maintain adequate standards of safety. The ferries to Brooklyn and Staten Island were a "public nuisance" with no guard rails, no life preservers, and a very high accident rate. The *Herald* recommended that the city impose and enforce strict safety regulations. The Camden and Amboy Railroad in New Jersey and the Harlem Railroad were also unsafe and should be forced to improve. There was seldom a month in which the *Herald* did not report a bloody train wreck. [14]

The deplorable state of public health and sanitation also made life dangerous for New Yorkers of the mid-nineteenth century. This alarmed Bennett, especially in the summer of 1849, when a cholera epidemic crossed Europe and seemed certain to strike America. The city did not take adequate precautions; it cleaned the streets only in the fashionable neighborhoods, not in the areas where the poor were crowded. Cholera struck New York in late June, and by July it was taking a deadly toll. Bennett saw a correlation between filth and cholera, castigated the nonprofessional Board of Health and the city government for their "culpable neglect," urged calmness, and noted the anomaly of deaths among the respectable classes; cholera was supposed to be connected to poverty and vice. It seemed a "just retribution" when it spread from "the huts of poverty" to the "palaces of the rich." When the epidemic subsided in mid-August, the editor pointed out the miserable state of medical knowledge and education in the United States.[15]

The city learned nothing from its experience with cholera in 1849. The streets remained filthy, the worst of any city in America. The fault, according to the *Herald,* was the city council's refusal to enforce the regulations. Only clean streets would prevent an annual summer epidemic. Bennett recommended a new city charter that would remove the street commissioners from politics and a professional board of health composed of physicians. One bright spot was the opening of Women's Hospital in 1855 to train women doctors, which the *Herald* approved. New York was becoming the center of medical learning in the nation.[16]

Bennett was an ardent supporter of building a great central park in Manhattan for reasons of both public health and beautification. "Give us oxygen. Give us that great central park." After years of discussion and delay, the park was finally authorized in 1853, but by 1856 construction had not begun. The *Herald* opposed efforts to curtail the size of the park, which should be a legacy to future generations of New Yorkers. If the original plan was implemented, the park would be "one of the noblest and most beautifully laid out gardens in the world." But the park commissioners were incompetent, the project was enmeshed in politics, and vast sums were being wasted. By 1860 enough progress had been made to raise property values in the adjoining areas, and the park had become a favorite spot for Sunday diversions.[17]

The *Herald*'s concern for the downtrodden included the immigrant poor. Bennett was an immigrant himself, of course, and except for a brief flirtation he did not succumb to the nativism of many New Yorkers. Despite the residue of anti-Catholicism that he retained, Bennett was tolerant of Catholic immigrants, perhaps reflecting his Scottish Enlightenment education. The *Herald* championed equal rights for all immigrants, and very early it criticized Whig hostility to newcomers. Bennett was usually a severe critic of Whig Governor William H. Seward, but in 1840 he supported him during the public school controversy, favoring the diversion of some of the public school fund to Catholic parochial schools. But he was critical of Seward's ally, Roman Catholic Bishop John Hughes, who Bennett believed was trying to establish a Catholic political party, a blend of politics and religion that would be fatal to republicanism. The Native American Republican party was formed in 1843 in reaction to Hughes's efforts. "Two wrongs can never make a right," the *Herald* editorialized. "All attempts to destroy the spirit of toleration as to a man's religion or birthplace, should at once be denounced, come from what quarter they may." If the nativist movement succeeded, Bennett warned, "we shall have again the glorious days of the sixteenth and seventeenth centuries, when they burned old women for witches in Salem — banished the Quakers from Boston to Providence — and punished the barrel of beer in Connecticut for working and fermenting on the Sabbath day."[18]

Less than six months after this ringing declaration, Bennett threw his support to the Native American Republican party in the city elections of 1844. The shift was caused, he said, by his disillusionment with the corruption of both major parties in the city and by Bishop Hughes's efforts to form a Catholic party. The nativists won, electing publisher James Harper as mayor, which the *Herald* hailed as a victory for reform. When nativist riots broke out in Philadelphia a few months later, Bennett blamed Bishop Hughes and the Irish: "By attempting to govern political results, as a distinct race or class, their conduct has aroused the opposition of the whole American people."[19] Part of the problem was that Bennett expected immigrants to assimilate and become part of the American mainstream, as he had done himself. He disliked the separatism of any ethnic group.

Bennett's support of nativism was short-lived. By the summer of 1844 he was disappointed in the failure of the nativists and Mayor Harper to carry out their promised reforms and for reviving bigotry to cover up their shortcomings. Bennett was positive about the benefits immigration brought to the nation, and he opposed a state head tax on immigrants, although he did support better health inspection at the ports of entry. While he remained critical of Bishop Hughes (accusing him of luxuriating in the safety of Saratoga Springs during the 1849 cholera epidemic), he became almost lyrical at the swelling tide of immigration. Most of these immigrants "became at once active producers of the wealth and resources of the country," he wrote in 1851. "Our railroads and canals are so many monuments of Irish and German industry. . . . We have room enough, and work enough, and bread enough, to share them with the industrious that have come or may come. Let them come."[20]

Surely they should be allowed to enjoy their Sunday respite from a week of hard toil. The *Herald* was vigorous in its opposition to blue laws, which would restrict the saloons and beer gardens. A Sunday closing law (which the *Herald* said violated religious liberty) was passed by the Republican legislature in 1859. By this time Bennett was critical of all Republican measures, but he urged the Germans to take note in their 1860 ballots that the Republicans were animated by a persecuting puritanism. A vote against the Republicans was a vote against Sunday closing.[21]

The local issues to which Bennett and the *Herald* devoted much of their attention were corruption and inept city government broadly, and more specifically lawlessness and the police system, what today would be called the "law and order" issue. In that sense the preoccupations of the popular press have not changed very much in the last century and a half. Because the local political parties were so corrupt, Bennett took an independent reformist position in local elections, usually favoring the ouster of whatever party happened to be incumbent until the 1850s, when the charismatic Fernando Wood emerged to command Bennett's consistent support.

The law and order issue stemmed directly from corruption in business and government. Exposures of corruption were always a staple of sensational journalism, and Bennett never tired of his brand of muckraking. The corruption of the New York Custom House was an early target, hit again during the depression of the late 1830s, and still a problem twenty years later because of the Tammany Hall patronage system.[22]

Much of the corruption in business centered on what Bennett called the "Wall Street clique," an amorphous group of Whig businessmen, bankers, politicians, and editors. One of their schemes was to construct a railroad across the southern tier of the state. This was "a visionary project . . . calculated to be a dead weight . . . to the community at large, without one redeeming quality or advantage." The money would be better spent, the *Herald* argued, in improving the railroad from New York to Albany and in repairing New York's harbor facilities. The same Wall Street clique was promoting extravagant enlargement of the Erie Canal system, which would end in "one of the most splendid financial revulsions that the world ever saw." Manipulations by the same group were responsible for the failure of the Manhattan Bank in 1840, which led Bennett to write a series of articles exposing the shortcomings of the state's free banking system.[23]

The city government was the hub of the corruption and the most frequent target of Bennett's muckraking. Soon after its establishment, the *Herald* noticed a proposal to increase the salaries of the mayor and the common council. It asked: "Pray what is the use of letting the public purse get rusty and too full? We support all the principles of modern patriotism, which mainly consists in taking care of one's self. While they are once in office, they are perfectly right to fleece as much as they can." Bennett joshed the Whig aldermen a few months later: "The truth is, the Whigs do not deserve success, because they want the roguery to win it. They talk of principle and virtue — (antiquated nonsense!) when they should be swallowing spoils and practicing cheatery."[24]

Bennett believed that New York was the worst governed city in the world and so he was always an advocate of charter reform to create greater responsibility and efficiency, leading to reduction of taxes. The city government should be patterned after that of the nation, with a two-house council in the same relation to the mayor as the Senate and House were to the president. But he despaired of any such reform. "We have carefully watched Common Council after Common Council," he said in 1850, "city government after city government, for more than a quarter of a century past, and we candidly confess that the present Common Council outstrip, in an infinite degree, all their predecessors."[25]

There was a brief moment of euphoria in 1853, when a new city charter was approved in a referendum. "Public profligacy and misgovernment are utterly routed. Reform is triumphant." But the state legislature would not approve the changes. There was hope again in the legislative session of 1855, when a new charter was proposed based on the principle of the responsibility of the mayor and the centralization of power in his hands. Again the legislature refused to approve. Then in September 1855, a grand jury indicted six members of the common council for bribery and corruption, which dramatized the need for reform and for the separation of city affairs from partisan politics. The financial condition of the city was grave; the income from a crushing taxation was outstripped by extravagant expenditures.[26]

Charter reform took a wrong turn in 1856, in the *Herald*'s view, and a new issue emerged — home rule. The need was to centralize power and responsibility in the mayor's hands, but the Republican minority on the council was proposing that its Republican friends in control at Albany weaken the mayor's power, especially over appointments. This scheme, directed against Mayor Fernando Wood, would effectively disfranchise the city by giving the governor power to appoint most of the municipal officials. The measure passed the legislature in April 1857. Bennett termed it unconstitutional. It would enable the Republicans to loot the city treasury, and the result would be heavier taxes, dirtier streets, less police protection, and wasteful expenditures on public works. He reminded his readers that Governor John King, the leader of the Republican conspiracy—what else?—was the son of Federalist Rufus King, one of the authors of the hated Alien and Sedition Acts. The new city charter was an even greater deprivation of liberty.[27]

It was no surprise to the *Herald,* then, that the city remained as corrupt and misgoverned as ever. Even the school system was being despoiled by the Board of Education. Taxes were increasing, street repair contracts were corruptly awarded, and the police were ineffective. The need to concentrate power and responsibility in the mayor's hands seemed obvious. A taxpayers' party pledged to vote only for honest men of good reputation did not offer much hope because the good citizens were apathetic.[28]

Bennett continued to stress the twin themes of the need for centralized authority and home rule. The Republicans at Albany considered New York City a rich field for patronage, and Brooklyn, Albany, and Troy lost their home rule to the state legislature in 1859. The problem could not be solved because of the apathy of the well-to-do. By 1860 the *Herald* saw little change in the quality of city government in three decades. "Our city legislators' . . . only aim in attaining power is to consummate schemes for their own aggrandizement and pecuniary gain."[29]

The corruption-related issue that most affected the *Herald*'s readers was the increasing lawlessness and the inept police system. From its inception the *Herald* had emphasized sensational crime coverage, and very early it criticized the city police: "Without check, without system, without liberal salaries, without any regulation, our Police Department have become mere loafers on the public—selling their duties to the highest bidder—and only suppressing crime or catching rogues when private individuals come forward to offer money for the performance of public duties." How could the police be reformed? "Increase the police officers—pay them a liberal salary—double your watch—when criminals are courted let them be punished—do not permit social or political ties to defeat the execution of the law—select fearless judges and make them independent—invoke seldom the pardoning power." The crux of the law and order problem was "the corrupt social and more corrupt party systems which interfere in the administration of justice and prevent its execution."[30]

Reform was not achieved. In 1843 the *Herald* again lamented the "bribery and corruption" underlying the fee system by which policemen were paid by the case. "Put trust in self-interest, and not in honesty, especially when under powerful temptation." Crime was increasing at an alarming rate by the 1850s and there still was no police reform. Again in 1853 the

Herald pleaded for the end of appointment of policemen by aldermen, the uniforming of the police, and an educational requirement.[31]

Through its sensational treatment of crime stories such as the murder of gang leader and boxer Bill Poole at Stanwix Hall in 1855 the *Herald* was able to keep the police reform issue before its readers. That year the issue became enmeshed with the home rule question. The Republican state legislature threatened to remove control of the police from the mayor and vest it in a board of police commissioners appointed by the governor. That prospect terrified Bennett.[32]

The feared metropolitan police bill passed the state legislature in the spring of 1857, and Bennett threw himself behind Mayor Fernando Wood's efforts to resist it. The *Herald* hoped that the measure would be declared unconstitutional. The legislature that passed it was "without question the most corrupt set of politicians we ever had," and the measure "will ever be known as the INFAMOUS ACTS of 1857."[33] But the court of appeals upheld the law, and the consequence, as the *Herald* saw it, was a rise in lawlessness and bloodshed in New York City. Disrespect for the law, which was devastating to business, was a direct result of the police legislation, but the only hope for a remedy was at the ballot box.[34]

Worsened by elected political judges and misplaced executive clemency, the law and order crisis was so acute by 1858 that Bennett recommended local vigilante committees to administer private justice, on the model of San Francisco. Despite a legislative investigation that revealed scandalous misconduct and corruption as a result of the metropolitan police act, there was no improvement by 1860. Crime was increasing, criminals were operating with impunity, and the police had lost the respect of the people.[35]

Because of its focus on the corruption of the city government and the local political parties, the *Herald* took an independent position in local politics. Bennett would no doubt have liked to support local Democrats, but he detested the Tammany machine, which paid no attention to his suggestions. Until 1839, and again in 1849, the *Herald* refused to support any of the candidates for mayor. During the decade of the 1840s (with the exception of backing the winning nativists in 1844), it supported the outs (usually Whigs) against the incumbents (usually Democrats backed by Tammany Hall). The Whigs were defeated, Bennett argued, both because of electoral corruption and because the Whig candidates were burdened by support by the Wall Street clique and the Whig press.[36]

Fernando Wood emerged on the local political scene in 1850, and from that point Bennett consistently backed him. The *Herald* found Wood, the 1850 Democratic nominee for mayor, "talented, discreet, sensible, active, and reliable," a reform-minded businessman who could bring harmony to the Democrats and honesty to the city government. His losses in 1850 and 1851 were attributed to Tammany's opposition and resulting Democratic defections. The domination of Tammany Hall must end if the party was to recover, the *Herald* warned: "The Democrats of New York have never in any manner or by any act vested in the Tammany Society to prescribe rules for their government in matters of political organization."[37]

Finally, Wood was elected during the chaotic party reorganization of 1854. Bennett was elated at the prospect for the long-awaited reform:

> For the first time for many years a Mayor has been found with suffi-
> cient nerve to point to the true cause of our municipal troubles, and
> to claim for himself a measure of authority commensurate with the re-
> sponsibility of his office, and the necessities of the city. . . . Mr. Wood
> intends to exercise a co-ordinate authority with the heads of depart-
> ments over every department of the city government, thus restraining
> the Comptroller from paying men who have earned no pay, and com-
> pelling the Commissioner of Streets to have the mud removed. . . . If
> Mr. Wood perseveres, it is possible that New York may be better gov-
> erned under his mayorality [*sic*] than it has been for years.[38]

All the signs seemed favorable to the *Herald* as Wood began the task of reform and retrenchment. As Bennett viewed the city, the streets were clean and well lit; all expenditures were scrutinized carefully; gambling was suppressed. Wood vetoed a council resolution curtailing the size of Central Park; he reformed the police department to neutralize the influence of rowdies; there was a marked improvement in sanitary conditions; and he reformed the method of tax collection. Unfortunately, the common council was contemptuous of most of the mayor's suggestions.[39]

Despite an occasional misgiving, the *Herald* supported Wood's renomination and reelection. Most of the mayor's failings, it argued, were the result of the atrocious city charter and the corrupt partisan politics of the council. His election, without Tammany's support, proved Wood to be the only viable Democratic leader in the city.[40]

Wood led the fight against the Republicans in the state legislature who were trying to curtail home rule, and his vetoes checked the corrupt spending schemes of the council. His renomination by a united Democratic party in 1857 was well deserved, the *Herald* said, and his reelection was certain because he was popular among the merchants, the workingmen, and the Irish alike. To Bennett's surprise and consternation, Wood was defeated by Republican William Tiemann.[41]

The city went from bad to worse during Tiemann's administration. Again the *Herald* stressed the need for centralized authority, and again it suggested an independent taxpayers' party, but the public remained apathetic to the governing of the city by a mobocracy. Each party seemed to select its worst men as candidates for the council.[42]

By 1859 Wood had created his own anti-Tammany organization, Mozart Hall, and the *Herald* praised his nomination as an independent Democrat. This support reflected some self-interest. Wood appointed a relative of Mrs. Bennett, Abe Russell, as a city judge despite Russell's reputation for incompetence, and in 1860 Russell ran on Wood's Mozart Hall ticket for recorder. This was the price Wood had to pay for the *Herald*'s support. But the public was told that Wood was superior to either the Tammany or the Republican candidates and that his election would mean the triumph of respectability over rowdyism, and of practical municipal reform. When the 1860 elections arrived, Wood had another asset: he was the only candidate who was not strongly antislavery, the only conservative Union nominee. Wood's election in 1860 no longer had much local importance, Bennett said, because the mayor was so severely restricted by the charter, but it had great national importance as a blow to antislavery extremism. Much of Wood's appeal to Bennett was his pronounced prosouthernism.[43]

Bennett's course in national and local elections had been erratic, but on the state level it was much straighter. During the decades of the 1840s and 1850s, he leaned to the Democratic party in state elections, and when Democratic factionalism became intense, to the conservative or Hunker Democrats. One reason for his consistency was the prosouthernism of the Hunkers. Another was his passionate antagonism to the antislavery views of Whig and Republican state leader William H. Seward. Thus in 1840 Bennett backed Whig William Henry Harrison for president but not the Whig state ticket. When he supported Whig Zachary Taylor for president in 1848, he campaigned vigorously against the Whigs on the state level. Again, while backing Republican John C. Frémont in 1856, he opposed the Republicans at Albany.

National issues and the position of state candidates on them was the overriding concern to the *Herald*, at least after slavery expansion became a prominent issue in the mid-1840s. Opposition to the Wilmot Proviso and support of the Compromise of 1850 and the Kansas-Nebraska Act were more important to Bennett than a state candidate's position on state concerns. Aside from the general theme of corruption at Albany, only a few strictly state issues received much attention from the *Herald:* the antirent controversy, revision of the state constitution, prohibition, and enlargement of the canal system. His support of Democrats because of their moderation in the sectional controversy and his opposition to the antislavery views of state Whigs and Republicans reflect Bennett's fundamental moderation and Unionism. The Democrats' lack of success in state elections — during the two decades after 1842 they occupied the governor's office for only six years — increased Bennett's frustration and his growing monomania about the threat to the Union of Seward's antislavery radicalism.

Until 1842 Bennett and the *Herald* kept their distance from both state parties, not very enthusiastic about Martin Van Buren, the state Democratic leader, and after 1837 very critical of Van Buren's handling of the depression. In 1838 Bennett supported William H. Seward for governor against Democratic incumbent William L. Marcy, the only time he backed the Whig leader. (He did recommend scratching Seward's running mate because the abolitionists endorsed him.) "The Democratic party, for its ignorant, headstrong, wicked tampering with the currency for the last eight years deserves a check — a defeat — a total overthrow." The *Herald* interpreted the Whig victory as a rebuke to Van Buren and his financial proposals.[44]

For the next two years Bennett held aloof from state politics. He was critical of the influence of the Wall Street clique on the Whigs, and he took no stand in the 1839 legislative elections or the 1840 gubernatorial contest, surprised at the closeness of Seward's reelection. The *Herald* had become disenchanted with Seward and his ties to the Wall Street clique, critical of Whig financial mismanagement and the growing state debt and of his pardoning an "enormous" number of convicts. His 1841 annual message was "the worst," "a most miserable affair," "a mess of trash."[45]

Then a national question intruded into state affairs. The state Whig leadership (like most northern Whigs) broke with the new president, John Tyler, whom the *Herald* warmly supported. The state Whigs were courting political suicide, it predicted, by deserting the president on the bank issue. Another factor in declining Whig fortunes was Seward's alliance with Bishop Hughes, who had become his "mere tool." When the Democrats swept the 1841 legislative elections, the *Herald*'s lead headline read: "Total Overthrow of the Bank Whig Party in the State of New York."[46]

By 1842 Bennett and the *Herald* were in the Democratic fold to stay, on the state level. The differences between the two New York parties were clear: "The policy and principles of the Whigs lead to speculation, high prices, expansions, credit, genteel piety, courtly extravagance, luxury, elegance, and fashion. The tendency of the democratic party is to cash business — low prices, restricted credits, moderate habits of life, low priced breeches and so forth. The manufacturers and financiers prefer the Whig party — the mechanics and laborers the democratic." Andrew Jackson could not have said it better.[47]

So in 1842 Bennett supported Democrat William C. Bouck in his successful campaign for governor, but he saw the overriding issue as national: a rebuke to Henry Clay's presidential ambitions and support of Tyler's policies. Bouck's message to the legislature in 1843 was "quite an old-fashioned affair — sound, sensible, unpretending, and giving a round, unvarnished tale of the assets and liabilities of the state." Again in 1844 the *Herald* backed the winning Democrat, Silas Wright, and again the main concern in the state election was national — Polk's expansionism.[48]

The Democrats swept the legislative elections in 1845, giving a further boost to expansionism, but Bennett was disturbed about one result of the election — the victory of many antirent candidates. Tenants in the Hudson and upper Delaware valleys since colonial times had been subject to a feudal system of land tenure in which annual quitrents in kind had to be paid to the landlord. After several years of rumblings, violence broke out in 1841, when tenants on the Van Rensselaer estates refused to pay their customary rents or back rents that had accumulated for many years. The Helderberg Hills became a battleground as sheriffs tried to collect rents from defiant farmers disguised in calico dresses and Indian paint.[49]

When the antirent troubles started in 1839 with nonviolent protests, Bennett was critical of Governor Seward for not intervening, but the *Herald* was surprisingly quiet during Bouck's Democratic administration despite an increase in disturbances that were becoming violent. When Wright became governor in 1845, the antirent issue was acute. Bennett blamed it on the inflammatory land reform ideas of Horace Greeley's *Tribune;* the next step would be to divide the public lands among the landless and the abolition of rents, leases, and title deeds, which would throw back society to its original savage state.[50]

When a group of antirenters led by "Big Thunder" were tried at Hudson in March 1845, Bennett sent a special *Herald* reporter to provide a full account of the proceedings. It predicted, accurately, an acquittal and then "a fresh outburst of disorganization, rebellion, and outrage, far more extended and serious than any that has yet been exhibited." It was now up to Governor Wright: "The most decided and vigorous action is imperative. Every manifestation of rebellion, and refusal to pay rent, ought to be promptly and effectually crushed . . . and the ringleaders . . . tried by jurors whose feelings have not been affected by any association with this wicked and dangerous movement."[51]

But another trial of antirenters in the fall at Delhi resulted in the conviction of their leaders and a life sentence for "Big Thunder." The *Herald* cheered this check to "disorganization, anarchy, and ruin." Could Wright resist the tremendous pressure to pardon those convicted? His 1846 message to the legislature raised doubts. On the anti-rent issue "he seems to combine whining apologies . . . for both parties, the effect of which will be to embitter both towards each other. This will widen the breach and increase the momentum of the anti-rent movement."[52]

The 1846 state election, then, concerned purely state issues, a rare occurrence in the *Herald*'s coverage of state affairs. To oppose Silas Wright the Whigs nominated John Young, an antirent radical. Young was elected, in a "Waterloo defeat" for the Democrats.[53] The issue was settled when Young pardoned the antirent rebels and constitutional revisions in 1846 eliminated the feudal land tenure relics they had fought.

This revision of the state constitution was an important issue in the 1846 election, entangled with the antirent question. In 1844 Bennett had supported a proposal for a state constitutional convention, but a year later he changed his mind, fearing that radicals would control it. Soon after he reversed course again, noting with approval a Louisiana convention that had restricted banking incorporation and set limits on the state debt.[54] But when the question of calling a state convention was placed on the ballot in the fall of 1845, the *Herald* urged its rejection. Greeley, the abolitionists, the antirenters, and other radicals favored the convention. Although the question carried, Bennett was delighted with the special spring elections, which gave the Democrats control of the convention, the result, he said, of their opposition to the extension of Negro suffrage.[55]

The new constitution produced by the convention provided for a popularly elected judiciary, the election of many officials who had previously been appointed, antirent restrictions on feudal land tenure, and a state debt ceiling. Removal of the property qualification for Negro suffrage was submitted to the voters as a separate question. Bennett urged support for the new constitution and rejection of the Negro suffrage proposal, and the voters satisfied him on both counts.[56]

That 1846 election was the last in New York's antebellum period in which the *Herald* focused on state issues. From that point on, state elections were important to Bennett because of their influence on national affairs, and he supported state candidates because of their stand on national concerns, especially the expansion of slavery. As New York produced a national antislavery leader in William H. Seward, opposition to Seward engrossed Bennett to the exclusion of everything else. Sewardism became *the* issue, and Bennett became a monomaniac on the subject.

This monomania is easier to describe than to explain. It can be argued that the threat of Sewardism was more rhetorical than real in view of Bennett's support of Seward as secretary of state during the Civil War. Sewardism became a code word for disunion, abolition, and corruption at Albany. It was the polar opposite of the moderation that Bennett believed to be the only safeguard of the Union.

The issue of Sewardism emerged during the 1848 election. Although the *Herald* supported Whig Zachary Taylor for president that year, Bennett was concerned about the Whig state victory, with Hamilton Fish elected governor, because the new state legislature would elect a United States senator early in the session, and Seward seemed assured of victory. This was dangerous for several reasons. Seward was the ally of corrupt Whig boss Thurlow Weed and of the Wall Street clique. He was a radical "demagogue" supported by abolitionists, antirenters, and Bishop Hughes's Irish party. Seward's election to the Senate, then, "would be one of the most unfortunate events for the peace and permanence of the Union that could possibly take place at the present crisis." He was "treacherous, double-faced . . . and utterly unfit" for the Senate. But the Whigs controlled the legislature, and Seward was duly elected, "the leading abolitionist agitator of this great state." The New York Whigs had "absorbed abolitionism, antirentism, Fourierism, socialism and all the *isms* and schisms and fag ends and scraps of all parties, of every complexion, as circumstances have required."[57]

Seward's opposition in the Senate to the Compromise of 1850 led Bennett to step up his attacks on the antislavery Whigs and to praise Whig compromisers. The New York Whigs had split: moderates supported Webster, Clay, President Millard Fillmore, and the compromise; the other wing was "a socialist organization, imbued with all the wildest isms of the day, and running riot in favor of Negroes, Senator Seward, a division of property, abolition of slavery, of the Sabbath, and of many of the old doctrines of Christianity." The split was widened in the 1850 state convention at Syracuse. When the convention refused to support the compromise and passed resolutions endorsing Seward's conduct, Bennett cheered when moderates walked out. Their separate convention was termed the "National Whig Convention" by the *Herald,* while the regulars were the "Abolition Convention." But Bennett was disgusted when both groups named the same state ticket, headed by Washington Hunt for governor.[58]

It was crucial in the 1850 state election that all Unionists support the Democratic state ticket led by Horatio Seymour. The *Herald* was convinced of the preponderance of Union and conservative feeling in New York City. The election of Hunt would mean an endorsement of nullifying the Fugitive Slave Law. "What we want . . . is the last vestige of Sewardism rooted out of the state." In a close contest, the Whigs won. The *Herald* blamed President Fillmore for not using patronage against the Sewardites. "A withering imbecility seems to hang over the White House."[59]

This "Triumph of Sewardism" had two other unfortunate results, in the *Herald*'s analysis: the selection of a second Sewardite, Hamilton Fish, for the United States Senate and the probability that Seward would be the abolition-Whig nominee for president in 1852. The Democrats were powerless to stem the Whig tide in New York because they were divided. Radical Barnburners and conservative Hunkers refused to reunite. Bennett advised: "The only way in which the party can be united, is for . . . [the Barnburners] to cease their assaults on the South, to abstain from irritating and insulting their Southern brethren, and striving to deprive them of their rights under the Constitution. . . . Let those who strayed from the right patriotic path [and defected to the Free Soil party in 1848], not be taken back until they are thoroughly purged and purified." Democratic reunion would have to be on the Hunker's terms.[60]

It was no consolation to Bennett that his appraisal of Senator Hamilton Fish was correct; he was a puppet of Seward and his "higher law" doctrines and did not understand that "his official oath binds him to protect this right of the South against the abolitionists." Although most New Yorkers favored "peace, the Union, and the compromises as they are, the Empire State throws her whole weight in the Senate in support of incendiaries who openly proclaim their object to be the abolition of slavery and the dissolution of the Union."[61]

Although most of the *Herald*'s attention in 1852 went to the defeat of Winfield Scott, Seward's candidate for president, the paper was pleased with the gubernatorial election, a rematch of 1850, but this time Seymour defeated Hunt. Now the divisive issue for the Democrats was the degree of enthusiasm with which they welcomed back the Barnburners who had defected to the Free Soil party in 1848. The "Hard Shells," with whom Bennett sided, were critical of President Pierce's New York appointments and would punish the Barnburners; the "Soft Shells" would forgive and forget.[62]

The state political situation was even more confusing by 1854 because of northern opposition to the Kansas-Nebraska Act, the emergence of a new nativist party (the Know-Nothings), and an attempt to impose prohibition on the state. Four candidates ran for governor: Whig Myron Clark, a tool of both Seward and the prohibitionists; Governor Seymour, a Soft Shell backed by the Pierce administration and the liquor interests; Know-Nothing Daniel Ullmann with support from conservative Whigs; and Bennett's choice, Greene Bronson, the "sound and conservative" Hard Shell. The *Herald* saw the issue as preservation of the union, which could be achieved only by the defeat of Clark and the Sewardites. But Clark beat Seymour by a hair, the result (the *Herald* believed) of Seymour's veto of a prohibition law.[63]

The new state legislative would select a United States senator early in 1855. Seward desired reelection, and Governor Clark and Thurlow Weed were ruthless in their efforts to attain that end. Seward's platform was "the improvement of rivers and harbors on a grand scale by the federal government, a high tariff of special bounties for the enrichment of manufacturing corporations, and war without quarter against the South, the extermination of slavery, and the disruption of the Union." Only the Know-Nothings at Albany stood in his way, but although they were aware of his alliance with Bishop Hughes they abandoned their principles and supported his election to another term in the Senate.[64]

The prohibition issue, which proved so disruptive, had been present for several years. New York prohibitionists wanted to adopt a version of Maine's law, which forbade the sale of liquor in retail quantities. Bennett had always opposed prohibition as a violation of individual liberties; if the state could prescribe what a person could drink, it could also prescribe what he could eat or wear. And prohibition would not work: "As well might laws be passed to make men and women angels." A better approach would be stricter enforcement of the licensing laws. When the legislature passed a prohibition bill, Bennett lauded Seymour's veto.[65] But the veto cost Seymour reelection, and the new legislature passed a prohibition law in 1855 which Governor Clark signed. The law was unconstitutional, the *Herald* charged, and unworkable, ruinous to business in New York City and a boon to wet New Jersey. Maine had repealed its own model law because it was unworkable. When the court of appeals invalidated the New York law in 1856, Bennett cheered the decision. It should teach the legislature a lesson about trying to legislate morals.[66]

The political reorganization that followed the Kansas-Nebraska Act attracted most of the *Herald*'s attention during the mid-1850s. The Sewardite state legislature was regularly scored for corruption. Its extravagant spending on canals threatened to bankrupt the state, and now it proposed to tax the railroads to keep the canal system solvent. Worse, it passed a personal liberty law with the effect of nullifying the Fugitive Slave Law. Now, the *Herald* warned, "every man may as well resolve at once whether he is for the Northern or the Southern Confederacy, for it must speedily ripen into secession and disunion."[67]

By mid-1855 Seward's antislavery coalition was formidable under the banner of the Republican party. Still, Bennett refused to support a Democratic reunion except on Hard Shell terms. The Hard Shells were the "Simon Pure Democracy" and had nothing to gain from a surrender to the Softs. The state Hard convention was termed the "national Democracy," and the Know-Nothings were urged to support its ticket in the 1855 state elections. The Republican state convention, in contrast, was "the Simon Pure negro worshippers," an "indescribable coalition of demagogues and fanatics, white, yellow, and black." The Whigs who supported the Republicans were Seward's "political stool pigeons," "his procuresses."[68]

The *Herald*'s rhetoric continued to escalate. The issue in these off-year state elections was abolition versus the Constitution. Seward was the worst traitor since Benedict Arnold. Republican Governor Clark could do nothing right. He was extravagant ("Sewardism is anything but retrenchment"); he was abusive of the pardoning power; he was the tool of the New York Central Railroad. Bennett was backing Republican presidential nominee John C. Frémont in 1856, but he refused to support the Republican state ticket. Instead, he urged the election for governor of Judge Amasa J. Parker, the choice of the temporarily reunited Democrats, against the eventual victor, John A. King, the tool of Seward and the New York Central.[69]

Buchanan's triumph over Frémont brought new patronage problems to the feuding Democrats. The New York party, Bennett lamented, was a "mere democratic scarecrow. It is ragged, filthy, hungry, down in character, down in principle, down in the mouth, down in the heel, and down in the dust." Therefore, he was willing to support a compromise dividing the patronage between Hards and Softs. Any move that would hasten reunion was necessary because the Republican legislature was the "most corrupt, rascally, unscrupulous body" in New York's history.[70]

Democratic unity was more apparent than real as the 1857 legislative elections approached. Bennett saw only two political forces: those who supported Buchanan's honest and conservative national administration and the railroad oligarchy supporting the Seward-Weed machine at Albany. Sewardism came increasingly to mean corruption. When the Democrats won the 1857 legislative elections, the *Herald* took credit for the victory. It had, it said, persuaded ten thousand Frémont voters from 1856 to cut loose from Seward, and it interpreted the results as an endorsement of both home rule for New York City and Buchanan's policy in Kansas.[71]

The *Herald*'s equation of Sewardism with corruption came to focus on the state canal system. Bennett had always opposed adding to the state debt to enlarge the canal; only such enlargement as could be financed from the canal revenues should be undertaken. It was clear by 1858 that New York was losing much of its western trade to Canada by the St. Lawrence River route, but to arrest the trend by enlarging the canal would cost $4 million. New York could raise this sum by a direct tax, Bennett argued, or else sell the canal system as Pennsylvania had done. The Republicans had so mismanaged the canal fund, threatening to bankrupt the state, that by 1860 he was convinced that the state would remain solvent only by selling the canal system.[72]

The *Herald*'s rhetoric rose to a higher pitch in the 1858 elections. The

Republican candidate for governor, Edwin D. Morgan, was, predictably, a tool of Seward, "the arch-fiend of American politics." Again, the issue was national: a vote of confidence in the moderate policies of Buchanan. More ominously, Seward's 1860 presidential hopes rested on a Morgan victory. Bennett was pessimistic about Democratic chances because a conspiracy — again — of Douglas Democrats was working against the Democratic ticket. Although a vote for Morgan was a vote for Seward's "irrepressible conflict" doctrines, a vote to carry fire and the sword into the South, he was elected handily. Another step had been taken to force the South to secede.[73]

Maneuvering for the 1860 presidential nominations dominated state politics for the next two years. The corrupt Republican lobby and legislators at Albany were doing everything in their power to secure Seward's nomination. The continuing feud between Hards and Softs reflected a difference in presidential preferences; the Hards, with Bennett's blessing, backed Governor Henry A. Wise of Virginia, while Soft leader Horatio Seymour was a stalking-horse for Stephen A. Douglas. In New York City, Tammany Hall favored Douglas and Fernando Wood wanted Wise. But the real issue was Seward. The stake was momentous in the 1859 legislative elections: Seward and irrepressible conflict or conservatism and the Constitution.[74]

The Republican victory was a catastrophe; it was "a direct triumph for the shrewdest demagogue and traitor whom the country has ever produced, and, fearful as that prospect is, he must inevitably be the next Presidential candidate of the black republican party." The main business of the 1860 legislative session would be to secure his nomination by plundering New York City, especially in the award of street railway franchises (the newest focus for Republican corruption) and an attempt to remove property qualifications for Negro voting. The latter move was in keeping with the doctrine of the Republicans, "who claim for the black race perfect equality in all things with the whites."[75]

Hysteria had become the *Herald*'s normal tone. This was a strange state of affairs for a man who so strongly favored moderation, but Bennett was apoplectic when the legislature passed a Negro suffrage amendment to submit to the voters in 1860. "It remains to be seen whether a sufficient number of white men can be found in this State willing to consummate the act of self-degradation which will bring them down to the level of blacks, to the same political status as the niggers of the Five Points. We cannot believe it."[76] The outlook seemed as grim for the city and state as for the Union as 1860 closed with moderates and Unionists in disarray, Sewardism apparently triumphant, and prospects for civil war a common topic of conversation.

7
Covering the Civil War

The Civil War brought no fundamental changes to the *Herald* or other metropolitan newspapers. It accentuated developments already under way. The *Herald*'s format remained the same, although it printed more maps and used bolder column heads, and it often expanded from the normal eight pages to a twelve-page triple sheet. Its news-gathering efforts were heightened; many new correspondents were hired; and the telegraph was used more extensively than before. The *Herald* continued its exhaustive coverage of foreign policy, and its expansionism was unabated. Bennett was still erratic although generally Democratic in his politics — racist, pro-slavery, and antiabolitionist. The two controlling political issues, in his view, were slavery and postwar reconstruction. The *Herald*'s military coverage was extensive and enterprising, but biased; General George B. McClellan, its hero, could do no wrong, and Secretary of War Edwin M. Stanton and the antislavery forces in the administration could do no right. Despite the prominence of national war-related news, the *Herald* continued its sensational coverage of local crime news and its city boosterism. But the war was a time of great stress. The performance of the *Herald* in the Civil War, then, is a case study of a mature metropolitan newspaper operating in unusual times.

As sectional tensions heightened, threatening civil war following Lincoln's election in late 1860, a visitor to the *Herald*'s office at the corner of Fulton and Nassau streets would have found a hubbub of activity. Managing editor Frederic Hudson was hiring new staff, writing southward to enlist correspondents, fretting over the lack of office space, and reading Timothy Dwight's *History of the Hartford Convention* as background to the secession crisis.[1]

For over a decade Hudson had handled the daily operations of the *Herald* as the first managing editor of an American newspaper. The youngest of ten children, Hudson was born in 1819 in Quincy, Massachusetts, attended the town school at Concord, and at age seventeen joined his brothers William and Robert in New York City, taking charge of the reading room at Hudson's News Room in 1835. Bennett met him there on his daily news-gathering rounds in 1836 and took a liking to the young man, who had furnished him with many news tips. On January 18, 1837, Hudson joined Bennett as his second full-time employee, in charge of collecting shipping and foreign news. Except for six months in 1838 when he helped edit the *New York Daily Whig,* Hudson remained with Bennett for three decades until his retirement in 1866.[2]

There was a perfect meeting of minds between the two, and Hudson was completely loyal to his employer and the *Herald.* In 1846 Bennett made Hudson the managing editor, feeling confident enough to leave the *Herald*'s direction to him during his own long absences. During the 1850s Bennett went to Europe at least once a year, and on one occasion he remained abroad for eleven months. Hudson held Bennett's power of attorney at such times. By 1861 Bennett spent little time at the newspaper office; his appearances were rare enough that Hudson noted them in his diary.[3]

Hudson was described by a contemporary as "long and solemn of face ... [with] lank and wiry length of limb—the sleek dark hair and closely shaven cheeks, the sad and bitter scrutiny of his glance, and the mysterious solemnity enveloping the man's whole appearance and movements." He dressed jauntily but in outdated clothes, immaculate in a blue jacket with brass buttons, polished boots, and a shiny black stovepipe hat. "In all matters relating to the *Herald* he is a walking file, talking proof-copy and automation index," the description continued, concluding that Hudson was "very uncompromising in his belief that the *Herald* and its various issues form the first and most sacred aspects of merely human exertion."[4]

The *Herald* was Hudson's life. Seven mornings a week at 9:30 Hudson left his house on East Twenty-second Street to walk to his office on the third floor of the *Herald* building. He remained there until four, walked home for dinner, and returned at eight to work until at least ten and often far into the night. "To manage a paper properly," he wrote, "one must work steadily and perseveringly. There is no let-up—no rest—no play that is not mixed up with business." His brother noted that Hudson "never voted. Had no political prejudices. Had no hobbies, no church, no club."[5] Indeed, he spent his retirement years on the only subject that interested him, writing a monumental and still valuable history of American journalism.

Hudson, commented historian Louis Starr, "devoted himself with manic single-mindedness to implementing James Gordon Bennett's dream of publishing the biggest, sauciest, newsiest newspaper the world had ever seen." The reporters he directed admired him. One wrote: "Much as Bennett was the *Herald* and the *Herald* Bennett, we who know understand very distinctly that Hudson was the *Herald* too; yet he will go down unhonored in the next generation as he was unsung in this." He was not unsung to his contemporaries. Henry Watterson described him as "the head and front of journalism"; Samuel Bowles believed that Hudson "did more than any man to organize and stimulate the collection of news." His ace Civil War correspondent Sylvanus Cadwallader, an unblushing admirer of General Ulysses S. Grant, gave Hudson the ultimate accolade: "Great hearted, chivalrous, magnanimous Fred Hudson! I cannot write of him, even at this distant time, with dry eyes. He was to Mr. James Gordon Bennett, Senior, what Rawlins was to Grant, which exhausts human praise." Bennett paid Hudson a salary of $10,000, the highest in the business, and he was worth it.[6]

By the 1850s both journalists and politicians recognized that Hudson was in practical control of the daily operations of the *Herald* while Bennett directed its editorial policy. Hudson's days, as reflected in his diary, were busy. Politicians called on him at the office or invited him for confidential talks: Stephen A. Douglas, army and navy officers, congressmen, diplomats, Mayor Wood, Governor Seymour, the district attorney, and many others. He took time for the required reading of political speeches and government reports. Hudson represented the *Herald* on the executive committee of the Associated Press, another time-consuming task. He had to investigate new press technology, attend meetings with managers of other dailies to concert action on prices, and explore possible amelioratives to the rising price of paper. He also had to attend to labor relations, not always a pleasant job, as when he had to reprimand and almost fire Bennett's brother-in-law Robert R. Crean for neglecting business.[7]

The secession of the states of the Deep South brought a crisis to the *Herald*'s editors and added a heavy burden to the already overworked Hudson. The *Herald* had vigorously opposed Lincoln's election in 1860, supporting first Breckinridge and then Bell as the best hope of defeating the northern sectional candidate. Many of the *Herald*'s prosouthern, proslavery, anti-Republican editorials since 1858 had been written by Malcolm Ives, the impetuous son of a New York physician who had an aura of European learning about him, a former Roman Catholic priest, he claimed, who joined the *Herald* after working briefly for the *New York Times* and *Journal of Commerce* and for Fernando Wood at the New York Custom House. Ives has been described as an "accomplished journalistic fraud . . . whose past was so checkered it was impossible to be sure of anything in it. His present was clear enough. He was a smooth, plausible, unconscionable liar [and] . . . con man." The editorials dealing with the secession crisis, whether written by Ives, Bennett, or Hudson, became increasingly strident.[8]

From the start, the *Herald*'s solution was a compromise, a constitutional amendment protecting slavery against federal interference and calling out sixty thousand militia to protect Washington against the ultras. The Crittenden proposals would be acceptable, or a constitutional convention of the states, and the *Herald* was optimistic that the Lincoln administration would support such a solution. News from the South was carried on page 1 in a column headed "THE REVOLUTION," but after South Carolina fired on the *Star of the West* in early 1861, the *Herald* conceded that Buchanan had done all he could. The question was now in the hands of Congress and the incoming Republican administration. Should all else fail, the *Herald* hoped for peaceable separation. It continued to press for compromise, but it was not optimistic.[9]

By late January the range of options had narrowed. Bennett feared that Lincoln, pressured by the abolitionist fanatics in his party, would coerce the South, which would mean war, even though nine-tenths of the northern people favored compromise. Separation into two confederacies would be tolerable; there was little doubt that Canada would join a northern confederacy in the future, more than balancing the loss of the Deep South. The future national capital would probably be St. Paul, Minnesota.[10]

The organization of the Confederate States of America in February at Montgomery, Alabama, by the seven states of the Deep South filled the *Herald* with gloom. New York City would be ruined by a civil war; terrible commercial convulsions threatened the North; southern preponderance in militia meant that military action would be disastrous to the Union. The only hope was that Lincoln would assert Unionist sentiments and support the Crittenden Compromise. He must reject the radical war program of the ultras and rally Unionist support. George Templeton Strong, who despised Bennett, despaired in his diary: "Were we of the North only united, of one mind, loyal to the government, I should not fear civil war. But there are the New York *Express* and the New York *Herald* and the like."[11]

Lincoln's inaugural address bothered the *Herald:* it was too vague, too cunning. The abolitionists were pressing the president for war, the final consequence of their "nigger worship." There was little doubt that Virginia and the border states would secede unless Lincoln decided to abandon Fort Pickens and Fort Sumter. The president should listen to the Confederate commissioners in Washington and recognize Confederate independence as a lesser evil than civil war. The economic issue was raised again; civil war would ruin northern commerce. Already the high Republican tariff had disrupted trade; Secretary of the Treasury Salmon P. Chase was trying to borrow $25 million; the regulations closing southern ports could be enforced only with military power.[12]

By April it was clear to the *Herald* that war had been Lincoln's intention all along and that the president was determined to hold Fort Sumter at any cost and was preparing an expedition to reinforce Fort Pickens. The paper editorialized on April 9: "It is becoming too evident that, so far as a vicious, imbecile, demoralized administration possesses power, the hideous horrors of civil war are about to be forced upon the country." Although a majority of northerners favored the evacuation of Fort Sumter, the administration would not budge. By April 12 news from Charleston was headed "The Impending War" and the *Herald*'s front page contained illustrations of the batteries at Charleston. Strong captured some of the excitement in his diary: "*War* has begun, unless my extra *Herald* lies, and its Charleston dispatch is bogus. Busy downtown. . . . Walked uptown. . . . The streets were vocal with newsboys — "Extra — a *Herald*! Get the bombardment of *Fort Sumter*!!!" We concluded it was probably a sell and that we would not be sold, and declined all invitations to purchase for about four blocks. But we could not stand it longer. I sacrificed sixpence and read the news."[13]

The news from Charleston came from Felix Gregory de Fontaine, a personal friend of General P. G. T. Beauregard, the Confederate commander there. On April 13 page 1 featured a map of Charleston harbor and news under the head "The War Begins." But the paper was curiously silent editorially, leading Strong to comment: "The New York *Herald* is noncommittal this morning. It may well be upholding the administration and denouncing the Democratic party within a week. It takes naturally to eating dirt and its own words (the same thing.)"[14]

On April 14 the *Herald* carried the first dispatch of the firing on Fort Sumter and the start of the Civil War. Fontaine had telegraphed from Charleston at 3:00 P.M. on April 12:

> Civil War has at last begun. A terrible fight is at this moment going on between Fort Sumter and the fortifications by which it is surrounded. . . .
>
> Breaches, to all appearances, are being made in the several sides [of the fort] exposed to fire, portions of the parapet have been destroyed. . . .
>
> The soldiers are perfectly reckless of their lives, and at every shot jump upon the ramparts, observe the effect, and jump down again cheering. . . .
>
> The excitement of the community is indescribable. With the very first boom of the gun, thousands rushed from their beds to the harbor front, and all day every available place has been thronged by ladies and gentlemen, viewing the solemn spectacle through their glasses.

The edition sold 135,000 copies, "the largest issue of any newspaper that has ever been printed," the *Herald* claimed, and there was such a crush in front of the office that the police had to barricade the street and re-route the traffic.[15]

The next day the surrender of the fort and Lincoln's proclamation of a rebellion and call for seventy-five thousand volunteers were announced. The *Herald*'s lead editorial that day supported Lincoln's action, leading Strong to remark that the "New York *Herald* is *in equilibrio* today, just at the turning point. Tomorrow it will denounce Jefferson Davis as it denounced Lincoln a week ago." Indeed it did. It lauded Lincoln's vigorous course and criticized Buchanan for not having done the same months ago. The time had passed for peace meetings and compromise talk. Strong could not resist another dig at Bennett:

> The conversion of the New York *Herald* is complete. It rejoices that the rebellion is to be put down and is delighted with civil war, because it will stimulate the business of New York, and that is what "we" (the *Herald,* to wit) have been vainly preaching for months. The impudence of old J. G. Bennett's is too vast to be appreciated at once. You must look at it and meditate over it for some time (as at Niagara and St. Peter's) before you can take in its immensity. His capitulation is a set-off against the loss of Sumter. He's a discreditable ally for the North, but when you see a rat leaving the enemy's ship for your own, you overlook the offensiveness of the vermin for the sake of what the movement indicates. This brazen old scoundrel was hooted up Fulton Street yesterday afternoon by a mob, and the police interfered to prevent it from sacking his printing office. Though converted, one can hardly call him penitent. St. Paul did not call himself the Chief of the Apostles and brag of having been a Christian from the first.[16]

The mob Strong mentioned had gathered in front of the *Herald*'s office, stimulated by an attack on Bennett as a rebel and traitor in Raymond's *Times,* and it refused to disperse until an American flag was hung from an upper floor window. No doubt this demonstration influenced Bennett's turnabout.[17]

The conversion was complete. The South was treating the North like a hostile power; therefore, "we must fight." The border states were urged to remain in the Union, but when Virginia seceded and mobs rioted in Baltimore to prevent the passage of troops to defend Washington, the *Herald* was concerned. Lincoln was not acting decisively enough. "Oh, for ten days of staunch old Andrew Jackson," the *Herald* pined. "A million dollars would be cheap for a President with a backbone—a man of the stamp of Andrew Jackson, who, being first sure he was right, would take the responsibility and go ahead, looking danger and death in the eye." Although the war would be a salutary one, purifying the country of its corrupt political parties, and would bring a return to reason after a few battles, Bennett was supporting merely the administration, not its party backers. The Republicans and their bloodthirsty press, the Marats and Robespierres of the North, remained the enemy.[18]

The president took the initiative in Bennett's conversion to support his war policies. The administration was especially concerned with what it perceived to be the *Herald*'s large influence in Europe. When Lincoln brought the matter before the cabinet, Seward urged that Thurlow Weed, the Albany Republican leader and Seward's longtime crony, be given the mission of appealing to Bennett. "It was a bitter errand," comments Weed's biographer, "this being sent to woo a man with whom he had not been on speaking terms for years, but Weed undertook the job." Lincoln gave the assignment to Weed, he said, because of Weed's "considerable experience in belling cats." Weed left on the next train to New York to see his old political enemy. A meeting was arranged by Richard Schell, a mutual friend, and Weed was invited to dine with Bennett at the editor's Washington Heights home. After a quiet meal, Weed revealed the purpose of his mission. He then listened to a ten-minute denunciation of the abolitionist Republicans who had brought on the war. Weed responded with his interpretation of the slave power conspiracy and the deliberate southern disruption of the Democratic party. Bennett reflected on this for a few minutes and then changed the subject. They parted amicably, Weed reported, with Bennett promising nothing about the future course of the *Herald*. But the paper immediately came to support the government against the rebellion. The reason was clear to Weed: "Bennett's judgement and . . . sense of duty as an influential journalist to the government and union. That appeal, direct and simple, was successful." Bennett offered his son's yacht to the revenue service and obtained a lieutenant's commission for yachtsman James Gordon Bennett, Jr.[19]

The conversion cannot be explained by Weed's intercession alone or the commission for Bennett's son. Surely Bennett sensed the change in public opinion in New York now that the war had come and compromise options had failed. Bennett had always been a chauvinist, and patriotism demanded that he support his country in its moment of peril. He was a moderate, not a revolutionary. He could foresee that opposition to the war would cost the *Herald* dearly in circulation and influence. Strong did not have to be a soothsayer to predict Bennett's conversion to the administration's war effort.

Bennett's changed attitude disrupted his relations with the former president. When Buchanan left office, he asked Bennett to send the *Herald* to his Lancaster home, saying, "I am quite lost without it." He was grateful for "the able and powerful support which you have given me almost universally throughout my stormy & turbulent administration." But Bennett's criticism of Buchanan after Fort Sumter outraged the former president. "The *Herald*," he complained, "from a spirit of malignity, & supposing that the world may have forgotten the circumstances, takes every occasion to blame me for my supineness. It will soon arrive at the point of denouncing me for not crushing out the rebellion at once, & thus try to make me the author of the war." He threatened to indict Bennett for libel and sought advice from his old friend Edwin M. Stanton but was dissuaded from initiating a suit. "The public mind is too much excited on other topics," Stanton wrote, "to give attention to the past and it would only afford occasion for fresh malignant attacks upon you from Bennett. His day, I think, is passing."[20]

While Bennett was involved in these political machinations, Hudson had to make arrangements to cover the war.[21] J. Cutler Andrews identified sixty-three *Herald* reporters as being in the field during the war. Thomas W. Knox served as a western correspondent for several eastern papers before coming to New York in early 1861 to seek a job from Hudson. The busy managing editor paused long enough to tell Knox: "A long and bloody war is upon us, in which the whole country will be engaged. We shall desire you to take the field, probably in the West. It may be several weeks before we need you, but the war cannot be long delayed." When Knox returned for final instructions, he found that Hudson "had determined upon a vigorous campaign. Every point of interest was to be covered, so that the operations of our armies would be fully covered from day to day. . . . I was instructed to watch the military movement in Missouri, and hastened to St. Louis as fast as a team could bear me."[22]

Henry Villard, who had been sending dispatches to the *Herald* about Lincoln's activities in Springfield, came to Washington in early 1861 to furnish news to several papers as a supplement to the inefficient Washington office of the Associated Press. The *Herald* was one of these papers, and it paid Villard $25 weekly (soon raised to $35) despite Villard's Republican sympathies. The reporter was on personal terms with Lincoln and Chase and provided inside information that Bennett relished. Villard drifted into army correspondence for the *Herald*, first covering the camps around Washington and then going to Louisville, where he was able to acquire southern newspapers from travelers. "With clippings from them, which I accompanied by proper comments, I made up regular budgets of Southern news, which became a highly-prized feature of the *Herald*." Villard left Bennett's employ a few months later for the more politically congenial *Tribune*.[23]

Good correspondents were hard to find. Knox, the chief western reporter by mid-1862, complained that "I have been most troubled about someone to send to Halleck's army. I had a man engaged several days ago but he backed out on account of his wife having some absurd prejudice against his going to the army & getting killed. . . . Journalists that are worth an army ration are exceedingly scarce in the West at present." The Washington bureau chief remarked that it was difficult "to manage correspondents after they get into the field. They become so much absorbed with what they see they forget to relate it."[24]

Bennett was willing to pay for talent and spared no expenses. He paid the best salaries and provided the best equipment. George A. Townsend, then working for the *Philadelphia Press*, was dazzled enough by the accoutrements of a *Herald* correspondent to switch to Bennett's employ. "His saddle was a cushioned McClellan," Townsend wrote admiringly of the *Herald* man, "with spangled breast-strap and plump saddle bags, and his bridle was adorned with a bright curb bit and twilled reins. He wore a field glass belt about his body and was plentifully supplied with money to purchase items of news, if they were at any time difficult to obtain. I resolved . . . to seize the first opportunity of changing establishments." The expenses for horses and campaign outfits were heavy; some correspondents used up as many as six horses a year, and if a man transferred from one army to another the equipment was usually abandoned. There was supposed to be a *Herald* correspondent with each army division, an ideal never reached, and a *Herald* headquarters tent and wagon with each army corps.[25]

In return for the high salaries and fine equipment, the *Herald* reporters were expected to be tireless in procuring the news. Bennett, Cadwallader said, "exalted late news above fine writing." A confidential *Herald* circular instructed the correspondents to furnish maps, plans, casualty lists, southern newspapers, biographical sketches of generals, and any secret military information they could acquire.

> In no instance and under no circumstances, must you be beaten. . . . You will have energetic and watchful men to compete with. Eternal industry is the price of success. You must be active — very active. To be beaten is to be open to great censure. . . .
>
> Remember that your correspondence is seen by half a million persons daily and that the readers of the Herald *must* have the earliest news. . . .
>
> Again bear in mind that *the Herald must never be beaten.*

If these instructions were followed, Cadwallader relates, "good service to the *Herald* insured good pay, rapid promotion, and a personal treatment by Mr. Bennett and Mr. Hudson, beyond computation in dollars and cents." As a result, "the *Herald* gathered around it, the ablest men in the country, any one of whom would risk his life in collecting valuable information, and transmitting it to the office in advance of all competitors."[26]

Politics was subordinated to the zeal for news-gathering. It was advantageous for a correspondent to be on intimate terms with generals, and many of them were, obtaining staff commissions (which also enabled them to avoid the draft): Cadwallader with Grant, Finley Anderson with Winfield Scott Hancock, Thomas Cash with Nathaniel P. Banks, T. M. Cook with Daniel Sickles, and Cash and Oscar G. Sawyer with David G. Farragut. Both Malcolm Ives and Cook seemed to have special access to Assistant Secretary of the Navy Gustavus V. Fox, and Washington bureau chiefs Simon P. Hanscom and L. A. Whitely had a confidential source in the War Department.[27]

The *Herald* also had an unusual confidential source in the White House, the first lady, Mary Lincoln. Bennett had cultivated her, sending her an occasional bouquet of flowers, and the *Herald*'s editorial columns defended her against criticism. She responded with a gushing letter of gratitude and an invitation to the Bennetts to the Grand Union Ball at the White House on New Year's Day 1862. Sometime *Herald* reporter Henry Wikoff, the "Chevalier," also courted Mrs. Lincoln and won her trust, culminating in Wikoff's scoop of the text of Lincoln's first annual message in December 1861. Wikoff would say only that the White House gardener had committed the message to memory, but the more likely assumption was that the first lady had given Wikoff access to the message.[28]

The *Herald* had a Washington bureau with a staff of four or five, supervised by Simon P. Hanscom until 1862 and after that by L. A. Whitely. This office sometimes channeled military news from reporters in Virginia to the New York office. In New York there was a southern department to collect and file all information coming from the South, especially from southern newspapers, which were procured from fugitive slaves, deserters, prisoners, and abandoned camps. Enough information was obtained from this desk to publish a nearly complete roster of the Confederate army on September 9, 1863. When a copy of it reached Richmond it caused a shakeup in the War Department, which assumed that one of the clerks had furnished the information to the *Herald*.[29]

Besides the correspondents' expenses, there were charges for increased use of the telegraph lines. Before the war the Herald had carried several columns of telegraphic news; now it ran to several pages. The telegraphic charge was $1,000, for example, for the *Herald*'s account of the capture of New Orleans. The *Herald*'s telegraph bill for the four years of the war was between $500,000 and $750,000.[30]

"From the start," Bernard Weisberger writes admiringly, "the *Herald*'s correspondents operated like a well-drilled team, amply backed by reserves. A mid-western editor visiting the capital in June of 1861 watched the Washington squad in action with helpless professional admiration. There were four of them, combing camps, office buildings, and 'public resorts' daily, with incidental expenses guaranteed and orders to send any copy, even 'in wads,' by wire." One minor naval engagement on the Potomac, for example, was covered exhaustively by three *Herald* reporters.[31]

A detailed examination of the *Herald*'s war reporting discloses that politics often colored its treatment of military news. Along with the rest of the northern press, the *Herald* expected a quick and decisive movement of all the Union armies, led by old General Winfield Scott, and the "utter extinguishment of the rebels at all points." Minor skirmishes early in the war in western Virginia and Missouri were touted as major routs for the Confederacy.[32]

The first major test of both the armies and the press was the Battle of Bull Run, and neither acquitted itself with distinction. Villard was the *Herald*'s correspondent with Irvin McDowell's army when it began advancing on July 16. That weekend the first large battle of the war was waged near Manassas amid great confusion. The first day's fighting was proclaimed a "BRILLIANT UNION VICTORY" in bold front-page headings in the *Herald*. "The Rebels Routed," the news columns said, and an editorial discussed the "grand victory." The story was correct as far as it went. But in midafternoon the tide of battle turned, and a Confederate counterattack led to a disorderly Union retreat. None of this was known in New York because the Washington telegraph office was closed. Villard's dispatch on its reopening on Monday morning was the first news of the defeat to reach New York. The account was so grim that Hudson refused to print it. The muted story on July 23 told of rebel reinforcements and the "Repulse of Union Troops by an Overwhelming Force." The *Herald* was enthusiastic about McDowell's replacement by young General George B. McClellan after the defeat, and it found a scapegoat in the Republican Congress. "The responsible parties . . . belong to that fanatical abolitionist clique who are laboring . . . to divert this war from its legitimate objective . . . into an exterminating crusade against Southern slavery."[33] These Republican "Jacobins" were the *Herald*'s scapegoat for all the reverses of the war that were to come.

Caught up in the general hysteria of the unexpected defeat, the *Herald* reported "Atrocities of the Rebels after the Battle." Louisiana Zouaves, it related, cut off the heads of Union wounded and kicked them around like footballs. But sanity soon returned to the paper. The *Herald* reported an inspiring rise in confidence when McClellan arrived to take command of the reinforcements pouring into Washington. The rebellion would be crushed by May 1862.[34]

The *Herald* also focused attention early in the war on Missouri, where General John C. Frémont had been appointed to command in mid-1861, to Bennett's satisfaction. The *Herald*'s Knox was one of the first reporters in the Missouri war zone and had accompanied General Nathaniel Lyon in several early skirmishes. He was with Lyon when the general was killed at the Battle of Wilson's Creek in August, the hardest fought battle of the early Missouri campaign. Knox's account appeared in the *Herald* on August 14, but it was not entirely accurate. He reported that Confederate General Sterling Price had been killed. Similarly, a month later, for a week, the *Herald* carried reports with "positive confirmation" of the death of Jefferson Davis.[35]

The other major news from Missouri was Frémont's proclamation freeing the slaves of rebels there, which surprisingly, the *Herald* supported as a military necessity occasioned by rebel atrocities. It soon changed its mind, lauded Lincoln's orders to rescind the proclamation and his rebuke to Frémont, rumored Frémont's removal, and cheered the affair as a setback to the abolitionists.[36]

McClellan's growing army in the Washington area was the major story of late 1861, with the *Herald* joining the rest of the press in regularly predicting its advance. Soon the *Herald* was defending McClellan's reluctance to move against the "On to Richmond" cries of the *Tribune* and the *Times*. By January the *Herald* forecast a winter campaign and supported McClellan's elaborate preparations, comparing him to Napoleon.[37]

This hero worship of McClellan, which continued throughout the war, was initially the work of Malcolm Ives. On January 15, 1862, Ives obtained an interview with McClellan, who took fellow Democrat Ives into his confidence. The general disclosed secret information about pending military movements in all the theaters and promised more. Why?

> After informing me that Mr. Hudson's name was a household word with some of his nearest friends . . . he added: — but I particularly wish to charge you with a message to Mr. Bennett — "Mr. Bennett had stood by me in the hour of the bitterest anxiety of my whole life. . . . He has done so disinterestedly, nobly, and with the whole force of his paper. He and he alone has upheld me, cheered me and encouraged me, when every other newspaper has heaped upon me calumny and abuse, at the

very time that I was saving them from the horrors of invasion. . . . I shall *never, never, never* forget his kindness, and I want him to know that I cherish him in my heart, and that I shall strive with all the energy that my Maker has given me to prove, as I have no doubt I shall, that his confidence has not been misplaced." He then rather apologized for saying that it was his duty to require a solemn pledge from me not only that what he was about to tell me [about pending troop movements] should be revealed to no living being, excepting yourself and Mr. Hudson, *exclusive of everyone else;* but also that we would not even let the fact of the possession of such knowledge be known.[38]

The day after this performance, remarkable both for his groveling to his employers and his inflation of his own role, Ives wrote to Hudson that Lincoln and the new secretary of war, Edwin M. Stanton, were happy with the reporting of the *Herald* and in a section marked "Private" warned the editor that McClellan "is as guileless and innocent as a child & we must be careful not to injure him even to promote *Herald* interests." Two weeks later Ives, now with a massive sense of self-importance, described visits to Stanton, Congressman Frank Blair, McClellan (who confided that his army would begin its advance in early March and the *Herald* would receive prior warning), Fox at the Navy Department (who promised more exclusives for the *Herald*), and Secretary of the Treasury Chase, who discussed at length both taxation and reconstruction, "which is considered by the President and his advisors, *the gravest question* now before them for consideration."[39]

Bureau chief Hanscom resented Ives's imperious posture and moved to destroy his rival. Hanscom told the War Department late in January 1862 that Ives had no connection with the *Herald*'s Washington bureau, and he began sending Hudson his own confidential information. Ives survived this sabotage for only another week. On February 10 he was arrested by the War Department and confined to Fort McHenry, charged with disclosing military movements to the enemy, with threatening the War Department with the *Herald*'s hostility if it did not leak secret information to him, and with being a Confederate sympathizer. (He had a brother in the Confederate army and was certainly proslavery.) The *Herald* disavowed him if he had used improper methods to gain information but affirmed his loyalty to the Union. Ives remained in confinement until late March, when he was released without being formally charged, his connection to the *Herald* severed.[40]

Meanwhile, the *Herald* remained optimistic that McClellan would soon advance to crush the rebellion. The paper credited victories in the West to his overall planning. Hanscom, still treated as a friend at McClellan's headquarters, began making arrangements to cover the advance. He estimated that he would need five or six reporters with the Army of the Potomac.[41]

There was good news early in 1862. An expedition in February to Roanoke led by General Ambrose Burnside was a "BRILLIANT" success, described to the *Herald*'s readers by John P. Dunn, as was the capture of Newbern in March. Again, the *Herald* gave much of the credit to McClellan's planning.[42]

At about the same time a more dramatic story arose from the four-hour naval battle off Hampton Roads, Virginia, between the ironclads *Monitor* and *Virginia* (formerly the *Merrimac*, scuttled at Norfolk and raised and rebuilt by the Confederates). There had been rumors that the *Merrimac* was being rebuilt for some time, and Hudson sent B. S. Osbon to investigate. At night in a small boat in October 1861 Osbon managed to slip past Confederate batteries and up the Elizabeth River to the *Merrimac*'s drydock. He escaped undetected and wrote an account for the *Herald* and an illustrated essay for *Harper's Weekly*.[43]

When the rebuilt *Virginia* emerged on March 8, *Herald* correspondent William H. Stiner at Fortress Monroe witnessed its destruction of the *Congress* and its threat to other ships, to the blockade, and perhaps to Burnside's Roanoke expedition. The arrival of the new Union ironclad *Monitor*, which fought the *Virginia* to a standstill, saved the day, and Stiner's account was featured for four days, on two of them filling the entire front page, with woodcuts and a battle map and with a reprint of Osbon's October story predicting the danger the ironclad posed.[44]

Osbon had missed the battle because he had joined the Gulf Squadron in January as Farragut's clerk. When they arrived in the Gulf, Farragut learned of Osbon's previous experience at sea and appointed him the signal officer of the squadron, an ideal position for close personal contact with Farragut and knowledge of the fleet's movements. Osbon witnessed the battering of the forts below New Orleans and the surrender of the city. His three-page account in the *Herald* on May 10 was the best and most detailed to appear, although he was beaten by a day by a *New York Times* reporter with news of the city's surrender.[45]

By this time the *Herald* had discovered another military hero to match McClellan — Ulysses S. Grant. The paper first noticed Grant at Paducah in September 1861. Then the *Herald*'s Frank Chapman was with Grant when he and Andrew H. Foote's gunboats captured two strongholds in February 1862, Fort Henry on the Tennessee River and Fort Donelson on the Cumberland. The *Herald* featured both victories prominently and credited both to McClellan's comprehensive planning. The *Herald* next expected the combined armies of Grant and Don Carlos Buell to attack Corinth and Decatur, where Confederate Generals Beauregard and Albert Sidney Johnston had concentrated their armies.[46] Instead, the Confederates attacked Grant's carelessly camped army at Pittsburgh Landing on the Tennessee River. The resulting Battle of Shiloh was the bloodiest of the war to date, and a great *Herald* beat on April 10. After the battle Chapman had gone upriver to Fort Henry and gotten access to the army telegraph on the pretext that he was on Grant's staff. The news reached New York late on April 9, and the next morning's *Herald* was the first account of the battle. It was read that day to both Houses of Congress.

The story, very inaccurate in overestimating the extent of the victory and the losses on both sides, began: "The bloodiest battle of modern times just closed, resulting in complete rout of the enemy, who attacked us Sunday morning. Battle lasted until Monday, 4.35 p.m., when the enemy commenced their retreat, and are still flying towards Corinth, pursued by large force of our cavalry. Slaughter on both sides immense. Lost in killed, wounded, and missing from eighteen to twenty thousand; that of the enemy is estimated from thirty-five to forty thousand." In an attempt to win Grant's favor, Chapman attributed some fictitious heroism to the general, crediting him with personally leading a charge that broke the Confederate advance on the second day. Again, the *Herald* gave credit for the victory to McClellan's planning.[47]

Within a week General Henry W. Halleck, the commander in the West, arrived at Grant's headquarters to take charge of the army. In April it began an agonizingly slow advance toward Corinth, where Beauregard had retreated. W. F. G. Shanks reported the movement and the eventual evacuation of Corinth in May; the *Herald* commented that "it needs but one more squeeze of McClellan's anaconda for the boasted Confederacy to vanish." But Halleck was overly sensitive to criticism from the press — none of it in the *Herald* — and he ordered the expulsion of unauthorized personnel from his army. The vague order was not intended to expel reporters with valid credentials, but soon after Halleck ordered all correspondents to the army's rear. They left in a body for Cairo, except for Shanks, who was too ill to leave his bed.[48] It made little difference because Halleck was soon called to Washington to assume overall command of the Union armies. Buell's army then returned to the Department of the Ohio to operate against East Tennessee; Grant's army was dispersed to garrison West Tennessee and northern Mississippi.

Thomas W. Knox of the *Herald* accompanied the navy in its bombardment and capture of Memphis, an important prize. For over a year after this, operations along the Mississippi were the dominant theme of reporting from the West. In the summer of 1862 the Union made preliminary movements against the two remaining strongholds on the river, Vicksburg and Port Hudson. Knox was with the unsuccessful Vicksburg expedition led by General William T. Sherman, and he wrote critically of Sherman's attempt. The general bristled at any newspaper criticism and decided to make an example of Knox. The reporter was arrested and tried by a military court-martial for giving information to the enemy, disobeying orders, and spying for the Confederacy. Convicted of the count of disobedience, Knox was expelled from Sherman's lines. The Washington press corps petitioned Lincoln to suspend the sentence, and he agreed to defer the decision to Grant, who in turn referred it back to Sherman, who was angry that Knox had not been convicted on all the charges and refused. The *Herald* was bitter, noting that this victory over the press was Sherman's only one.[49]

After that, the *Herald* devoted little attention to Grant's army. Banks's expedition up the Red River received more notice, and the campaign against Port Hudson was given elaborate coverage. The *Herald* did report the feat of the navy in running the batteries of Vicksburg in March 1863, which enabled Grant to ferry his troops across the river south of the city, but it was disappointed, overall, in the military prospects in the West.[50]

But a Confederate invasion of Kentucky by General Braxton Bragg had been repulsed, and there was hard fighting in Tennessee in late 1862 and early 1863. The *Herald*'s Shanks was with Buell as he tried to parry Bragg's Kentucky invasion, the campaign decided at Perryville in October. Shanks exaggerated the extent of the Union victory. The *Herald* was optimistic when General William Rosecrans arrived at Nashville to replace Buell, and at the end of the year Shanks was the first to learn of Rosecrans's advance against Bragg that culminated in the Battle of Murfreesboro at the New Year 1862–63. Shanks described the battle vividly and with the usual embellishments.[51]

Coverage from the West had been spotty. The paper was more concerned with the eastern theater and the activities of its hero, McClellan. The *Herald*'s Washington bureau had made elaborate preparations for the advance south from the Potomac, and when McClellan moved into abandoned Confederate positions without firing a shot, the *Herald* celebrated a great victory and predicted the collapse of the rebellion and the flight of the Confederate government from Richmond within two months.[52] The *Herald*'s reports and editorials regarding McClellan often bore little resemblance to reality.

McClellan was the *Herald*'s political as well as military hero. As a conservative he was hated by the Jacobins in the cabinet and on the Committee on the Conduct of the War. The *Herald* credited all Union victories to his master plan and blamed his defeats on inadequate support by Stanton and the War Department. McClellan was partial to *Herald* reporters. His chief of staff (and father-in-law) Randolph Marcy had once worked for Bennett and was a close friend of Hudson's.[53]

McClellan did not march south toward Richmond. Instead, he took his army by water to Fortress Monroe to approach Richmond by way of the peninsula formed by the York and James rivers. Fourteen *Herald* correspondents accompanied the Army of the Potomac on the peninsular campaign, but according to one of them, George A. Townsend, few were "fit to describe a fire":

> They were the usual run of forward, uneducated, often middle-aged, misplaced people, who had mysteriously gotten on a newspaper. They were capable of plenty of endurance, and would ride up and down, talk with great confidence, and be familiar with everybody, and then not know how to relate what they saw. . . . Whenever a big battle would start up, the *Herald* man would dash immediately for New York, and there portray a plan of the battlefield he had never seen, with all the worm fences and creeks running the wrong way in it. Instead of placing one or two well-equipped, well-mounted, well-behaved young men with the army, who should feel independent, gain the confidence of the general officers and make the reputation of the newspaper with their own, the work was all cut up, and any forward, tricky fellow could take the credit from all the modest ones — if there were any such.[54]

But Bennett and the *Herald* office had already decided that McClellan was invincible, and the accounts were rewritten to stress that point so it is doubtful if another system would have made much difference.

The first move on the peninsula, agonizingly slow, was against Confederate positions at Yorktown. The *Herald,* like McClellan, greatly overestimated the strength of Confederate numbers and fortifications there, hailing its evacuation after a month as a brilliant victory for McClellan. The rebels had been routed, and the road to Richmond was open. After this, a western correspondent at Yorktown seconded Townsend's complaints. The map of Confederate fortifications at Yorktown which appeared in the *Herald* was a "gross imposition." Bennett should *"quit his tricks at fabricating defenses* that don't exist and plans that never entered any head except his own. The Confederate entrenchments on the peninsula are strong, but that they are of such a character as the above map represents is preposterous."[55]

The War Department devised an elaborate system of censorship of news from the peninsula. To circumvent it, the *Herald* stationed a man at Fortress Monroe to forward the dispatches of *Herald* reporters to Baltimore, usually with the stewards of the Old Colony Steamship Line. If the packet was on time, the messages were carried by train and special messenger to New York. If the packet missed connections with the New York train, the dispatches were sent by telegraph.[56]

As McClellan edged up the peninsula toward Richmond, a battle was fought near Williamsburg. Again there were complaints that the *Herald*'s coverage was misleading, giving much of the credit for the victory to a regiment that was three miles from the battle and manufacturing a bayonet charge by Hancock's division. Attention was momentarily shifted to Stonewall Jackson's successful diversionary campaign in the Shenandoah Valley, which led the *Herald* to echo McClellan's call for reinforcements.[57]

Finally, at the end of May, after an uneventful march up the peninsula to the Chickahominy River a dozen miles from Richmond, desperate fighting began at Fair Oaks (or Seven Pines). The *Herald*'s reports were extensive, vivid, and timely; they hailed another splendid McClellan victory and again exaggerated Confederate strength. The New York office received the accounts quickly because the *Herald* chartered a tugboat from McClellan's base at White House to Fortress Monroe. But there were errors again: reports of great fighting on the next day, when all was quiet, and stories that the rebels had opened dams on the upper Chickahominy to flood the Union rear, which were complete fabrications.[58]

For the next three weeks McClellan's army remained in place, then in late June began to advance on Richmond again. After being attacked at Gaines Mill by Lee and Jackson, McClellan retreated to the James River and established a more secure base at Harrison's Landing. These movements were duly reported by Townsend and Anderson with the usual optimism. Then the fighting resumed again, the furious and bloody Seven Days. Despite tight censorship, the *Herald* carried a large front-page map of the battles before Richmond, the story headed "The Consummate Strategy of McClellan." The change of base to the James River had been a brilliant move; the administration should send reinforcements immediately; McClellan was heavily outnumbered, but he would be in Richmond any day. When the fighting at Malvern Hill ended, McClellan retreated back to his base at Harrison's Landing. The failure was caused by Secretary of War Stanton. The abolitionists in Congress had persuaded him to take control of the campaign away from McClellan. If Stanton had given McClellan fifty thousand more men, he would be in Richmond. The cabinet must be reorganized, Stanton must be let go, and politics must be subordinated to the capture of Richmond.[59]

The *Herald* had been the first New York paper with the news of Malvern Hill because of the resourcefulness of B. S. Osbon. When a train carrying reporters from the peninsula broke down near Philadelphia, the correspondents decided to stay overnight in the city. But Osbon went on by foot, persuaded a farmer to drive him through a pelting rainstorm to the West Philadelphia station, and chartered a special train to Jersey City, where he was met by a group of *Herald* compositors. The *Herald*'s extensive story combined Osbon's early account and later details from Townsend.[60]

A Cincinnati reporter was critical of the *Herald*'s bias toward McClellan. The *Herald* correspondent wrote, he said,

> on that terrible Tuesday, after the doubly decimated army had changed
> its base and reached Malvern Hill . . . that the soldiers were recovering from their fatigue and were in the jolliest of spirits, and unbounded
> in their confidence in their general. . . . The army's confidence in Gen.
> McClellan was required to be put in at stated intervals in their letter.
> So in the Herald office it was kept standing [in type], to be inserted in
> the correspondence at stated intervals, that Gen. McClellan was on the
> field in the thickest of the fight, inspiring the troops with the utmost
> enthusiasm.[61]

The *Herald* continued to support McClellan as he remained inactive for several weeks. His escape from disaster had been masterly; his estimates of rebel strength had been accurate, and he had been outnumbered by two or three to one. All he needed to take Richmond was equal numbers with the enemy, but until reinforcements arrived he would be unable to move forward. There was a new concern. Stonewall Jackson was back in the Valley operating against the new army of General John Pope. The *Herald* was optimistic that Pope and McClellan would cooperate closely; it sent correspondents to the Valley, and they reported a Union victory at Cedar Mountain with Jackson retreating toward Richmond. The report was the work of Frank Chapman, in charge of the *Herald* reporters with Pope as a reward for his Shiloh beat. When Townsend saw Chapman's account and his map of the battlefield, he was astonished; it bore no resemblance to the battlefield. Chapman, he wrote, was "not a bad fellow. He had simply defined the loose way things were running on the *Herald,* and had made up his mind to be in on the big events, whether there or not. I do not think he was anywhere near the battle of Cedar Mountain."[62]

Within the next week McClellan's army abandoned its base at Harrison's Landing and was brought back to the Potomac to join Pope. While McClellan's army was in transit, Lee was able to rush his and Jackson's armies north to attack Pope on the site of the old Bull Run battlefield. The *Herald* was hopeful that with Congress not in session and Halleck in overall command there would be no radical political interference. The *Herald*'s accounts of the Second Battle of Bull Run were inaccurate and misleading, but understandably so because of the tight censorship imposed by Pope. The paper's headlines first reported a "Rebel Raid on Manassas," then "The Enemy Thoroughly Routed," then "Pope's Splendid Achievements" and "Brilliant Operations" in a crowning victory that immortalized the old battlefield. When Pope's defeat and retreat became clear, it was blamed on his being heavily outnumbered. When McClellan arrived with his troops and took command, the *Herald* was confident that Lee's probable invasion of Maryland would be a Confederate disaster.[63]

McClellan began his pursuit of Lee on September 5. The censorship remained in place. Although the *Herald* had several correspondents in units of McClellan's army, its account of the Battle of Antietam was two days later than the *Tribune*'s. Its joy at McClellan's success was unbounded. The battle was a rebel rout, the death blow to the rebellion. Lee would be destroyed. When McClellan did not pursue, the blame was placed on the administration's refusal to send reinforcements.[64]

Antietam had broken the backbone of the rebellion, and the *Herald*'s cry was "On to Richmond." McClellan delayed only for want of supplies. The *Herald* hoped the rumors were true that Halleck would be sent back to the West and Little Mac would again be given command of all the Union forces. The paper was still confident of McClellan's cautious but certain advance on Richmond.[65]

But on November 9 the *Herald*'s favorite was removed and replaced by General Ambrose Burnside. The administration had caved in to pressure from the radicals. McClellan had been cautious but safe, the *Herald* argued; his removal would make him the next president, the most renowned military hero since Andrew Jackson. But Burnside would also do the job, as he began to move on Richmond by way of Fredericksburg. There would be no more disappointments.[66]

The *Herald* reported the preliminaries to Burnside's attack on Lee at Fredericksburg, but strict censorship prevented accurate knowledge of the situation. On December 12 the paper reported that Burnside had captured Fredericksburg. It hedged the next day but still expected Lee to retreat, and not until December 17 did it report "the disaster" to Burnside. Again the blame was placed in Washington, with Stanton and the radicals, but the ultimate cause of the disaster had been the removal of McClellan. He should be recalled to command.[67]

As usual, the *Herald* had inflated the strength of Lee's army to two hundred thousand, three times its actual size. General George G. Meade complained to his wife that the *Herald* reported that his men ran at the first fire. "This is the harder, because I saw a *Herald* correspondent on the field, and he might have known and indeed did know better." But General David Birney wrote that Finley Anderson's account was "a very true one."[68]

An attitude of uncertainty and gloom settled over Washington following the Fredericksburg disaster. The *Herald* editorialized, again, that the real fault was in the administration, that Stanton, Chase, Gideon Welles, and Halleck should be removed and McClellan restored to command. It was apprehensive when Burnside was replaced by General Joseph Hooker, a favorite of the radicals. It expected little without McClellan, compared him to Wellington, and lashed out at the Committee on the Conduct of the War for its abuse of him. Hooker seemed capable only of staging grand reviews. When would the army move?[69]

Hooker did move, finally, in late April 1863, and the result was Chancellorsville, another disaster. Censorship was imposed and so the initial accounts were inaccurate, indicating "a crowning Union triumph along the whole line." Not until May 8, three days later, did the *Herald* report Hooker's retreat, which caused a "profound sensation of disappointment and despondency." Hooker, one of McClellan's critics, had been put to the test and found wanting. He would be replaced, but not by McClellan, who was too smart to serve "under poor Stanton's blundering, imbecile administration. The conservative masses of the country want General McClellan for the great political campaign in November 1864. They cannot spare him to prop up Stanton, Halleck and Company."[70]

After his victory, Lee began moving his army north into Maryland, with Hooker following on an inside line. Lee's destination after provisioning in Pennsylvania would be Washington, the *Herald* speculated. A terrible battle was in the making, with an opportunity to administer a death blow to Lee, if only the administration would remove Hooker.[71]

Hooker was replaced by Meade on June 23, and the *Herald* was delighted; Meade was not involved in politics. On June 29 much of page 1 contained a map of the Harrisburg area with the forecast of a decisive battle there that would determine America's destiny for centuries to come. On July 1, when the fighting started at Gettysburg, there was a map of the Gettysburg area on page 3, but with suggestions that Lee was moving to avoid a battle, an opinion repeated the next day. The first news in the *Herald* of the terrible fighting at Gettysburg was on July 3, with indications that Meade would win. On July 4 it carried a banner head, "A GREAT VICTORY WON!" and anticipated Lee's annihilation. On July 6 there were three large maps of the battlefield and details of the second and third days of fighting. The editorial cried "Victory! Victory! The Dying Struggles of the Rebellion." Meade was the man for the crisis and would not allow Lee to escape.[72]

The *Herald*'s reports were not entirely accurate, but they were the first of the battle to appear in New York. The paper had established a special relay of horses to carry dispatches to the Baltimore telegraph office, but on the morning of July 4 Frank Chapman reached Baltimore ahead of the other correspondents, awakened the superintendent, and began sending his copy over the wires to New York. He held the line the entire day; when rival reporters arrived and he ran out of fresh copy he began transmitting the Bible.[73]

The same day that the Battle of Gettysburg was concluded, July 4, 1863, the Confederate stronghold of Vicksburg surrendered to Grant. The *Herald* had been following Grant's efforts closely, and when Grant ferried his army across the river to a position south of Vicksburg, the *Herald* contrasted his decisiveness with Hooker's failures in the East. It covered Grant's campaign in detail: his capture of Port Gibson, the siege of the "Rebel Gibraltar" (with a front-page map), and the city's final surrender reported on July 8, with an editorial singing Grant's praises. By late July the *Herald* believed that the rebellion was crushed in the West.[74]

In contrast to the success of Grant and Meade, General William Rosecrans's army in Tennessee had done nothing for most of 1863. Pressure from the War Department finally forced him to move against Chattanooga in the late summer, accompanied by Shanks of the *Herald*. Rosecrans was tricked by Bragg into the mountains near Chattanooga and into the ensuing Battle of Chickamauga on September 30. Shanks was no admirer of Rosecrans and correctly interpreted the result as a Union defeat, a narrow escape from disaster. Editorially, the *Herald* again apportioned blame: the administration's order to Rosecrans to advance while refusing him reinforcements and the general incompetence of Stanton. Rosecrans was still in a good position; Bragg had not dislodged him from Chattanooga. Rosecrans's replacement by General George B. Thomas was attributed to his disagreements with the bunglers in the War Department.[75]

The armies in the West were then placed under the overall command of Grant, who arrived in Chattanooga to take charge. After reopening his supply lines, Grant carefully prepared an attack on Bragg's positions around the city. The battle began on November 23; the first accounts appeared in the *Herald* on November 25, hailing the battle as another brilliant victory for Grant and another fatal blow to the rebellion. Shanks's account of the fighting on Missionary Ridge was spectacular.[76]

Back in the East, after Gettysburg and Lee's escape, Meade's army had

done little. In March 1864, after Congress voted to commission a lieutenant general, Grant was brought east and made general in chief of all the
Union armies. Halleck remained as chief of staff, administering the Washington office, while Grant made his headquarters in the field with Meade's
Army of the Potomac. Sherman was left in Tennessee in command of the
western armies.

The *Herald* was delighted with the changes; Grant was fast eclipsing
McClellan as its favorite general. Grant's record was one of uninterrupted
success, the paper pointed out. On March 18 three seperate editorials lauded
Grant, "The Man on Horseback at Last." Nothing would stop him except
administration treachery. The coming campaign in Virginia would determine the future of free government. If Grant succeeded, he was certain
to become president.[77]

To cover the campaign, Bennett and Hudson made far-reaching changes
in their reporting arrangements. Sylvanus Cadwallader, who had been reporting on Grant's army in the West for the *Herald,* the *Chicago Times,*
and other papers, had quit and gone home. An urgent telegram from Hudson summoned him to New York in April 1864. Cadwallader was given
an independent position to cover Grant for the *Herald;* the general had
become his personal friend. He was to remain with Grant and submit his
dispatches directly to New York, responsible only to Hudson. There would
be a large salary and liberal expenses. Cadwallader arrived at Grant's headquarters in early May and soon completed arrangements to get the dispatches through the War Department censorship. After buying "the most
stylish horse in the Army of the Potomac," he hired three special messengers to carry *Herald* dispatches from Grant's headquarters at City Point
to Baltimore and two others to carry them from there to New York. The
combination sea and rail route left City Point at ten each morning and
arrived in New York by evening.[78]

Frank Chapman was left in charge of the other *Herald* correspondents
for another month, when, following the Battle of the Wilderness, he was
replaced by Cadwallader and banished to the routine at Cairo, Illinois.
The resourceful Finley Anderson, recently released from a Confederate
prison camp, was also assigned to the Army of the Potomac. Wounded
at the Wilderness, Anderson became a member of General Hancock's
staff.[79]

The army began to move south on May 4. The *Herald* arranged to use
the messengers or, because of Cadwallader's personal connections, Grant's
private mailbag. "On to Richmond," the *Herald* cried on May 7, the same
day Grant was checked by Lee at the Wilderness and furious fighting took
place on the old Chancellorsville battlefield. Cadwallader was organized

and energetic; by noon he had rounded up all that the *Herald* correspondents had written and had compiled a casualty list. Getting the account
to New York was harrowing. He was captured by John S. Mosby's Confederates, bribed his way out without the dispatches, got to Washington
by raft, and holed up at Willard's Hotel. There he dictated all night for
the telegraph and then took the train to New York, where he continued
to dictate to Hudson until he was on the verge of collapse. But the *Tribune*
had already broken the story. Until Cadwallader's account, the *Herald's*
news of the Wilderness had been meager.[80]

Bennett was furious at being beaten by the *Tribune*. Cadwallader was
put in complete charge and told to hire a good chef — he got the one from
Willard's — and to open a *Herald* center at Grant's headquarters where he
could entertain in style. Cadwallader claimed that in his three tents with
three servants his dinners rivaled Grant's.[81]

Grant's and Lee's armies continued to encounter each other daily as
Grant tried to outflank Lee on the way to Richmond. Each move by Grant
was parried by Lee, and the casualties of the daily contact were enormous.
The *Herald's* reports were optimistic, tended to minimize the losses, re-
posed confidence in Grant's leadership, and by June 1 noted that Richmond was in sight.[82]

By early June Lee had pulled back to defensive lines around Richmond
and Petersburg, and a partial siege of the rebel positions began. When Grant
boldly changed his base of operations to the James River, the *Herald*
cheered, and on June 18 it very prematurely announced the fall of
Petersburg. The city's surrender was only a question of time, the *Herald*
believed, but Grant's job was made more difficult because of the incompetent generals (such as Franz Sigel and Benjamin F. Butler) that the administration had forced upon him.[83]

Attention was diverted from the Richmond area in July when rebel
General Jubal Early's cavalry in the Valley began moving north in a diversionary move that seemed to threaten Baltimore and Washington. The
Herald minimized the threat. Even though Early came within sight of
Washington, causing panic in the capital, the *Herald* assured its readers
that the city was safe, that Early's retreat was certain, and that the diversion was of little importance. To end the Confederates' use of the Valley,
General Philip Sheridan's cavalry was sent in pursuit of Early, and by October the Confederates were badly beaten. Now there would be nothing
to distract Grant in his pressure on Lee.[84]

By August the *Herald* was calling Petersburg another Vicksburg. All
that Grant needed to complete his encirclement was more men. The *Herald's* readers became familiar with the Richmond-Petersburg area through

many front-page maps. By early 1865 the end seemed near. Lee was ex-
hausting his men and rations; there was a clamor in Richmond for Jefferson Davis's removal. On March 2, 1865, the *Herald* reported rumors of
the flight of the Confederate government.[85]

Sheridan's cavalry was in Lee's rear by this time, threatening his com-
munications and supply lines. The Confederacy would collapse without
another battle; the choice at Richmond was evacuation or starvation. Grant
tightened his grip on the rebel capital, and on April 4 the *Herald*'s head
was "Richmond Ours." The editorial called the Union victory "the grandest triumph that has crowned human efforts for centuries." Lee's flight and
the Union pursuit were detailed by Cadwallader's men and, on April 10,
"THE END." Lee had surrendered his army to Grant at Appomattox Court
House.[86]

There had been, in the meantime, a sideshow in the eastern theater involving General Ben Butler, in command of the Army of the James at Fortress Monroe. Here two *Herald* correspondents were able to use to their
advantage the favoritism Grant had shown to Cadwallader. William H.
Stiner and William Merriman were great favorites of Butler, puffed him
shamelessly, and secured a pledge from Hudson not to attack Butler editorially. But another *Herald* reporter, Oscar G. Sawyer, was stationed at
the headquarters of Butler's corps commander, General Quincy A. Gilmore, who detested Butler. Sawyer's dispatches were fulsome in praising
Gilmore but failed to mention Butler. "It was evident," comments Bernard A. Weisberger, "that editorial consistency was not going to deny a
clear track to any *Herald* correspondent moving in on a firsthand story."[87]

When Butler mismanaged a combined operation with the navy off North
Carolina late in 1864 he was removed by Lincoln after pressure from Grant.
The *Herald* scored another beat. Cadwallader learned the news at Grant's
headquarters and army censors permitted only him to telegraph the news
to New York. The *Herald* puffed its beat, but Butler was furious. When
the North Carolina operation succeeded the next week without him, his
fate was sealed.[88]

More important operations were taking place in Georgia. As Grant was
moving south against Lee and Richmond, General William T. Sherman
and his western army launched a drive from Chattanooga to the Atlantic
through Georgia. Sherman was outspokenly hostile to reporters, but along
on his drive to Atlanta were *Herald* correspondents D. B. R. Keim, on
James McPherson's staff, T. M. Cook, secretary to Sickles, and David P.
Conyngham. It was a campaign similar to Grant's against Lee. Sherman
would try to outflank Joseph E. Johnston, and the Confederates would
make the appropriate countermove as they zigzagged toward Atlanta with

almost daily contact. It was all covered in detail and with front-page maps in the *Herald* until the city fell to Sherman in September 1864.[89]

The fall of Mobile to Admiral Farragut was also given vivid treatment by the *Herald*. Oscar G. Sawyer was along as the admiral's secretary on his flagship; Cook, recently transferred from Sickles's staff, was on another ship. Gustavus V. Fox of the Navy Department considered Cook's account of the battle the best.[90]

When Sherman set out from Atlanta on his march to the sea, about ten reporters accompanied his army, two of them from the *Herald*. Few facts were available in New York, but the *Herald* was optimistic. Typical heads were "Sherman's Grandest Campaign" and "Rebel Panic in Georgia." Numerous maps showed Sherman using the "Grant system" to cut through the heart of the rebellion; Georgia corn fields were Sherman's base of supplies. John B. Hood's campaign at Sherman's rear was hopeless. At Franklin and Nashville Hood was annihilated by Thomas.[91]

The *Herald* reported Sherman in front of Savannah on December 13, in touch with the navy, and the city fell as a Christmas gift to the nation. At the start of 1865 Sherman began moving north to join Grant, and the *Herald* documented his rapid progress: the capture of Augusta, the occupation and burning of Columbia, the surrender of Charleston, and on April 24 from North Carolina the news of Sherman's "Rash Armistice" terms and the surrender of the last Confederate army in the East. The war was over.[92]

The *Herald* demonstrated great zeal and efficiency in its coverage of the military side of the war, enterprising in its news-gathering and willing to spend as much money as necessary to get the war news first. Its corps of correspondents, the largest in the country, scored an impressive number of beats and provided some vivid and accurate battle accounts. But too often, accuracy was sacrificed for speed or, more reprehensible, it was sacrificed for politics. McClellan and, later, Grant could do no wrong; Stanton and the radicals were to blame for all the military failures. But the paper's record on the home front was worse. Its irresponsible criticism of the administration did little to contribute to support of the Union.

8

War and Postwar Politics

When the Civil War ended, Bennett pointed proudly to the "large corps of trained and able men," thirty or forty of them, who had brought the war to the breakfast tables of the *Herald*'s readers. What should be done with them? "We shall send them as our Ambassadors to all the great capitals of the world. . . . Just as there is a *Herald*'s headquarters tent with every army . . . so shall there be a *Herald* legation in all the chief cities from Melbourne to Spitsbergen" so that each morning Bennett's readers would get "a complete photograph of the world of the previous day."[1]

The *Herald* had not slighted world news during the war. Issues not related to the Civil War such as the Paraguayan War in South America and the Prussian conquest of Schleswig-Holstein were adequately reported, with illustrative maps. But the major focus was on the international ramifications of the American Civil War.[2]

Bennett became a steadfast supporter of Secretary of State William H. Seward (only recently the "arch-fiend") on both foreign policy and political matters, despite earlier political differences. This rapprochement cannot be explained with precision, but it resulted from Bennett's recognition that Seward (despite the *Herald*'s rhetoric during the 1850s) was a conservative force in the administration, a buffer to the "Jacobins," and from Seward's aggressive and expansionist ideas of foreign policy, which were similar to Bennett's. With Seward at the helm, the *Herald* predicted, there would be "no blunders to regret, and certainly no timidity to deplore." When England proclaimed her neutrality in May 1861, recognizing Confederate belligerency, Bennett supported Seward's vigorous protest and blamed the British action on the need for southern cotton.[3]

The tension with England reached a crisis in late 1861 over the *Trent* affair, when the Union navy removed from a British packet off Cuba the Confederate envoys James M. Mason and John Slidell. The *Herald*'s initial reaction was subdued; it opposed the return of the two diplomats but stressed that Captain Charles Wilkes had not been authorized to make the seizure, which violated the long-standing position of the United States about the right of search. It predicted that the administration would disavow the action and apologize to England. But the paper soon became more bellicose. Wilkes had merely followed the expanded view of belligerent rights that England had championed for so long. The captives would not be returned, and England would not risk a war with the United States over the matter.[4]

Then, after insisting that there would be no surrender of Mason and Slidell, the *Herald* did a spectacular reversal. On December 21, 1861, the paper predicted and justified the return of the southerners, disappointing to popular sentiment but necessary if the Union was to bring all its military power to bear on the rebels. But future revenge was promised; "as Rome remembered Carthage from the invasion of Hannibal . . . so will the people of the United States remember and treasure up for the future this little affair."[5]

Although the crisis had passed, the danger remained that the aristocrats in control of the British government might intervene to break the popular institutions of the United States and crush a commercial rival. To the *Herald* there was no question but that Britain would aid the Confederacy by building ships to break the blockade in return for southern cotton. To retaliate, reparations should be filed away for the future, most likely the seizure and retention of Canada "until full and satisfactory retribution be made."[6]

The continuing British interference in the war, along with European intervention in Mexico, led the *Herald* to warn the powers that when the war ended American hegemony in the Western Hemisphere would be complete. "We cannot brook the interference of any European power on this continent, and those who take advantage of our present troubles to intrude, will someday reap the whirlwind they are surely sowing."[7]

This bellicosity toward the powers was nothing new for the *Herald,* but it should not be dismissed as mere rhetoric. One authority on the diplomacy of the American Civil War calls the *Herald*'s position "the most articulate":

> The *Herald,* so often dismissed in the commentaries as an unrepresentative and irresponsible troublemaker in the international arena, in fact offered some of the more perceptive analyses of power realities in the new world, and of ideological possibilities in the old. Its attitudes were probably more deeply symptomatic of embedded American values than Americans would like to admit. But it moved in a world of harsh real-

ity. Spirited, aggressive, bigoted, cynical of motives, often wild and careless of consistency, the *Herald* stirred the pot.[8]

The *Herald*'s overriding concern for hemispheric hegemony derived as much from European intervention in Mexico as from British interference in the Civil War. The *Herald* had warned of European designs in Mexico in late 1861, with a long account of the joint seizure of Vera Cruz by the British, Spanish, and French. When England and Spain withdrew from the joint debt-collection venture, leaving only the augmented French army of Napoleon III, the *Herald* said that Mexico would prove fatal to the emperor. His conquest of Mexico was the most glaring abuse of power in history, and surely the United States would call him to account and reestablish the Monroe Doctrine.[9]

Troubles in Europe and a depleted treasury would force Napoleon to abandon his comic opera in Mexico. An American empire was an absurdity, and the Mexicans did not want Maximilian as emperor. His rupture with the reactionary Mexican Catholic church would be his undoing. As soon as the Civil War ended, the United States would assert the Monroe Doctrine and force a bloodless French withdrawal. "After Mexico will come Canada, and after Canada will come Cuba." The European powers would be gone from America.[10]

But the *Herald* was not optimistic about Mexico's future even after the restoration of Juarez and the republicans. The Mexicans were "not up to the mark, not yet sufficiently civilized to control their own destinies. . . . They need policing, and they shall have it; . . . and if we choose we can do it just as well as France. . . . Our sympathies . . . are enlisted on the side of American governmental ideas and principles, and not purely and simply on that of the Mexican people, who are as dust on the scale."[11]

When the Civil War ended, the *Herald* became less bellicose toward the European powers but still confident of American hegemony. No longer did the paper advocate the seizure of Canada and Cuba or armed intervention in Mexico. "Our wisest statesmen prefer a slower, but more peaceful process of reunion. . . . We do not want Canada any more than we want Mexico; but the point is to have the European powers withdraw. . . . As for Spain, we would pay her a round sum for Cuba, as we bought Louisiana from France. Thus the whole matter could be peaceably and satisfactorily arranged and the Monroe Doctrine vindicated without a war."[12]

All of this was so hypothetical that it signaled no basic change in policy. The *Herald* remained expansionist. It praised the purchase of Alaska, and it continued to press for the annexation of Canada, "our natural and most necessary complement." Monarchy there was "irritating to our republican institutions and an obstacle to the realization of the manifest destiny of the American republic." Manifest Destiny was not dead, the *Herald* argued in 1870: "The revolution in Cuba, the insurrection in the Winipeg [sic] country, the application of the people in British Columbia for annexation, the chronic disorders of Mexico . . . and the condition of the West Indies . . . show that our republican empire must become continental."[13]

These foreign policy attitudes are not surprising in light of the *Herald's* similar positions before the war. Nor were its wartime political positions much of a change. They continued to be erratic, with an eye to the main chance, and the issues that dominated Bennett's political choices were emancipation and reconstruction.

Bennett had always denounced the abolitionists. Abolition was first raised as a war issue in the late summer of 1861, when General John C. Frémont issued his proclamation freeing the slaves of those engaged in rebel activities in turbulent Missouri. The guerrilla atrocities of the rebels had driven Frémont to this extreme, the *Herald* explained, warning the South that only a speedy return to the Union would prevent similar proclamations. The purpose of the war was not to end slavery but to put down both secession and abolition. Happily, Lincoln took an antiabolitionist position in revoking Frémont's proclamation. Bennett detected an abolitionist conspiracy pressing Lincoln to make emancipation a war aim. The orchestrated protests of the radicals after Lincoln's removal of Frémont was proof of the conspiracy.[14]

Congress was wasting too much time on the "nigger question" and neglecting the financial crisis. The meddling of the "Jacobin Conspiracy" (the *Herald's* name for the Committee on the Conduct of the War) was demoralizing the government and the army and increasing the threat of European intervention. The Jacobins were out to destroy the Constitution in the South and then force racial equality on the North. The result would be the ridiculous spectacle of black congressmen and, ultimately, racial amalgamation resulting in an inferior strain of Americans.[15]

Lincoln's moderate course on emancipation won the *Herald's* support, in contrast to the unconstitutional confiscation bill of Congress. The president would provide financial aid to the border states if they would gradually, and with compensation, end slavery. But this approach would ruin the cotton states of the Deep South, as Jamaica had been ruined by emancipation. In contrast to Jamaica, both Brazil and Cuba had retained slavery and were prospering. Bennett was confident that Lincoln would veto a bill for emancipation in the District of Columbia unless it was modified to include approval by the voters of the District and compensation to the owners.[16]

The *Herald* did not expect emancipation to benefit the slaves. The fugitive contrabands who entered the Union lines were useless, too lazy to work, incapable of learning, and dangerously swelling the black populations of Ohio, Indiana, and Illinois. The *Herald* ridiculed the efforts of philanthropists working with the freedman at Port Royal; they were teaching the blacks that they did not have to work for a living.[17]

In the spring of 1862 General David Hunter in the Carolinas issued a proclamation similar to Frémont's. The *Herald* urged Lincoln to disavow this "Bombshell"; it was the work of Secretary of War Stanton, the only cabinet member still engaged in the "nigger business." Fortunately, the president squashed the proclamation, although the *Herald* continued to abuse Hunter and Stanton. The charge of Stanton's complicity led Lincoln to write a vigorous denial to Bennett.[18]

A few months later, Congress passed the Confiscation Act, which the *Herald* likened to the English confiscations in Ireland. Ill-timed and revolutionary, the act would transform the southern labor system. Lincoln, happily, refused to sign it without modifications. Without these, the act would have stiffened southern determination and lengthened the war so it was a stunning triumph for the president over the Jacobins.[19]

The text of the preliminary Emancipation Proclamation was printed on the *Herald*'s front page on September 23, 1862. Bennett interpreted the proclamation as a warning to the Confederacy; the seceded states must return to the Union before January 1, 1863, to escape this revolution in their labor system. But he recommended that Lincoln postpone implementation of the proclamation. State elections in October in Ohio, Indiana, and Pennsylvania demonstrated that northern sentiment was against emancipation.[20]

Implementation was not postponed, and the proclamation became effective on January 1, 1863. It was "unnecessary, unwise and ill-timed, impracticable, outside of the Constitution, and full of mischief" in the *Herald*'s opinion. It would unite the South toward greater resistance and possibly turn the country into another Santo Domingo. The *Herald* was apprehensive about the Jacobin influence over Lincoln, demonstrated in proposals to enlist Negro soldiers to which the *Herald* was unalterably opposed.[21]

Bennett opposed Lincoln's reelection because he believed the president was the captive of the abolitionists. A war for emancipation would drag on for twenty years. The sensible policy, as Seward had proposed, was a speedy reconciliation under the present Constitution and a general amnesty for all except a few rebel leaders. Then the army would be free to deal with the provocations of England and France. The war should be ended and slavery left to its natural consequences. It was already dying in the upper South so there was no need to force emancipation, which would bring to southern blacks "those doubtful blessings of indolence, destitution, disease and death."[22]

The only legal method to effect emancipation, the *Herald* argued, was by a constitutional amendment that would allow compensation of loyal owners. Such an amendment (but without compensation) was in the Senate judiciary committee, and Bennett supported it. The measure did not pass during that session, but Bennett continued to back it as the only solution to a political problem. For the slave, it would only mean "exchanging his easy fetters for bullets or starvation." Border state resistance was futile; the question was decided. When the Thirteenth Amendment passed Congress, the *Herald* pressed for quick ratification, hoping that New York would lead the way.[23]

The "nigger question" was settled, but now the Jacobins were pressing for Negro suffrage. The *Herald* could not care less. "If all the negroes on earth should vote, they could not give us worse government than we have had for twenty years, whether national, State, or municipal." If the Negro was not fit, then he would not use the gift of the vote.[24]

Reconstruction was the other controlling issue responsible for the *Herald*'s political preferences during the Civil War era. The *Herald* was consistent during the war in supporting a mild reconstruction policy and opposing harsher radical proposals. In early 1862 Bennett cheered Lincoln's amnesty proclamation and rejected the conquered province theory of Senator Charles Sumner. The way to restore the Union was to reinstate the rebellious states with all of their rights unimpaired. Seward and Montgomery Blair in the cabinet seemed to be in favor of such a moderate settlement, and as a result the administration had the *Herald*'s support until late 1863.[25]

But Lincoln's announcement of his presidential reconstruction plan in late 1863 caused Bennett some concern. The president was trying to ride both the radical and conservative horses at the same time, but the radicals were ahead. It was "confusion worse confounded" and would cause a rupture between radical and moderate Republicans.[26]

The radical plan in the Wade-Davis Bill, with its new constitutional doctrine that the governments of the rebellious states had been destroyed by the war, was merely an extension of Lincoln's unconstitutional plan, a tinkering with percentages. The Wade-Davis Manifesto castigating Lincoln's pocket veto of the measure was more bitter than any Copperhead denunciations of the administration. The Republican split over reconstruction made Lincoln's reelection impossible.[27]

After Lincoln's reelection, and with the end of the war in sight, Bennett swung back to support Lincoln's more moderate reconstruction policies against the harsher proposals of the radicals. A magnanimous policy was the only constitutional one because the rebellion had not removed the southern states from the Union but had only suspended the authority of the government and the enforcement of the laws in the South. General Grant indicated his support of this policy in the surrender terms he gave to Lee. The rebel leaders should be pardoned so as not to make martyrs of them. Lincoln's policy, announced in his last public speech on April 12, 1865, was magnanimous and conciliatory, "a liberal, easy, comprehensive and conservative policy" that would allow the states discretion about their labor systems and the political status of blacks.[28]

When Andrew Johnson became president after Lincoln's assassination, the *Herald* backed his continuation of Lincoln's moderate policies until after the election of 1866. It welcomed the formation of a constitutional party sustaining Johnson. (Bennett was one of the sponsors of a mass meeting on February 22, 1866, at Cooper Union, where Seward spoke in support of Johnson's veto of a bill to extend the Freedmen's Bureau.) The paper supported the Fourteenth Amendment as a moderate rejection of the more radical plans of Thaddeus Stevens. But Bennett was never one to back a loser, and when the voters rebuked Johnson in the 1866 elections, and when Johnson opposed the Fourteenth Amendment, the *Herald* deserted the president.[29] By this time Bennett had retired and his son was running the paper.

The *Herald*'s rather erratic support of Lincoln and Bennett's desertion of the president before the 1864 election are explained by the editor's perception of the administration's positions on slavery and reconstruction. Bennett regarded the abolitionists as equal enemies with the Confederates. He wanted both pro-Confederate newspapers and abolitionist ones, including Greeley's *Tribune,* barred from the mails. There was no concern for freedom of the press where the Jacobins were concerned.[30]

Bennett could best be described as a War Democrat. He supported the war to restore the Union as it was, and he criticized Republican attempts to broaden its scope. But he rejected the Copperheads at the other extreme. He supported candidates he considered to be moderates, regardless of their party, but more often Democrats than Republicans, both in New York and nationally.

Early in the war the *Herald* had supported most of the Lincoln administration's measures in Congress: the Pacific railway bill, the Morrill Tariff (which was a declaration of economic independence from Europe), and the issuance of treasury notes as "the national popular loan." But it viewed Secretary of the Treasury Salmon P. Chase as a dangerous radical and often opposed his recommendations. The nation should not be saddled with a permanent national debt to finance the war.[31] The main danger was from the "Satanic Abolition" element in Congress, and Bennett cheered Lincoln's ouster of Secretary of War Simon Cameron as a repudiation of the abolitionists. The war should be fought with vigor, and the *Herald* supported the draft and measures to enforce it; Bennett believed the abolitionists were laggard in volunteering.[32]

Lincoln demonstrated that he could manage the abolitionists during the cabinet crisis of mid-1862. Seward, the *Herald*'s favorite conservative in the administration, was not forced out; unfortunately, neither were radicals Chase and Stanton. Seward was "the only member of the Cabinet who has done his job thoroughly, efficiently, and successfully."[33]

Because Bennett believed that the war was a conservative measure with the sole purpose of restoring the Union as it was, he worked to reorganize New York's politics and to form a conservative party, even making overtures to his old nemesis Thurlow Weed to form an antiradical coalition. Although generally supportive of Republican Governor Edwin Morgan, a conservative, the *Herald* wanted to ensure that the succession went to a conservative in the 1862 election. Its choice was a War Democrat, General John A. Dix, whose nomination would be a rebuke to radicalism, and it was disgruntled when the Democrats chose Horatio Seymour instead. But Seymour was preferable to the Republican nominee, General James Wadsworth, a radical firebrand who had been one of the plotters against McClellan. The *Herald* hoped that Seymour would withdraw in favor of Dix, but against Wadsworth, Seymour began to appear better and better. As the paper viewed the situation, "Mr. Seymour thinks we should fight for the nation, and let the negro take care of himself; Mr. Wadsworth believes we should fight for the negro, and let the nation take care of itself." The conservative Democratic victories in New York and many other states — Seymour was elected by a large majority — marked a "tremendous revolution in public sentiment," "the finishing blow to radical abolitionism." The Republicans had lost because they had not cooperated with Lincoln and his moderate program. The result of the radical defeat would be a Unionist reaction in the South and a speedy end to the rebellion.[34]

The *Herald* was optimistic about the administration's success when Congress convened in late 1862, despite the Emancipation Proclamation and McClellan's removal. Bennett continued to call for the dismissal of the radicals from the cabinet, and he was very critical of Chase's expansion of the currency, although he supported the National Banking Act as a necessary evil. But the *Herald* feared that the radicals were scheming to make Chase the party nominee in 1864. Lincoln's reelection, then, seemed necessary to save the nation from the extremes of radicalism and Copperheadism; he was the only candidate able to hold the Republican party together.[35]

Bennett's support for Lincoln's reelection eroded by the end of the summer of 1863. The *Herald* continued to warn that public opinion would not sustain radical measures, and it pointed to Seward's dwindling influence and the emergence of Chase and Frémont as radical candidates to oppose Lincoln. At least Frémont's candidacy might kill Chase's hopes because there was room for only one radical candidate. Chase was spending his time on the presidential race rather than on the war effort. If he was not removed, a popular military chief would be elected president.[36]

Bennett began to take this line on December 15, 1863, pushing General Grant as the "popular candidate" unconnected to corrupt party machinery, in the tradition of Jackson, Harrison, and Taylor. Within a few weeks the *Herald* was convinced that Grant would run and be elected, in the process destroying the old political parties and the abolitionists. Grant, not Lincoln, was the man to end the war quickly and bring about a quiet and orderly reconstruction of the nation.[37]

The leading antagonist continued to be Chase, who was blamed for the corruption in the administration. Lincoln had demonstrated no capacity as commander in chief, and only Grant could save the day. The level of the *Herald*'s rhetoric began to escalate. "Certainly it would be the last evidence that we were a besotted and blinded people if, with a man like General Grant within our reach, we should coldly pass him by to re-elect the imbecile joker who has dragged the country into the slough of slaughter and corruption." "Wanted — A New Set of Statesmen," the *Herald* headed its editorial on March 2, 1864. Three days later: "Give us a change and give us a practical military man." With Frémont to run as a radical independent, and with McClellan the probable Democratic nominee, Lincoln had no chance. Better that he should withdraw and give both Frémont and McClellan active field commands so that all parties could fuse behind Grant and a speedy termination of the war.[38]

The planned nominating conventions should not be held; rather, a Union fusion ticket should be adopted by a congressional caucus, the original nominating procedure that was better than the managed conventions. Chase had to be removed, but even without him the Lincoln administration would destroy the nation. Lincoln was "claiming credit for carnage, and trying to make capital out of wholesale slaughter"; he was the "head ghoul."[39]

The *Herald*'s advice was not taken, and it was disappointed in the results of the three nominating conventions. The radicals met first; they did not transform themselves into a people's party and nominate a ticket of Grant and Frémont, as the *Herald* urged. They nominated Frémont, with the sole object of defeating Lincoln, but at least they had cleared the track so that the Democrats could choose a conservative Union ticket headed by Grant.[40]

Bennett hoped that the Republican (or Union) convention would reject Lincoln in favor of Grant to avoid certain defeat. But "King Shoddy rules," and the gathering adopted a radical platform and renominated Lincoln. Lincoln was bound to lose because he was unable to end the war. There was one bright spot; soon after the convention Chase resigned. Lincoln could redeem himself if he would replace Stanton with McClellan. He did not, and Chase's successor, William P. Fessenden, was another dangerous radical.[41]

The Democratic convention was the only hope. If it rejected a Copperhead platform and nominated either Grant or McClellan, victory was certain. But their zeal for spoils resulted in a deal, with McClellan nominated on a Copperhead platform. The *Herald* urged him to reject the platform; he was "not large enough to cover out of sight all the bad points" in it. Now there were three candidates who were all failures; the only candidate who might succeed—Grant—had been ignored.[42]

Describing McClellan as a failure indicates Bennett's cooling toward his former hero. Grant had certainly eclipsed McClellan militarily, and he remained nonpolitical. In contrast, McClellan was too eager, too partisan, too willing to deal with the Copperheads. Unlike Grant, he was not willing to wait in the wings for the call.

With the real choice between Lincoln and McClellan, the *Herald* gave a cautious nod to the general. He was not so complete a failure as Lincoln; Grant, Sherman, and the soldiers preferred him; he repudiated the Copperhead planks; and the Democratic platform had less of the "nigger" than the Republican one. After Frémont withdrew in September, there was neither an abolitionist nor a Copperhead candidate. The choice was between Lincoln and McClellan.[43]

In late October the *Herald* shifted to a neutral position and printed a platform of its own. It would support any candidate who would stand on it. It was, says Allan Nevins, "the kind of straddle that appealed to every corner-grocery loafer with bellicose prejudices." Bennett proposed a complete military victory to achieve reunion; the readmission of southern representatives to Congress; ultimatums to Napoleon III to vacate Mexico and to Britain to pay for her "piratical depredations"; and a Supreme Court review of the unconstitutional acts of the abolitionists. This remained Bennett's position, but he had no takers. So the choice was between Lincoln and McClellan, both of whom stood for the same policies. Neither's election would ruin the country. But the best course would be for the presidential electors, who could legally vote for whomever they pleased, to reject both Lincoln and McClellan and vote for Grant.[44]

The *Herald* explained after Lincoln's reelection that it had been expected. McClellan was a victim of Copperhead influence and management. The Democratic party was dead, and there would be a new set of issues for 1868. Lincoln had a great opportunity if he would reconstruct the cabinet and adopt the *Herald*'s platform. Peace was near, and the paper hoped that Lincoln would be generous in his terms.[45]

Some scholars have contended that Lincoln bought Bennett's shift from opposition to neutrality. David Quentin Voigt has documented overtures by the administration to Bennett as early as July 1864, through Abraham Wakeman, the Republican postmaster of New York City. Nothing very specific was put on paper; the language is cryptic. Bennett apparently wanted something more definite. Lincoln kept Seward and the cabinet in the dark and used William O. Bartlett as his agent to Bennett. Bartlett was a prominent New York lawyer and occasional editorial writer for the *Tribune,* the *Evening Post,* and the *Herald.* He visited Bennett in September and again in October. Bartlett told the president that Bennett expected Lincoln to win, "but by a very close vote. He said that puffs did no good and he could accomplish most for you by not mentioning your name." A week later, on October 26, Bartlett nudged Lincoln to make a definite commitment to the editor, successfully it would appear, for on November 4 Bartlett told Bennett that he was "fresh from the bosom of Father Abraham" and that Lincoln said "he *expected to do that thing* (appoint you to France) *as much as he expected to live.*" McClellan had also visited Bennett in a bid for his support, and the editor's neutrality put him in the enviable position of being able to claim a reward from whichever candidate happened to win. On February 25, 1865, Lincoln offered Bennett the mission to France, which the editor declined two weeks later. "I am sorry to say that at my age I am afraid of assuming the labors and responsibilities of such an important position. Besides, in the present relations of France and the United States, I am of the decided opinion that I can be of more service to the country in the present position I occupy."[46]

Certainly Bennett craved the recognition and respectability the offer of the French mission brought him. Turning down the reward gratified him even more. He had been offered a higher political post than Greeley, Webb, Raymond, or Bryant, but he told the president he could be of more service to the country in his present position. The offer had much to commend it. Bennett spoke French fluently and had visited France many times; the *Herald*'s major European bureau was in Paris, and his family lived there much of the time. Moreover, the leading issue with France was the intervention in Mexico, and Bennett was America's most uncompromising champion of the Monroe Doctrine. Napoleon III could not mistake the message. Indeed, even Greeley's *Tribune* (in an editorial written by Bartlett) lauded the appointment of the first editor since Benjamin Franklin to the French mission.

The administration's pessimism in the summer and fall of 1864 about its ability to carry New York turned out to be exaggerated. Lincoln's election was not as close as feared, but he did not have the historian's benefit of hindsight. There is another problem, however, in dealing with the offer of the French mission. At the time that Wakeman and Bartlett were making overtures to Bennett, the French mission was not vacant. There were no apparent plans to recall the incumbent, William L. Dayton, although Lincoln may have decided to dump him after the election. Conveniently, Dayton died suddenly on December 1, 1864, creating the vacancy.[47]

The support purchased by the offer of the French mission remained lukewarm. The *Herald* was shocked by the nomination of Chase as chief justice. "A worse selection could not be made." It disagreed with Lincoln's insistence on emancipation as a condition for peace, and it deplored continued mismanagement in the Treasury Department. Why was the war being prolonged to end slavery when the institution was doomed by constitutional amendment?[48]

But by Lincoln's second inaugural, and after the offer of the French mission, Bennett's support became warmer. The president was "a most remarkable man," "the keenest of politicians, and more than a match for his wiliest antagonists in the arts of diplomacy." The second Inaugural Address, however, contained too many generalities and gave little indication of future policy.[49]

There was no future policy. Lincoln was assassinated the following month. The details, the funeral preparations, reflections on Lincoln's place in history, and estimates of Andrew Johnson filled the *Herald*'s pages for the next few weeks, until the funeral train arrived in Springfield.[50]

In a remarkable example of eating crow, the *Herald* rhapsodized about the man who only a few months earlier had been the "head ghoul," "the imbecile joker."

He will take his place in a sphere far higher than that accorded to any mere conqueror; and, indeed, without speaking profanely, we may well say that, since the foundation of the Christian era, no more remarkable or pregnant passages of the world's history have been unfolded than those of which Mr. Lincoln on this continent has been the central figure and controlling influence. . . .

While we must all mourn with sad and sickened hearts the success of the great crime which has removed our beloved and trusted President from the final scenes of the contest he had thus far conducted to a triumphant issue, let us not forget that by the circumstances of death the seal of immortality has been stamped upon his fame; nor is it any longer in the power of changing fortune to take away from him, as might have happened had he lived, one of the most solid, brilliant and stainless reputations of which in the world's annals any record can be found — its only peer existing in the memory of George Washington.[51]

The *Herald* returned rather quickly to the business at hand. It was convinced that Jefferson Davis and other Confederate leaders were accomplices of the assassin John Wilkes Booth. But it was confident that Andrew Johnson would do well in the place of the martyr — a Joshua to Lincoln's Moses, it said — in the firm but patriotic tradition of an earlier Tennessean, Andrew Jackson. He would lead "the ruling party of the future."[52]

The most important local story of the war years was the New York City draft riots of July 1863, and Bennett's role in them has been a source of controversy ever since. Some authorities argue that his "reaction to the riots was not so admirable." The other Manhattan papers put the riot story on their front pages, but the reports in the *Herald* "were brief and somewhat disconnected, running on an inside page. Obviously . . . he had given orders to play down one of the greatest news stories, perhaps the most remarkable, he would ever see in his city — and this from the man who boasted that the news came first." Douglas Fermer, on the other hand, in his exhaustive study of Bennett's editorial opinions during the Civil War era, describes the *Herald*'s "fully detailed coverage" of the riots and argues that "there was no justification for charges that it directly condoned bloodshed and the destruction of property in the period immediately preceding the riots or during them."[53]

The riots were the result of the imposition of the draft in New York City, which began without trouble on Saturday, July 11, 1863, a week after the Battle of Gettysburg. Bennett supported the draft and denounced the Copperheads who opposed it; he especially attacked Governor Seymour for an Independence Day speech in the city in which he said that the "revolutionary doctrine of public necessity can be proclaimed by a mob as well as a government." The *Herald* that appeared on the streets on Monday morning, July 13, just as the rioting was beginning, gave editorial support for conscription and assurances that the populace was supportive of this necessary effort to win the war.[54]

During the three days of rioting, in which at least 105 persons were killed, the *Herald* provided detailed coverage in its local news columns, although it reserved editorial judgment apportioning blame until the rioting was over. Both the *Times* and the *Tribune* attacked Bennett's detachment (especially the *Herald*'s description of the rioters as "the people" rather than "the mob"), and Bennett responded in kind. He found it a delicious irony that the mob had surrounded and threatened Greeley's *Tribune* office; Greeley had been delighted when a mob threatened the *Herald* in April 1861. The *Herald* apportioned blame equally among the Copperheads and "niggerheads," but especially it charged that the abolitionists had made the draft as harsh as possible to stir up resistance that would lengthen the war until the entire South was abolitionized. It defended the Irish of the city against Republican attacks, conceding that the Irish had been prominent in the rioting but pointing out that there were many Irish among the city police who suppressed the disorder. On balance, the *Herald* can be indicted for misconduct only indirectly. Its antiabolitionist, Negrophobic editorials had made the point unmistakably in the months before the riots that the "northern abolition traitors . . . are responsible for the rebellion and for the success it has achieved [and must] be held to strict and final account." The mob had listened.[55]

Bennett spent little time at the *Herald* office during the war years, leaving Hudson in almost complete charge. The *Herald* emerged from the war as the leading daily in the city and nation. Its receipts for the year ending May 1865 were $1,095,000, equal to the combined totals of its five leading rivals. Its circulation during the last week of the war, it claimed, was 131,000 daily, larger than the combined circulations of all other New York City dailies. These were, Bernard Weisberger comments, "bonanza figures for the sixties. They were the seals on a diploma certifying big-city journalism's graduation from the class of small business; they were also an impressive vindication of the strenuous methods which Bennett had brought to the newspaper profession."[56]

The gains were reflected in mechanical improvements and expansion of the physical plant. In July 1861, the *Herald* began to stereotype its forms, speeding up the compositors' work and making possible the inclusion of later news. Then in 1863 it bought four adjoining buildings to house five new ten-cylinder presses. When Barnum's Museum on Broadway burned down, Bennett bought the site and built, in 1866, a new white marble structure to house the *Herald,* "a conspicuous monument," George Templeton Strong grumbled, "proof of the profit that can be made out of this people by unprincipled, demoralizing journalism."[57]

Bennett had been easing gradually into retirement, and since 1862 he and Hudson had been training James Gordon Bennett, Jr., to take over the helm. In the spring of 1866 Hudson took a year's leave of absence because of his wife's poor health, moving to Concord, Massachusetts. He never returned, resigning officially in July 1867, and devoted his remaining years to writing his *History of Journalism in the United States,* in which Bennett and the *Herald* figured prominently. (He had rejected an offer from Henry J. Raymond to manage the New York *Times.*)[58]

Young Bennett, twenty-five years old, took over effective management of the *Herald* in the spring of 1866. He had spent most of his youth with his mother in France, educated by private tutors and attending the Ecole Polytechnique in Paris for a time. He returned to the United States in 1861 to serve in the revenue service, with his yacht *Henrietta,* during the first year of the war. He was not very familiar with American affairs. A spoiled playboy who moved in the fast set of young New York bachelors, he was much too erratic to manage the newspaper with a steady hand.[59] Hudson was gone, but most of the staff remained, and his father was close by for guidance, which must have been offered freely. The editorial opinions remained about the same, as did the *Herald*'s reliance on sensationalism.

The *Herald* supported the reconstruction policies of Andrew Johnson as long as they had some hopes of success—until the fall of 1866. The senior Bennett became an influential spokesman for the president, a loud and persistent Johnson supporter through the *Herald*'s editorial writer W. B. Phillips. The president, in turn, was gratified and gave Bennett's advice careful consideration, writing the editor a note of thanks.[60]

Part of the advice was that Johnson not compromise with the Republican Congress, but Bennett was uncertain of Johnson's policies. The *Herald* at first had no objection to Negro suffrage in the South but soon abandoned the position when Johnson was opposed. It approved of Johnson's veto of the Freedmen's Bureau bill in February 1866 but believed that civil rights could not be denied the freedmen. The *Herald* hoped and expected that Johnson would sign the Civil Rights Act—"We can find in it nothing conflicting with the Constitution as it now stands, and nothing in conflict with the declared opinions and policy of President Johnson"—but then supported the veto as "an emphatic declaration of war against the radicals."[61]

There were three other recommendations which the *Herald* made to the president. The first was to use patronage to remove all "hostile radicals" and replace them with "Conservative Union Administration men." The second was to exploit economic issues, especially the national banking system and the vulnerability of Republican financial policies. The third, and most significant, was to form a new national conservative party organization.[62]

The 1866 congressional elections were critically important to Bennett, even more important than the election of the first Congress in 1788. He expected conservative Johnson supporters to win and Johnson to support the Fourteenth Amendment, which the *Herald* considered to be a reasonable compromise, very close to the president's position. The paper championed the Union Convention of Johnson supporters at Philadelphia and ridiculed the rival Southern Loyalist Convention as one of the "Nigger-worshippers. . . . Such an aggregation of the freaks of nature, physically and mentally, in the shape of humanity, was never seen before."[63]

But after reporting Johnson's "swing around the circle" in support of conservative congressional candidates in "the most meticulous and glowing detail," the *Herald* began to waver in mid-September after Republican victories in Vermont and Maine. "We regard the contest between the President and Congress as virtually decided by Maine. We bow to the judgement of the mighty North, and we trust that the President will shape his course accordingly." Johnson's defeat was caused by his refusal to "take up" the Fourteenth Amendment and by the widening of his conflict with the radicals into a broader conflict with Congress.[64]

When Bennett dropped Johnson he did not drop his racism or his hatred of the radicals. The *Herald* continued to castigate black suffrage, and it celebrated Republican defeats in the 1867 elections, especially Thaddeus Stevens's defeat for a seat in the United States Senate. When Stevens died in 1868, the *Herald* gave the radical his due: "It was his marvelous obstinacy, his Hannibal-like animosity against the South, which postponed the settlement of our national differences. His death . . . sounds the death knell of the extravagant hopes of the radicals. It was he alone whose firm will held together the most refractory among his partisans."[65]

The *Herald* "cautiously" sided with Johnson when he was impeached in 1868, predicting early his acquittal by the Senate and warning of the dangers of his removal. "The extreme radicals, who have worked their way into the foreground, will rule in every department of the government."[66]

Bennett was more concerned with president-making than with Johnson. The *Herald* toyed with the idea of promoting Grant for the Democratic nomination in 1868 and even an "experimental sectional reconciliation ticket of General Grant and General Lee." It did not discourage New York's Samuel J. Tilden from making the race. But Bennett's real choice, surprisingly, was Chief Justice Salmon P. Chase, so often abused in the *Herald* in the past. The reason he gave was expediency; Chase could attract the votes of moderate Republicans and southern Negroes. Perhaps his role in saving Johnson from removal in his trial before the Senate, presided over by Chase, was another factor.[67]

When the Democrats rejected Chase in favor of Horatio Seymour, the *Herald* supported Grant, the Republican. (George Templeton Strong, a Grant supporter, regarded this as "a bad sign. . . . It is almost always on the losing side.") Grant's victory was interpreted as a triumph of moderation. The voters were tired of radicalism and had voted for sectional peace. This was Bennett's last venture into presidential politics. He was dead before the 1872 elections.[68]

How can one appraise the *Herald*'s editorial performance during an era of great national trauma? It is a mixed balance sheet of credits and debits. Its news-gathering record at the front was also mixed. It was always enterprising in Washington and scored several impressive beats, most notably Wikoff's procuring (probably from Mrs. Lincoln) of the president's annual message.

The *Herald*'s political position contributed little to national unity in support of the war effort. It was a carping critic of Lincoln and all things Republican, and its racist defense of slavery was unrestrained. It was not very consistent, and the war saw some spectacular turnabouts. It was not, then, a very responsible newspaper in its politics, although this was partly offset by its vigorous defense of American national interests in foreign policy.

Its enterprise and self-promotion paid financial dividends. The *Herald* emerged from the war as the nation's largest and most prosperous daily, with its news budget almost unlimited. No cost was too high to obtain news, and this attitude stimulated its rivals to do better. It was a valuable property that Bennett turned over to his son to run, and ruin.

9

Bennett in Retrospect

George Templeton Strong was unforgiving to the end. "Old James Gordon Bennett is reported dead or dying," he noted in his diary on June 1, 1872, after Bennett had suffered two heart attacks a week earlier. "During a period of about thirty-seven years, he has done more than any living man to debase American journalism."[1]

The funeral was held at Bennett's home on Fifth Avenue and Thirty-eighth Street, delayed to enable Bennett's family to arrive back from Europe, where the editor had planned to join them for a summer vacation. The occasion was a who's who of New York journalism and politics. The vicar general of the Roman Catholic diocese presided — Bennett had been reconciled with the church in his old age, and Archbishop John McClosky had administered the last rites — and the pallbearers were Horace Greeley of the *Tribune,* Charles A. Dana of the *Sun,* George W. Jones of the *Times,* William L. Stone of the *Journal of Commerce,* Erastus Brooks of the *Express,* Hugh J. Hastings of the *Commercial Advertiser,* Robert Bonner of the *Ledger,* J. M. Bundy of the *Evening Mail,* George A. Childs of the *Philadelphia Public Ledger,* and Fred Hudson. In attendance were General Banks and General Frémont, former governor Washington Hunt, most of the New York congressional delegation, and most of the city government. The city courts were closed out of respect.[2]

Strong was furious. "Old J. G. Bennett was buried today under a volley of eulogistic paragraphs and resolutions of dolorous and deep affection," he wrote in a rage. "Flags at half mast! This community is devoid of moral sense. It has proclaimed an extra Beatitude of greater practical influence than all the others together, namely, 'Blessed are the smart.'"[3] Strong was correct. Most of the obituary eulogies by Bennett's colleagues and former rivals were laudatory and uncritical. But most of them struck the same common themes, and they are a useful starting point in assessing his importance as a journalist.[4]

All of his peers counted Bennett an "unqualified professional success," as the *Sun* put it, and attributed the *Herald*'s triumph to Bennett's personal genius. Bennett was credited with launching the newspaper revolution with its twin themes of news-gathering enterprise and independence from party dictates. These points were stressed in most of the obituary judgments.[5]

Although it was natural for the journalistic profession to close ranks at the loss of one of its own, the sameness of these eulogies from cities large and small in all parts of the country is striking. They all credit Bennett with creating the modern newspaper, independent and enterprising. None credit Bennett's editorial opinions with being a useful force. The few that were not wholly laudatory made this point.

He could be vindictive and merciless toward his foes, one noted. Another agreed: "Fools were his playthings; and solemn and respectable humbugs he loved to pounce upon and tear to pieces." He was too negative, his *Herald* too "excessive in its pugnacious patriotism to be a leader of public opinion," it was noted. From Philadelphia: "He was not, as Mr. Greeley was, a champion of right against any odds."[6]

Greeley's *Tribune* had the most balanced and the most critical estimate:

> It was as a collector of news that Bennett shown conspicuous. Editorially he was cynical, inconsistent, reckless, and easily influenced by others' opinions, and by his own prejudices. But he had an unerring judgement of the pecuniary value of the news. He knew how to pick out of the events of the day the subject which engrossed the interest of the greatest number of people, and to give them about that subject all they could read. The quality might be bad, and generally was; but it suited the multitude, and the quantity at any rate was abundant. . . .
> He developed the capacities of journalism in a most wonderful manner, but he did it by degrading its character. He made the newspaper powerful, but he made it odious.[7]

The *Herald* itself had surprisingly little to say on the death of its founder. Within its mourning bands on June 2 it stated:

> His career as a journalist is before the world and is public property. It will be commented on, wherever civilization reaches, by friends and enemies; for no man could hold in his hands for nearly forty years so formidable a power as a fearless, independent press and hope to escape the latter. His death will be mourned by all who regret the passing away

of the sterling benefactors of the human race; for no one will gainsay the benefits conferred upon mankind by the genius, energy and liberality of the deceased. To him more than to any other individual the American newspaper owes its present high and honorable position.[8]

The following day, as the *Herald* began to print comments from other newspapers, it noted "how cheerfully they do justice to his energy, enterprise and power. The highest praise that can be bestowed upon the founder of the HERALD is the acknowledgement of those who have been his colaborers and competitors that he leaves this stamp of his genius upon the press of the nation."[9]

A week later the *Herald* devoted nine full columns, a page and a half, to an article titled "The Results and Lessons of Mr. Bennett's Career as a Journalist." There were no surprises here. Bennett, it said, was "universally recognized as the originator of the present newspaper system." His "ideal of a metropolitan daily newspaper," the article continued, was "independent in politics, uncontrolled in its financial article by the operators on 'change; cheap in price; compact in size; with new elements of popularity and a competition for news such as had never before been contemplated." The *Herald*'s mission was "to revolutionize the existing management of newspapers, to release the country from political thralldom; to break up the close corporation of financial power; to correct the glaring vices of society; to raise labor to its proper equality with capital; to protect conscience against fanaticism; to spread intelligence among the people; to develop the resources and aid the progress of the young and vigorous republic."[10]

The *Herald,* it argued defensively, did have a political platform and an editorial policy that was consistent and responsible. It was simply "the support of the constitution under whatever government; the advocacy of all wise and liberal measures by whoever originated; the judgement by its acts, and not by the standard of party; the encouragement of all projects calculated to stimulate the growth and prosperity of the United States and of the city of New York as the commercial metropolis of the Union." Six months later, when Frederic Hudson's *Journalism in the United States from 1690 to 1872* was published by Harper and Brothers, Bennett's contemporaries in the press were afforded what amounted to a second round of obituaries because, not surprisingly, Bennett's former managing editor emphasized the news-gathering function of the press over its analytical and opinion-molding function. If Hudson's history has a hero, it is Bennett, and the *Herald* was the standard by which metropolitan journalism was judged. The culmination of the work, the sixth and last era in Hudson's chronological organization, is "The Independent Press," which followed the *Herald*'s establishment in 1835.[11]

The theme of several book reviews in the New York press, as well as of three obituaries on Hudson's death in 1875, was that Hudson had misconceived the role of the press and as a result had misused the *Herald* as a role model by overemphasizing the reportorial function and financial success and not paying attention to the analytical editorial function of interpreter and formulator of public opinion. Hudson, by using the *Herald* as a model, had exaggerated the role of the newspaper as an informer and neglected its role as a teacher. The *Herald,* to these critics, was too sensational, too anti-intellectual to serve as a worthy model by which to measure journalistic progress.[12]

The judgment of Bennett's peers on his contribution to journalism was, then, mixed. But the criticisms all focused on the same theme: the neglect of the editorial, opinion-forming, teaching role of the press. This was not a function Bennett considered important. As the *Tribune* put it, "a public conscience, a personal earnestness, a freedom from private ends, and a respect for the dignity of human nature . . . [Bennett] considered outside the sphere of journalism."[13]

What was the judgment of the *Herald*'s readers? The best answer is the circulation figures. Bennett's audience was anonymous. He claimed that it was because of this anonymity that the *Herald* could be politically independent, "simply because it is subservient to none of its readers — known to none of its readers — and entirely ignorant who are its readers and who are not."[14]

The historian would like to know. Who read the *Herald?* Why? Unfortunately, there is no evidence to answer these questions. There were no market research surveys in the mid-nineteenth century. Aside from a small proportion of mail subscribers, the bulk of the *Herald* was sold by newsboys on the street. No business records have survived from Bennett's years on the *Herald,* and almost no useful information can be extrapolated from the extant records of other newspapers. There are very good business and circulation records, for example, for M. M. Noah's *Evening Star* for the 1830s, which have been used very effectively by historians of that paper.[15] But Noah's paper was a Whig mercantile sheet with a small circulation, sold by subscription and not by the cash-and-carry methods of the popular press. Its records do not provide many useful hints to the historian of the mass circulation popular press.

The *Herald* had the largest circulation in Europe of any American paper. Many politicians in Washington, New York, and Albany read it. So did southern politicians, who liked its racist, proslavery stance. Presidents read the *Herald*. George Templeton Strong read it, perhaps to satisfy some masochistic urge. Beyond this, the historian must speculate. An analysis of advertising, sampling a week of the *Herald* every five years, indicates a universal appeal, something for everyone. Bennett himself made this point in 1848 when he instituted the policy that advertisements would have to be resubmitted daily. The advertisements, he said, were "the most interesting and practical city news. They are the hopes, the thoughts, the joys, the plans, the shames, the losses, the mishaps, the fortunes, the pleasures, the miseries, the politics, and the religion of the people."[16]

The news stories also had a universal appeal. Dan Schiller in a brilliant and provocative account, *Objectivity and the News* (a book that is long on speculation and short on evidence), argues that because workingmen constituted almost half of New York City's wage-earning population in the mid-1830s when the penny press was founded, "most readers must have been drawn from the ranks of artisans and mechanics" initially. Then, after its commercial success was established, the penny press attracted readers from "many levels of the social scale."[17]

There was a vigorous labor press in the 1830s, Schiller says, but it did not survive the Panic of 1837 and ensuing depression. The new popular press stepped into the vacuum, claiming "to speak alike to the politicized and the less politicized, the journeyman and the merchant, and which appropriated and softened the anger of the labor press into a blustery rhetoric of equal rights, enlightenment, and political independence."[18]

Bennett's *Herald* was in the forefront of these papers, Schiller continues, espousing "a variant of entrepreneurial equal rights." It championed the cause of the journeymen not only in its rhetoric but also in its exposés of violations of the standards of equal justice. The focus of the *Herald*'s crime news was not sensationalism but to expose the unequal effects of the law on different social classes. Indeed, this was the point of the *Herald*'s coverage of the Robinson-Jewett case, the exposure of a conspiracy by men in high places, of a cover-up by men of wealth.[19]

An essay by Alexander Saxton makes a similar claim. In what he calls the "first wave" of penny dailies, those born before the Panic of 1837, most of the publishers were artisans, eight of the ten, Saxton suggests. Many of them, including the publishers of the *Sun* and the *Daily Transcript* in New York and the three partners who established the *Philadelphia Public Ledger* and *Baltimore Sun*, had close connections to the workingmen's movement in New York. The appearance of the new penny dailies of the first wave "coincided with the formation of the Democratic party. . . . Initiated by artisan printers, they propagated an urban artisan ideology that was rationalist and secular in tone, democratic in politics, expansionist in aspiration, and ferociously white egalitarian in its identification. Pioneers of the new press included influential veterans of the Workingmen's parties of the late 1820's." Bennett, of course, does not fit this artisan model of the first-wave publisher, and Saxton concedes as much. "Yet like the others, Bennett was a wage earner," he says. This is questionable. Bennett had no connection with the artisan tradition; he never worked with his hands. His education in Scotland was surely the equal of an American college education. His antilabor views also differentiate him from his fellows in the first wave. In every respect Bennett resembles Saxton's model for the "second wave" of popular publisher, Henry J. Raymond of the *Times*. The second wave was those popular papers established after the Panic of 1837 reduced sources of credit and advertising revenue for artisan printers and after improved technology raised the price of entry into newspaper publishing to a figure artisan printers could not afford. But Raymond's background and education were similar to Bennett's. Raymond had a University of Vermont education and, like Bennett, for many years was a "wage earner" although, like Bennett, he never worked with his hands in the artisan tradition. Although much of Saxton's analysis is insightful, he is no more successful than Schiller in explaining the *Herald*'s audience and appeal.[20]

Perhaps Bennett did consciously seek a workingman's audience for his paper and try to retain it by shaping his editorial policy and news coverage to suit. He wanted, of course, as wide a readership as possible. The argument is plausible, but there is no evidence to prove it. The *Herald*'s audience must remain anonymous to the historian.

Another provocative analysis, by sociologist Michael Schudson, attempts to explain the newspaper revolution as the result of the growth of a democratic market society centered in the cities where the penny press originated, "an egalitarian market democracy, where money had new power, the individual new standing, and the pursuit of self-interest new honor." In this setting, "the penny papers expressed and built the culture of a democratic market society, a culture which had no place for social or intellectual deference."[21]

The *Herald*'s appeal, Schudson claims, was to the practical needs of New York's well-to-do population. This was especially true of the *Herald*'s money articles and Wall Street reports. To substantiate this theory, first he cites the *Herald*'s own claims (in 1835) that it was "calculated to circulate among all ranks and conditions" and (in 1840) that no other paper "has ever attained so extensive a circulation or is read by so many of the business, educated, and intelligent classes." Second, he uses both the

Herald's claims (in 1837) that commercial newspapers in other cities were using its commercial reports and the statement of the *Albany Argus* that nearly all of the *Herald*'s regular subscribers bought the paper for its money articles. Third, the Moral War indicated that Bennett had gained the middle-class audience he sought; when Webb and his allies urged respectable men and women not to read the *Herald* and hotels and reading rooms to exclude it, the inference is that respectable people did read it in respectable places.[22]

Again the historian must respond—perhaps. Schudson's argument, which runs counter to Schiller's, is based on a few self-promotional quotes from the *Herald* and some inference. The best that can be concluded about the audience is that Bennett's paper had a large circulation and that its contents had a wide and diverse appeal. It is doubtful if the editorials were a very large part of this appeal, except perhaps for Negrophobes, southerners, and doughface politicians. More likely, as Frederick Merk has argued in reference to the *Herald*'s jingoistic expansionism, New Yorkers bought the *Herald* in spite of rather than because of its editorial policy.[23]

The editorials were heavy-handed and vituperative, stirring up emotions, strident and tasteless in the use of code words such as "nigger worshipper" for Republican. Bennett had a tendency to conspiratorial explanations that oversimplified issues. Inflation was caused by conspiracies of landlords and food processors, panics by Wall Street conspiracies (with the mercantile press as co-conspirators), unsatisfactory election results by political conspiracies, sectional tension by an international abolitionist conspiracy, and Civil War reverses by a War Department conspiracy, to cite some of the more obvious examples. There was nothing unusual about this "paranoid style"; Richard Hofstadter and David B. Davis have demonstrated that it has always been present in Amerian politics, but in the middle third of the nineteenth century it was the most common. Andrew Jackson made it part of his political style, and in many ways Bennett can be viewed as the prototypical Jacksonian, an elitist entrepreneur who exploited the masses as much as he served them.[24]

The writing in the *Herald* was not distinguished. Whether in early editorials written by Bennett, or later when Hudson and others did more of the writing, the style was too breathless and emotional, too hyphen-laden, too simplistic, and too vulgar to rank with the editorials Greeley was composing for the *Tribune* or Bryant for the *Evening Post* or Raymond for the *Times*. *Thoughtful* is not a word that comes readily to mind in describing the *Herald*. Occasionally there was a telling phrase—in the attack on land speculation, the plea for "ploughing the soil instead of lithographing it," and on Soulé's mission to Spain, "We wanted an ambassador and we have sent a matador," are examples — but these are memorable because they are so exceptional.

Editorials aside, the *Herald*'s readers got reporting that was reasonably objective and as complete and as wide a coverage of the news as prevailing technology would allow. There was something for everyone in the *Herald,* or for everyone except New York's small Negro population. Bennett's news-gathering enterprise was a pace-setter for his rivals; he was quick to adopt innovative technology; he was zealous in his promotion of New York City's welfare; and he was fearless and independent, if often unwise, in his political opinions.

But the *Herald* could continue in such a fashion only with Bennett at the helm. Under his son's eccentric and absentee direction, the *Herald* continued to be sensational and erratic but lost much of its focus on news as news. Joseph Pulitzer and William Randolph Hearst were more direct legatees than Junior of what Bennett had created, in Hearst's case even including an irresponsible editorial policy, but in Pulitzer's case the more positive and responsible of Bennett's contributions. Horace Greeley most cogently expressed this legacy when he said of Bennett: "He was the first journalist who went to meet the news half-way."[25]

Notes
Bibliographical Essay
Index

Notes

1 — Learning Journalism

1. The following paragraphs are based on the *New York Herald* (hereafter *NYH*), Aug. 27, 28, 30, 1845, Sept. 11, 1848; and [Isaac C. Pray], *Memoirs of James Gordon Bennett and His Times by a Journalist* (New York, 1855), 460–65. The day is drawn primarily from *NYH*, Aug. 27, 1845. The reporter is quoted in J. Cutler Andrews, *The North Reports the Civil War* (Pittsburgh, 1955), 8.

2. The information on Bennett's first twenty-five years is from fragmentary autobiographical statements in *NYH*: "Sketches of My Own Life," Oct. 11, 1836; and travel letters from Scotland, Aug. 7, 8, 9, 10, 11, 1838. Oliver Carlson, *The Man Who Made News: James Gordon Bennett* (New York, 1942), 5–22, and [Pray], *Memoirs of Bennett*, 25–37, provide the fullest discussions of Bennett's twenty-five years in Scotland.

3. *NYH*, Oct. 11, 1836; Carlson, *Man Who Made News*, 27–48; [Pray], *Memoirs of Bennett*, 37–46.

4. Carlson, *Man Who Made News*, 47–60; *Charleston Courier*, Jan. 1, 1823. For Willington, see J. Cutler Andrews, *The South Reports the Civil War* (Princeton, 1970), 5–8; Herbert R. Sass, *Outspoken: 150 Years of the Charleston News and Courier* (Columbia, S.C., 1953), 116.

5. Perhaps he had financial problems. See Henry I. Mcgary [sp.] to James Gordon Bennett, Jan. 3, 1823, in Miscellaneous Papers, New-York Historical Society.

6. [Pray], *Memoirs of Bennett*, 49–62, 70–75; Carlson, *Man Who Made News*, 65–73; *Harper's Weekly* (July 10, 1858), 1–2.

7. [Pray], *Memoirs of Bennett*, 49–62; Carlson, *Man Who Made News*, 65–73. For Noah, see H. W. Schoenberger, "M. M. Noah," in Allan Johnson and Dumas Malone, eds., *Dictionary of American Biography*, 21 vols. (New York, 1928–44), 13:534–35 (hereafter *DAB*); Jabez D. Hammond, *The History of Political Parties in the State of New York*, 3 vols. (Cooperstown, 1846–48), 2:334; Isaac Goldberg, *Major Noah: American Jewish Pioneer* (New York, 1937); Jonathan D. Sarna, *Jacksonian Jew: The Two Worlds of Mordecai Noah* (New York: 1981); Frederic Hudson, *Journalism in the United States from 1690 to 1872* (New York, 1873), 286.

8. Carlson, *Man Who Made News*, 74–80; *New York Enquirer*, Jan. 5, Apr. 27, July 2, 1827.

9. *New York Morning Courier*, Dec. 1, 1827; Carlson, *Man Who Made News*, 80–84.

10. Carlson, *Man Who Made News*, 81–94; *Enquirer*, Jan. 8, 15, 22, Mar. 26, May 5, 1828. For Albany letters, see *Enquirer*, Mar. 1829.

11. James L. Crouthamel, *James Watson Webb: A Biography* (Middletown, Conn., 1969), 19-30. For the rivalry between Webb and Noah, see *Enquirer,* July 7, Oct. 25, 1828; *Morning Courier,* July 2, 8, 15, 22, Oct. 27, 30, 31, Nov. 3, 5, 7, 1828; James Watson Webb to M. M. Noah, Nov. 28, 1828, Webb items in Miscellaneous Papers, New York Public Library.

12. Crouthamel, *Webb,* 30-31; *Morning Courier and New York Enquirer* (hereafter *Courier and Enquirer*), May 21, 25, 1829. [Pray], *Memoirs of Bennett,* 105-6, credits Bennett with instigating the merger, which is plausible. See Charles King to Luther Bradish, Mar. 2, 1829, Luther Bradish Papers, New-York Historical Society.

13. Bennett to Jesse Hoyt, Jan. 20, June 7, 1829, in [Pray], *Memoirs of Bennett,* 106, 108-9; idem, June 11, July 20, 1829, in William L. Mackenzie, *Life and Times of Martin Van Buren* (Boston, 1846), 221-22; James Watson Webb to Azariah C. Flagg, July 3, 1829, Azariah C. Flagg Papers, New York Public Library.

14. Bennett to Nicholas Biddle, Apr. 2, 13, 21, 1829, Nicholas Biddle Papers, vol. 20, Library of Congress (hereafter Biddle Papers); idem, May 11, 1829, Greer Collection, Historical Society of Pennsylvania; idem, July 13, 1829, James Wright Brown Collection, New-York Historical Society.

15. *Courier and Enquirer,* Feb. 11, 1832, quoting *Washington Chronicle.*

16. Crouthamel, *Webb,* 28-33. The financial condition of the paper was established before a House committee investigating the bank. See *House of Representatives' Committee Reports,* 22d Cong., 1st sess., 4 (no. 460), 84-93 (hereafter *House Report 460*).

17. Jerome Mushkat, *Tammany: The Evolution of a Political Machine, 1789-1865* (Syracuse, 1971), 120; *Courier and Enquirer,* May 26, 1829, Sept. 6, 1833; Bennett to Jesse Hoyt, June 7, 11, July 20, 1829, in William L. Mackenzie, *The Lives and Opinions of Benj'n Franklin Butler . . . and Jesse Hoyt* (Boston, 1845), 91-92.

18. Carlson, *Man Who Made News,* 105-7; [Pray], *Memoirs of Bennett,* 117-20; Wallace B. Eberhard, "Mr. Bennett Covers a Murder Trial," *Journalism Quarterly* 47 (1970): 457-63.

19. *Courier and Enquirer,* May 18, June 3, 4, 18, 22, July 24, 26, 29, 30, 31, Aug. 2-7, 9-13, 1830.

20. Ibid., Aug. 6, 1830.

21. Ibid., Aug. 7, 9-13, 1830.

22. Walter Nelles and Carol W. King, "Contempt by Publication in the United States," *Columbia Law Review* 28 (1928): 421.

23. *Courier and Enquirer,* Aug. 24-31, Sept. 1-10, 1830.

24. Bennett to Biddle, Oct. 17, Nov. 9, Dec. 6, 1829, Apr. 9, May 30, Sept. 11, 1830, Biddle Papers, vols. 20-23; Thomas P. Govan, *Nicholas Biddle: Nationalist and Public Banker, 1786-1844* (Chicago, 1959), 146.

25. *Courier and Enquirer,* Nov. 30, Dec. 7, 1829; Ralph C. H. Catterall, *The Second Bank of the United States* (Chicago, 1903), 180-82.

26. Bennett to Biddle, Sept. 25, Oct. 22, Nov. 10, 1830, Biddle Papers, vol. 23.

27. Crouthamel, *Webb,* chap. 4; and "Did the Second Bank of the United States Bribe the Press?" *Journalism Quarterly* 36 (1959): 35-44. Bennett's own account is in *Courier and Enquirer,* Feb. 2, 1832. Webb's testimony to the House investigating committee makes it clear that Bennett wrote the antibank articles (*House Report 460,*77-83). See also Webb to Congressman C. C. Cambreleng, Mar. 19, 1832, in ibid., 75-77.

28. *Courier and Enquirer,* Feb. 5, 7, 16, Mar. 3, 1831.

29. Crouthamel, *Webb,* 37; *Courier and Enquirer,* Apr. 9, 1831.

30. Crouthamel, *Webb,* 38-39.

31. *Courier and Enquirer,* July 1831; e.g., July 22 with a letter of July 5 from Auburn;

James Gordon Bennett, "Diary of a Journey," June–July 1831, New York Public Library, entries of June 26, July 6; Bennett to Biddle, June 27, 1831, Biddle Papers, vol. 27.

32. Bennett, "Diary of a Journey," entries of June 22, July 17, 18, 1831.

33. *Courier and Enquirer*, Feb. 2, 1832.

34. Ivor D. Spencer, *The Victor and the Spoils: A Life of William L. Marcy* (Providence, 1959), 66-68; C. C. Cambreleng to Jesse Hoyt, Mar. 15, 1832, in Mackenzie, *Van Buren*, 234; [Pray], *Memoirs of Bennett*, 136-37; *Courier and Enquirer*, Jan. 27, Apr. 12, 1832.

35. Crouthamel, *Webb*, 34-35.

36. *Courier and Enquirer*, Apr. 2, May 2, 24, 25, 1832.

37. Crouthamel, *Webb*, 43-45; *Courier and Enquirer*, Aug. 23, 1832.

38. *Courier and Enquirer*, Sept. 1, 6, 1832.

39. [Pray], *Memoirs of Bennett*, 146-47; Hudson, *Journalism in the United States*, 409-10; *New York Globe*, Nov. 29, 1832.

40. Richard B. Latner, "A New Look at Jacksonian Politics," *Journal of American History* 61 (Mar. 1975): 953-54; Bennett to Biddle, Nov. 24, Dec. 1 (private), 1832, Biddle Papers, vol. 36; Bennett to Levi Woodbury, Dec. 4, 1832, Levi Woodbury Papers, ser. 1, vol. 12, Library of Congress; William E. Smith, *The Francis Preston Blair Family in Politics*, 2 vols. (New York, 1933), 1:111.

41. *Courier and Enquirer*, Feb. 3, 1833; *Pennsylvanian* (Philadelphia), May 24, June 4, 6, July 27, Oct. 11, 1833.

42. Charles McCool Snyder, *The Jacksonian Heritage: Pennsylvania Politics, 1833-1848* (Harrisburg, 1958), 23-32.

43. Bennett to William L. Marcy, Mar. 15, 1833, William L. Marcy Papers, vol. 2, Library of Congress; Bennett to Levi Woodbury, Apr. 6, 1833, James Wright Brown Collection, New-York Historical Society; Bennett to Jesse Hoyt, June 13, [1833], in Mackenzie, *Butler and Hoyt*, 93.

44. Bennett to Hoyt, July 27, Aug. 3, 15, 1833, in Mackenzie, *Butler and Hoyt*, 93-94.

45. *Pennsylvanian*, July 20, 26, 30, 1833; *Courier and Enquirer*, July 31, 1833; Amos Kendall to Bennett, July 31, 1833, in Hudson, *Journalism in the United States*, 447-48.

46. *Pennsylvanian*, June 21, July 30, Aug. 1, 5, 12, Sept. 6, 9, Oct. 25, 26, 31, Nov. 6, 13, 22, 1833; *Courier and Enquirer*, Sept. 16, 1833; *Washington Globe*, Sept. 7, Oct. 29, 1833; Snyder, *Jacksonian Heritage*, 32-33.

47. Bennett to Andrew Jackson, Sept. 10, 1833, Bennett to Levi Woodbury, Sept. 10, [1833], Levi Woodbury Papers, ser. 1, vol. 12; Andrew Jackson to Bennett, Sept. 12, 1833, in *Pennsylvania Inquirer* (Philadelphia), Dec. 6, 1833; Bennett to Aaron O. Dayton, Nov. 9, 1833, Simon Gratz Collection, Historical Society of Pennsylvania.

48. [Bennett to Biddle], n.d. [Aug. 1833]; n.d. [Sept. 17, 1833]; n.d. [Sept. 23, 1833]; Oct. 14, 1833; Biddle to Bennett, Sept. 17, 1833, Biddle Papers, vols. 31-32.

49. *Pennsylvanian*, Nov. 30, Dec. 2, 1833; *Pennsylvania Inquirer*, Dec. 2, 6, 1833; *Courier and Enquirer*, Dec. 11, 1833; Govan, *Nicholas Biddle*, 239.

50. [Pray], *Memoirs of Bennett*, 151-52; Mushkat, *Tammany*, 155; Bennett to Biddle, Apr. 4, 1834, Biddle Papers, vol. 37.

51. [Pray], *Memoirs of Bennett*, 186.

2 — Sensationalism and the Newspaper Revolution

1. Much of the discussion that follows is from James L. Crouthamel, "The Newspaper Revolution in New York, 1830-1860," *New York History* 45 (1964): 91-113.

2. Mary Alice Wyman, "Seba Smith," *DAB*, 17:345-46; Frank Luther Mott, *American Journalism*, rev. ed. (New York, 1950), 216-18.

3. Alfred M. Lee, *The Daily Newspaper in America* (New York, 1937), 383; Nelson F. Atkins, "William T. Porter," *DAB*, 15:107-8; Frank Luther Mott, *A History of American Magazines*, 4 vols. (Cambridge, Mass., 1938-57), 1:480-81.

4. Mott, *American Journalism*, 218-20; William Harlan Hale, *Horace Greeley, Voice of the People* (New York, 1950), 40.

5. Louis Dudek, *Literature and the Press* (Toronto, 1960), 101-2.

6. *New York Sun*, Sept. 3, 1833; Frank M. O'Brien, *The Story of the Sun* (New York, 1918), 1-24; Charles W. Levermore, "The Rise of Metropolitan Journalism, 1800-1840," *American Historical Review* 6 (1900-1901): 457-58; Harold A. Innis, *The Bias of Communication* (Toronto, 1961), 95.

7. Mott, *American Journalism*, 238; William T. Coggeshall, *The Newspaper Record . . .* (Philadelphia, 1856), 148; Dorothy Macgill Hughes, *News and the Human Interest Story* (Chicago, 1940), 10; Frank Luther Mott, "Facetious News Writing," *Mississippi Valley Historical Review* 29 (1942-43): 39; James L. Crouthamel, "James Gordon Bennett, the New York *Herald*, and the Development of Newspaper Sensationalism," *New York History* 54 (1973): 298.

8. Hudson, *Journalism in the United States*, 430-31.

9. Americans, as Harold Innis has pointed out, were literate but not book-bound, as Europeans were. Newspapers expanded more rapidly in areas that were not dominated by the book (*Bias of Communication*, 28).

10. *NYH*, May 6, 1835.

11. *NYH*, May 11, 14, 1835.

12. See Crouthamel, "Newspaper Revolution" and "Bennett and Sensationalism." Leonard L. Richards, *"Gentlemen of Property and Standing": Anti-Abolition Mobs in Jacksonian America* (New York, 1970), 71-72, has a stimulating discussion of the "revolution in printing" of the mid-1830s and its effects.

13. George Juergens, *Joseph Pulitzer and the New York World* (Princeton, 1966), viii-ix.

14. *Sun*, Sept. 5, 1833.

15. *NYH*, May 11-15, 19, 22, 1835.

16. *NYH*, May 28, June 17, July 11, 13, 15, Aug. 4, Nov. 19, 20, 1835, Feb. 6, 11-13, 1836.

17. *NYH*, May 11, July 22, 28, Sept. 16, 25, Nov. 10, Dec. 11, 12, 24, 1835.

18. *NYH*, June 18, 28, July 9, 1835.

19. *NYH*, Aug. 7, 31, Sept. 7, Oct. 19, Dec. 28, 1835, Mar. 10, 31, Apr. 9, 1836.

20. *NYH*, Oct. 10, 1835, Mar. 2, 1836.

21. *NYH*, Sept. 16, 1835.

22. *NYH*, May 12, 16, 23, 30, June 22, 25, Sept. 10, Oct. 8, 9, 17, 1835, Jan. 5, 1836.

23. *NYH*, May 19, Aug. 25, Sept. 2, Dec. 29, 1835.

24. *NYH*, Feb. 6, 1836.

25. *NYH*, Dec. 19, 21, 1835.

26. *NYH*, Dec. 9, 1835. It was reprinted Dec. 19.

27. *NYH*, Jan. 6, 7, Feb. 20, Mar. 23, 1836.

28. *NYH*, Apr. 11, 1836, reprinted on Apr. 12; all the stories about the case were reprinted on April 13.

29. Hughes, *News and the Human Interest Story*, 11-12, 197.

30. *NYH*, Apr. 12, 1836.

31. *NYH*, Apr. 13-15, 1836.

32. *NYH*, Apr. 16, 1836; Nils Gunnar Nilsson, "The Origin of the Interview," *Journal-*

ism Quarterly 48 (1971): 707-13; Lucy M. Salmon, *The Newspaper and the Historian* (New York, 1923), 233.

33. *NYH,* Apr. 11-19, 1836; *Sun,* Apr. 16, 18, 1836; *Daily Transcript,* Apr. 14, 16, 1836.

34. *NYH,* Apr. 30, 1836.

35. *NYH,* Apr. 25, 30, 1836.

36. *NYH,* June 2-10, 1836. Quote from June 8.

37. *NYH,* June 1, 11-13, 1836; Hughes, *News and the Human Interest Story,* 159.

38. *Sun,* Apr. 11-21, 26, June 2-11, 14, 20, 24, July 13, 14, 19, 1836; *Daily Transcript,* Apr. 11-16, June 2-11, 1836; *NYH,* June 2-11, 1836.

39. *Courier and Enquirer,* Apr. 11-13, June 2-11, 1836; *New York Evening Post,* Apr. 11-19, June 2-11, 1836; *New York Evening Star,* Apr. 11, 13, 18, June 2-11, 1836; *New York Commercial Advertiser,* Apr. 11, 30, June 2-11, 1836; *New York Journal of Commerce,* Apr. 11, 30, June 2-11, 1836; *New York American,* Apr. 11, 1836.

40. Two of these were in *NYH,* Oct. 7, 22-25, 1839, Mar. 25-30, 1840; and Dec. 31, 1843, Jan. 1-11, 21, June 27-30, July 2-6, 1844.

41. *NYH,* Sept. 15, 16, 1842; Oct. 7, 1839 (with long accounts of five fires); Jan. 5-9, 1839, Jan. 16-30, Feb. 7, 1840, Jan. 8-11, 1841; July 8, 10, 17, 20, 21, 1841; Sept. 16, 19, 1836; Sept. 2, 9, 10, 13, 14, 23, 1839; Jan. 5, 6, 15, 19, 21, May 7, July 14, Oct. 1, 2, 5-15, 1841. Bennett sent a special correspondent to cover the McLeod trial.

42. *NYH,* July 8, 10, 1844, Aug. 14, 1838, May 10, June 25, July 22, 1841, Nov. 4, 6, 12-14, 16, 1842.

43. *NYH,* Mar. 12, 1837.

44. Crouthamel, "Bennett and Sensationalism," 309-10.

45. Ibid., 310-11; *NYH,* Mar. 22, 27, 29, 1842. Quote from July 17, 1843.

46. *NYH,* Mar. 19, 1844; Frederick Merk, *Manifest Destiny and Mission in American History: A Reinterpretation* (New York, 1963), 56.

47. For example, *NYH,* May 23, 25, Aug. 18, Sept. 3, Nov. 21, 1836, Aug. 14, 1837, Oct. 26, 1838, June 1, 1839, May 12, 1840, Aug. 19, 1841, Apr. 26, 1842.

48. *NYH,* Nov. 26, 1841, May 8, 1837.

49. *NYH,* Oct. 11, 17, Dec. 1, 1836, June 5, 1837, Feb. 9, 14, May 6, 1838, July 17, 1839, Feb. 3, June 8, 1840.

50. *NYH,* July 16, 1836, Jan. 11, 1838, May 16, 1839, Aug. 3, 9, Oct. 13, 22, 1841, Sept. 14, 1842.

51. *NYH,* Apr. 20, 29, 1841, Sept. 14, 1842. The *Herald* usually referred to Greeley as a "galvanized squash" but sometimes as a "pumpkin" or a "miserable dried vegetable."

52. *NYH,* July 17, 18, 21, 23, 30, Aug. 16, Sept. 18, 20, 1840, for a sampling of Bennett's European society letters; Aug. 7, 1838, for an example of society in the regular Washington correspondence; Aug. 7-20, 1839, for Bennett's letters from Saratoga Springs; July 30-Aug. 22, 1840, for his letters from Niagara Falls; Jan. 4, 22, 29, 31, Feb. 1, 6, 22, Mar. 9, 1839, for his Washington letters dealing with society. The quote is in *NYH,* Mar. 17, 1837.

53. *NYH,* Oct. 17, 1840; Robert A. Rutland, *The Newsmongers: Journalism in the Life of the Nation, 1690-1972* (New York, 1973), 164. Respectable New Yorkers such as Philip Hone were shocked at Bennett's impudence in sending a reporter (Allan Nevins, ed., *The Diary of Philip Hone, 1828-1851,* 2 vols. [New York, 1927], 1:464-65).

54. *NYH,* Apr. 12, July 17, 25, Aug. 14, Sept. 15, Nov. 5, 1838, Mar. 11, 14, Aug. 13, 15, 27, Sept. 4, 11, 12, 22, 25, 26, Oct. 8, 22, 25, Nov. 25, Dec. 12, 1839. Later examples of illustrations in Mar. 26, May 5, June 6, 19, July 6, Aug. 14, 1840, Mar. 5, Nov. 29, 1841, Feb. 15, 16, July 17, Aug. 6, 1842. Later examples of maps in Mar. 19, 23, July 10, Oct. 19, 21, Dec. 6, 1841, June 4, July 13, 1842.

55. *NYH*, Dec. 7, 1836, Mar. 4, Sept. 1, 1837.

56. James Harvey Young, *The Toadstool Millionaires: A Social History of Patent Medicines before Federal Regulation* (Princeton, 1961), 80–87. Bennett's explanation for expunging Brandreth is in *Sun*, Mar. 24, 1837.

57. The abortion advertising will be discussed more fully in Chapter 3.

58. *NYH*, May 20, June 1–3, 1840; Merle M. Hoover, *Park Benjamin, Poet and Editor* (New York, 1948), 104–9.

59. *NYH*, May 10, 14, 16, 27, 1840.

60. Levermore, "Rise of Metropolitan Journalism," 463.

61. Crouthamel, *Webb*, 84–86; *NYH*, May 30–June 14, 1840; *Courier and Enquirer*, June 3–13, 1840; Lambert A. Wilmer, *Our Press Gang; or, a Complete Exposition of the Corruptions and Crimes of American Newspapers* (Philadelphia, 1859), 392–93. Hudson, *Journalism in the United States*, 460, lists the choicest epithets used by Webb to describe Bennett.

62. *NYH*, June 1, 8, 1840; [Pray], *Memoirs of Bennett*, 279–80.

63. *NYH*, June 3, 4, 6, 9, 13, 1840.

64. *NYH*, June 26, July 3, 7, 16, Aug. 31, Sept. 3, 21, Oct. 9, 27, 1840.

65. Hudson, *Journalism in the United States*, 453. Several authorities argue that the *Herald*'s circulation dropped by as much as five thousand daily and that it did not recover until 1844. See Hughes, *News and the Human Interest Story*, 221; Rutland, *Newsmongers*, 143; Hoover, *Park Benjamin*, 109; Willard G. Bleyer, *Main Currents in the History of American Journalism* (Boston, 1927), 194.

66. *NYH*, July 14, 1836; *American*, July 14, 1836; *Journal of Commerce*, July 16, 1836; *Sun*, July 16, 1836; *Courier and Enquirer*, July 18, 1836; *Commercial Advertiser*, July 19, 1836; *Evening Post*, July 1836.

67. *NYH*, July 13, 1843; *Courier and Enquirer*, July 14, 1843. A search of the *Sun, Express, Tribune, Journal of Commerce, American*, and *Evening Post* yielded nothing.

68. *NYH*, June 3, 21, 1837; *Express*, June 2, 3, 1837; *Sun*, June 2, 6, 1837; *Commercial Advertiser*, June 1, 2, 1837; *Evening Post*, June 1–3, 1837; *Courier and Enquirer*, June 1, 2, 1837. The *Journal of Commerce* printed neither race advertising nor results.

69. *NYH*, Oct. 17, 1840; *Courier and Enquirer*, Oct. 16, 1840. A search of the *American, Sun, Commercial Advertiser, Evening Post*, and *Journal of Commerce* yielded nothing.

70. *NYH*, Apr. 11, Nov. 1, 1859, Aug. 25, 1860.

71. *NYH*, Mar. 6, 1845, June 24, 1847, June 2, 4, 28, 1845, Aug. 10, 11, 1845, June 21, 1857, May 13, 1845, Mar. 8, May 30, June 24, 1858; Hughes, *News and the Human Interest Story*, 221.

72. *NYH*, June 9, 1855, devoted most of page 1 to the regatta of the New York Yacht Club; May 12–14, 1845, Sept. 17, 1855, Feb. 1, 1856, for horse racing; Feb. 9, 11, 1849, Nov. 26, 1857, Oct. 21, 22, 1858, May 8, 1859, Apr. 29, 30, May 2, 3, 1860, for prizefighting.

73. *NYH*, Apr. 13–15, July 20, 1845, May 19–22, 1849, Sept. 18–25, 1857, May 9–12, 1853, Jan. 10–12, 1856, July 1, Sept. 7, 8, 1855, Jan. 19, 1857.

74. *NYH*, May 1, 1850, Jan. 3, Mar. 10, 12, 14, 1855, Mar. 20, June 17, 1856, Aug. 2–4, 1857, Dec. 10–12, 1860, for a sample of murders; Mar. 20–31, Apr. 1, 2, 4, 6, July 3, 4, Aug. 31, 1850, for the Parkman murder.

75. *NYH*, Feb. 2–16, 22, Mar. 5, 10, 22, Apr. 2, May 7–11, 19, June 15, Aug. 5–8, 25, 26, 1857, for this Burdell-Cunningham case.

76. *NYH*, Mar. 1, 2, 4, Apr. 2–8, 17, 27, 1859. Sickles published a defense in *NYH*, July 20, 1858.

77. *NYH*, Aug. 7, 8, 1845, Feb. 25, 1855, for attacks on *Tribune;* Nov. 5, 1850, for attack on *Express;* Dec. 16-19, 1853, Feb. 18, 19, Mar. 5, 18, 19, Oct. 6, 1855, for the libel trial; Jan. 27, 1853, Mar. 8, 1855, for the biographies; Jan. 5, 1855, for the testimonial; Oct. 29, 1856, for his son.

78. *NYH*, May 1, 6, 9, 1855, May 25, 1859, May 31, 1860.

79. *NYH*, Sept. 1850, especially Sept. 2; criticism of Barnum's methods in June 7, 9, July 4, 1855. Barnum's side of the feud is in P. T. Barnum, *Struggles and Triumphs; or, Forty Years' Recollections* (Hartford, 1870), 665-75.

80. For example, *NYH*, Dec. 1-5, 1859, for art; Aug. 2, Sept. 22, 1855, for AAAS; Oct. 4, 1858, for the state fair.

81. *NYH*, Apr. 1, Nov. 26, 1850, Feb. 19, Mar. 26, Apr. 12, May 17, 24, 1851. When New York held its own world's fair in 1853, the *Herald* did better. *NYH*, July 13-15, 1853. For a complete discussion see Robert F. Dalzell, Jr., *American Participation in the Great Exhibition of 1851* (Amherst, Mass., 1960).

82. *NYH*, Dec. 15, 18, 19, 22, 1851, Jan. 1, 29, Feb. 2, 14, 16, 21, Apr. 1, 1852. For a detailed account see E. Maurice Bloch, "The American Art-Union's Downfall," *New-York Historical Society Quarterly* 38 (1953): 331-59.

83. *NYH*, Feb. 15, Sept. 6, 21, 23, 1846, for Mormons; Jan. 31, Feb. 1848, for Fré-mont; July 12, 25, Aug. 2, Sept. 1, 26, Oct. 12-20, 1860, for the Prince of Wales; May 6-11, June 17-22, 1860, for the Japanese.

84. *NYH*, Jan. 20-Feb. 16, 1851, Apr. 4, July 10, Sept. 1, 20, 24-26, 1858.

85. *NYH*, Jan. 1845 for Onderdonk; Feb. 1845 for series on Unitarians; Jan. 7, 22, 25, Apr. 1, 11, 14, 22, 1855, on Catholic issues; May 27, 28, 1858, on revivals.

3 — Technology and the News

1. For the development of printing, see Mott, *American Journalism,* 314-16; Richards, *"Gentlemen of Property and Standing,"* 71-72; Innis, *Bias of Communication,* 168; Robert Hoe, *A Short History of the Printing Press* (New York, 1902), which has illustrations of most of the presses mentioned below, and James Moran, *Printing Presses: History and Development from the 15th Century to Modern Times* (Berkeley, 1973). For a good survey of printing-related technology see William S. Pretzer, "The Quest for Autonomy and Discipline: Labor and Technology in the Book Trades," *Proceedings of the American Antiquarian Society* 104 (1968): 85-131.

2. *NYH*, Apr. 9, 12, 13, July 14, Nov. 21, 1836, Nov. 9, 1838, May 12, 1840.

3. *NYH*, Aug. 19, 1841, Feb. 1, Apr. 26, 1842.

4. *NYH*, July 7, 1848, Jan. 22, 1849, with an illustration and explanation of the lightning press; Oct. 22, 1850, Apr. 28, 1852, Jan. 5, Mar. 2, May 8, June 16, 1857, Mar. 27, 1859.

5. Innis, *Bias of Communication,* 158-60; Lyman Weeks, *A History of Paper-Manufacturing in the United States, 1690-1916* (New York, 1916), 195, 223-24; Dard Hunter, *Papermaking: The History and Technique of an Ancient Craft* (New York, 1943), 285-86, 362-63; Joel Munsell, *Chronology of the Origin and Progress of Paper and Paper-making,* 5th ed. (Albany, 1876), 81-82, 134-36, 140, 154-55; and the definitive David C. Smith, *History of Papermaking in the United States, 1691-1969* (New York, 1970). There are few accurate statistics on the price of paper used by newspapers before 1860 (letter of John J. Zima, statistician for the Newsprint Service Bureau, to the author, Jan. 9, 1962).

6. *NYH*, Aug. 30, 1845, Apr. 28, 1852, May 27, 1855.

7. Calder M. Pickett, "Technology and the New York Press in the 19th Century," *Journalism Quarterly* 37 (1960): 402–3; *NYH,* Dec. 5, 9, 1835.

8. *NYH,* Mar. 29, Dec. 8, 13, 1837, Mar. 13, 1838, June 3, 1839, Feb. 3, 1840; T. H. Giddings, "Rushing the Transatlantic News in the 1830s and 1840s," *New-York Historical Society Quarterly* 42 (1958): 47–59.

9. *NYH,* Jan. 25, Sept. 23–25, 29, 30, Oct. 3, 8, 10, 1840, May 8, Dec. 26, 1844, Jan. 6, 1845, Feb. 19–21, 1846, Nov. 27, 1847.

10. Innis, *Bias of Communication,* 167–70; Robert L. Thompson, *Wiring a Continent: The Telegraph Industry in the United States* (Princeton, 1947), chap. 14; Alvin F. Harlow, *Old Wires and New Waves: The History of the Telegraph, Telephone, and Wireless* (New York, 1936), 175–200; Oliver Gramling, *A.P.: The Story of News* (New York, 1940), 19–35; Victor Rosewater, *History of Cooperative Newsgathering in the United States* (New York, 1940), 70–72.

11. *NYH,* Nov. 15, 29, 1845, Feb. 24, 25, Mar. 9, 1846. Quotes from June 6, 1844, and Oct. 24, 1845.

12. *NYH,* May 1846, e.g., May 19, 25, 29; Rutland, *Newsmongers,* 156.

13. Hudson, *Journalism in the United States,* 611; Rosewater, *History of Cooperative Newsgathering,* 57–58; Gramling, *A.P.,* 119. These accounts are superseded by Richard A. Schwartzloze, "Harbor News Association: The Formal Origin of the AP," *Journalism Quarterly* 45 (1968): 253–60, and "Early Telegraphic News Dispatches: Forerunner of the AP," *Journalism Quarterly* 51 (1974): 595–601.

14. *NYH,* July 16, 1852, Sept. 9, 17, 1860.

15. Richard B. Kielbowicz, "News Gathering by Mail in the Age of the Telegraph: Adapting to a New Technology," *Technology and Culture* 28 (1978): 26–41.

16. *NYH,* Aug. 6, 1858; Allan Nevins and Milton H. Thomas, eds., *The Diary of George Templeton Strong,* 4 vols. (New York, 1952), 2:409. Webb of the *Courier and Enquirer* wrote that "the accomplishment of the European cable scheme, cannot fail to be the most disastrous to some of the Daily Press in this City. I fear its consequences greatly; because it is impossible to *conjecture* to what expense we may be put by it, while we know there can be no adequate return. . . . The Journal [of Commerce] & Courier will suffer most from it, because we are the commercial & morning papers, & live by advertising and *not* circulation" (Webb to William H. Seward, Aug. 6, 1858, William H. Seward Papers, Rush Rhees Library, University of Rochester).

17. *NYH,* Apr. 20, June 25, Aug. 21, 27, 28, 31, 1857.

18. *NYH,* Nov. 30, 1835, Jan.–Feb. 1836, Jan. 2, 5, 6, 10, 11, 20, Feb. 8, Aug. 28, Nov. 16, Dec. 8, 1837, Aug. 8, 1838; Nevins, ed., *Diary of Philip Hone,* 1:289–90.

19. *NYH,* Mar. 24, Apr. 24, 25, 30, May 1, July 17, Oct. 6, 10, 1838; Giddings, "Rushing the Transatlantic News," 47–49.

20. *NYH,* Jan.–Feb. 1839, e.g., Jan. 4, 17; Nov. 11, 1839, Dec. 5, 1840.

21. *NYH,* May 8, 24, 28–30, June 3, 5, 12, 14, 21, July 7, Dec. 2, 1841 (quote from June 5); [Pray], *Memoirs of Bennett,* 289–91; Ben. Perley Poore, *Perley's Reminiscences of Sixty Years in the National Metropolis,* 2 vols. (Philadelphia, 1886), 1:260–62; Frederick B. Marbut, "The United States Senate and the Press, 1838–1841," *Journalism Quarterly* 28 (1951): 342–50.

22. *NYH,* Sept. 29, Oct. 1–3, Dec. 9, 1842, Dec. 30, 1843, Aug. 6, 1848. There is an interesting and humorous account of how Attree had functioned as a correspondent covering the 1839 vacation trip of Martin Van Buren in Smith T. Van Buren to Angelica Van Buren, July 30, 1839, "Martin Van Buren's Journey Home in 1839: An Account by His Son," ed. Carol E. Kohan, *New York History,* 68 (1987): 93–99.

23. *NYH*, Sept. 4, 1847, May 1, 1849; Rutland, *Newsmongers*, 161.

24. Frederick B. Marbut, *News from the Capitol: The Story of Washington Reporting* (Carbondale, 1971), 85-93; Philip S. Klein, *President James Buchanan: A Biography* (University Park, Pa., 1962), 190-91; Milo M. Quaife, ed., *The Diary of James K. Polk*, 4 vols. (Chicago, 1910), 3:333-34, 353-56, 359.

25. *NYH*, Feb. 22, 25, Mar. 11, 13, 15, 16, 1848.

26. *NYH*, Apr. 1 (quote), 4, 6, 1848. For Polk's reaction, see Quaife, ed., *Diary of James K. Polk*, 3:396-410. Polk was convinced that Buchanan was the source of the leak.

27. *NYH*, May 3, 1848. Nugent stayed on as Bennett's trusted agent in Washington. Early in the Taylor administration Bennett recommended him warmly to Secretary of State John M. Clayton as a reliable person to whom State Department intelligence could be leaked (Bennett to Clayton, Mar. 7, 1849, John M. Clayton Papers, vol. 3, Library of Congress).

28. *NYH*, Jan. 5, Aug. 2, Oct. 21, 1855.

29. For example, *NYH*, Jan. 11, 1860, with special reports from Pennsylvania, Wisconsin, Illinois, and Louisiana; Henry Villard, *Memoirs of Henry Villard: Journalist and Financier, 1835-1900*, 2 vols. (Boston, 1904), 1:140.

30. Holman Hamilton and James L. Crouthamel, "A Man for Both Parties: Francis J. Grund as Political Chameleon," *Pennsylvania Magazine of History and Biography* 97 (1973): 470.

31. For example, *NYH*, Jan. 1, 1840, July 11, 1857.

32. For example, *NYH*, Mar. 25, 1836, Dec. 28, 29, 1838, Aug. 7-20, 1839, Jan. 13-18, July 30-Sept. 19, 1840, Feb. 13, 15, 19, 1841. President Van Buren was at Saratoga Springs at the same time as Bennett in 1839. Philip Hone, who detested Bennett, commented: "The President takes the head of one of the tables, and the *modest* Mr. Bennett of the *Herald* the other" (Nevins, ed., *Diary of Philip Hone*, 1:411).

33. *NYH*, May 1, July 14-Oct. 11, 1838, Aug. 5, 22, Sept. 6, 23, Oct. 6, 21, 23, 1843.

34. *NYH*, July 22, 1846-June 23, 1847 (e.g., Sept. 21, Dec. 7, 1846), June 19, 1847, Nov. 28, 1850, Jan. 5, Sept. 15, 1851. For Mrs. Bennett's letters see Dec. 22-24, 1846, Feb. 26, Mar. 2, 24, 27, Apr. 24, 27, May 2, 5, 20, 1847.

35. *NYH*, July 17, 1839, May 30, 1840, Aug. 19, 1841, Aug. 5, 1842, Aug. 28, 1852; George Alfred Townsend, "Recollections and Reflections," *Lippincott's Monthly Magazine* 38 (1886): 505-24; Julius Wilcox, "Journalism as a Profession," *Galaxy* 4 (1867): 797-805.

36. *NYH*, July 28, 29, Aug. 2, 1836, July 17, 1839, Aug. 2, 1842, Apr. 11, 28, 1852; Elizabeth Faulkner Baker, *Printers and Technology: A History of the International Printing Pressmen and Assistants' Union* (New York, 1957), 49-53; Ethelbert Stewart, "Documentary History of the Early Organization of Printers," *U.S. Bureau of Labor Bulletin*, no. 61 (Nov. 1905): 896-929. Sean Wilentz, *Chants Democratic: New York City and the Rise of the American Working Class, 1788-1850* (New York, 1984), 129-32, supports this dismal picture of printers' wages and documents the debasement of the printing trades. See also W. J. Rorabaugh, *The Craft Apprentice from Franklin to the Machine Age in America* (New York, 1986), chap. 4.

37. Frank Presbrey, *The History and Development of Advertising* (Garden City, N.Y., 1929), 187, 192-99; *NYH*, July 4, 1836.

38. Presbrey, *History and Development of Advertising*, 208, 233-45; *NYH*, June 24, 1836, Oct. 4, 1856. The *Herald* on May 6, 1858, contained seven pages of Bonner's "iterations" to announce a new adventure serial. Other examples of ways around the agate rule were Mathew Brady's 1856 ad for his photographic studio, which arranged the agate type in inch numerals to form 359, his address on Broadway, and a clothing merchant announc-

ing a Christmas sale by rearranging the word *overcoat* into the shape of a Christmas tree. See Daniel J. Boorstin, *The Americans: The National Experience* (New York, 1973), 138–44.

39. *NYH*, Aug. 14, 21, 1837, May 25, June 1, 4, 6, 1839, Feb. 10, 1840, Oct. 6, 1841, Nov. 8, 1842.

40. Presbrey, *History and Development of Advertising*, 210, 232; *NYH*, Mar. 14, 21, 1849.

41. *NYH*, Nov. 11, 1855, Apr. 10, 1856, Apr. 11, 1858; Michael Schudson, *Discovering the News: A Social History of American Newspapers* (New York, 1978), 19.

42. Marvin Olasky, "Advertising Abortion during the 1830s and 1840s: Madame Restell Builds a Business," *Journalism History* 13 (1986): 49–55, is a careful study of the topic. See *NYH*, Dec. 8, 1841, for three typical Restell ads; Sept. 17, 1852, for an ad for Lohman's book.

43. *NYH*, Aug. 18, Sept. 6, 7, Dec. 1 (quote), 2, 1836, Apr. 17, May 8, 23, Dec. 4, 1837, May 30, 1839, Oct. 20, 1841, Aug. 3, 1842, The evening edition (changed from the *Chronicle* to *Evening Herald* in July 1837) was discontinued on March 30, 1839 (Lee, *Daily Newspaper in America*, 277).

44. *NYH*, Nov. 20, 1839, May 5, Dec. 2, 31, 1841, Jan. 3–29, 1842; Lee, *Daily Newspaper in America*, 261, 391–92.

45. *NYH*, Feb. 3, 13, 1848, Oct. 20, 1853, Feb. 13, 1854, May 4, July 10, 1855, Aug. 6, Sept. 5, 1856, Mar. 19, Apr. 14, 1857, Sept. 16, 1859, Apr. 16, May 1, Nov. 8, 1860.

46. *NYH*, July 1, 1856, Jan. 1, 1857.

47. Allan Nevins, *Ordeal of the Union*, 2 vols. (New York, 1947), 1:88. The most recent estimate is 75,806 in December 1860, up from a 70,000 daily average in 1859. See Douglas Fermer, *James Gordon Bennett and the New York Herald: A Study of Editorial Opinion in the Civil War Era, 1854–1867*, Royal Historical Society Studies in History, no. 46 (New York, 1986), 324.

48. Crouthamel, "Newspaper Revolution in New York," 102–8, and *Webb*, 82–94.

49. Donald L. Shaw, "Technology and Conformity: A Study of Newsgathering in the American Press, 1820–1860," paper presented at annual meeting of Association for Education in Journalism, Aug. 1972, Carbondale, Ill., and "At the Crossroads: Change and Continuity in American Press News, 1820–1860," *Journalism History* 8 (1981): 38–50.

50. David C. Smith, "Wood Pulp and Newspapers, 1867–1900," *Business History Review* 38 (1964): 328–45.

4 — Editorial Jingoism

1. James Parton, "The New York Herald," *North American Review* 102 (1866): 418; Howard C. Perkins. "The Defence of Slavery in the Northern Press on the Eve of the Civil War," *Journal of Southern History* 9 (1943): 501–31.

2. Merk, *Manifest Destiny and Mission*, 56.

3. For the *Herald*'s overseas circulation see Fermer, *Bennett and The Herald*, 326, and Lee, *Daily Newspaper in America*, 383–84. On the *Herald*'s influence abroad, see Arnold Whitridge, "Anglo-American Trouble-Makers: J. G. Bennett and J. T. Delane," *History Today* 6 (Feb. 1956): 88–95, and Martin Crawford, *The Anglo-American Crisis of the Mid-Nineteenth Century: The Times and America, 1850–1862* (Athens, Ga., 1987). Several of the *Vanity Fair* cartoons are reprinted in Don C. Seitz, *The James Gordon Bennetts, Father and Son* (Indianapolis, 1928).

4. *NYH*, July 28, Oct. 1, Nov. 9, 24, 1835, May 18, 19, 1836, Aug. 10, 11, Oct. 11, 1837.

5. *NYH*, Apr. 13, Aug. 27, 1838, Feb. 25, Mar. 13, 15–17, 1842. See the comments

about the *Herald* in Howard Jones, "The Peculiar Institution and National Honor: The Case of the *Creole* Slave Revolt," *Civil War History* 21 (1975): 48.

6. *NYH,* Nov. 10, Dec. 17, 1841, July 17, 1843.

7. *NYH,* Oct. 12, Nov. 10, 1843; Duff Green to Abel P. Upshur, Aug. 3, 1843, in Frederick Merk, *Slavery and the Annexation of Texas* (New York, 1972), 224–25.

8. *NYH,* Mar. 1, 2, 5, 1844.

9. *NYH,* Mar. 9, 10, 18, 19, 1844; Julius W. Pratt, "John L. O'Sullivan and Manifest Destiny," *New York History* 14 (1933): 213–34, and "The Origin of Manifest Destiny," *American Historical Review* 32 (1926–27): 795–98.

10. *NYH,* May 1, 1844.

11. *NYH,* June 6 (quote), 14, July 28, 1844.

12. *NYH,* Aug. 2, 30, Sept. 22, 23, 25, 26, Nov. 14, Dec. 4, 7, 1844.

13. *NYH,* Dec. 9, 11, 21, 1844, Jan. 31, Feb. 2, Mar. 2, 1845.

14. *NYH,* Mar. 17, Apr. 29, 30, May 31, June 5, 6, 27, 28, July 2, 6, 1845.

15. *NYH,* July 20, Aug. 1, 3, 10, 17, 22–26, Sept. 2–4, 1845.

16. *NYH,* Sept. 7, 13, 1845, Jan. 11, Apr. 1, 1846. Quote from Jan. 20, 1846. See Frederick Merk, *The Monroe Doctrine and American Expansionism* (New York, 1966), 81–82, 158–60.

17. *NYH,* Sept. 25 (quote), 30, 1845, May 2, 1846.

18. *NYH,* Jan. 18, 22, 27, Feb. 2, Mar. 25, Apr. 9, 17, 18, 21, 23, May 12, 1846. On Mar. 15 the front page featured a large woodcut of Taylor's camp at Corpus Christi.

19. *NYH,* May 13, 14, June 4, 21–23, 1846.

20. *NYH,* June 5 (quote), Sept. 3, 17, 29, 30, 1846, Jan. 11, 1847.

21. *NYH,* Apr. 20, 1847; Merk, *Manifest Destiny and Mission,* 114; Anna Kasten Nelson, "Secret Agents and Security Leaks: President Polk and the Mexican War," *Journalism Quarterly* 52 (1975): 14.

22. *NYH,* July 27, 1846, May 15, June 16, 1847; Merk, *Manifest Destiny and Mission,* 123.

23. *NYH,* Sept. 22, Oct. 8, 10, 19, 24, 28, 1847.

24. *NYH,* Jan. 27, 31, Feb. 1, 3, 9, 12, 15, 22, 23, 26, Mar. 9, 12, 1848.

25. *NYH,* Mar. 13, Apr. 27, May 10, 12 (quote), 1848.

26. *NYH,* June 7, 1842, Mar. 9, 10, 1844; Bennett to James K. Polk, Mar. 10, 1846, quoted in David M. Pletcher, *The Diplomacy of Annexation: Texas, Oregon, and the Mexican War* (Columbia, Mo., 1973), 237.

27. *NYH,* Apr. 23, 24, 1845.

28. *NYH,* July 10, Oct. 10, 1845.

29. *NYH,* Feb. 5, 7 (quote), 10, Apr. 25–27, June 10–13, 19, 1846.

30. *NYH,* Jan. 3, 1846, June 3, 1847, Aug. 4, 1848 (quote).

31. *NYH,* Aug. 15, Oct. 22, 1848, Jan. 11, Apr. 4, 14 (quote), 1849. See Basil Rauch, *American Interest in Cuba, 1848–1855* (New York, 1948).

32. *NYH,* Oct. 20, Dec. 16, 1848, Mar. 27, 28, 1849; Merk, *Monroe Doctrine and American Expansionism,* 263–68.

33. *NYH,* Aug. 6, 15, 16, 18, 1849, Jan. 31, May 24–28, June 1, 16, 17, 1850, Oct. 28, 1851. See Robert E. May, *The Southern Dream of a Caribbean Empire, 1854–1861* (Baton Rouge, 1973).

34. *NYH,* Nov. 28, 1850, Jan. 8, 1851; Frederic Hudson Diary, Feb. 11, 1851, Frederic Hudson Papers, Concord, Mass., Public Library.

35. *NYH,* Aug. 2, 25, 26, 28, 31, Sept. 6, 7, Nov. 15, 1851, Mar. 8, 20, Oct. 11, 16, Nov. 20, Dec. 9, 1852.

36. *NYH*, Apr. 8, 9, 28, July 7, Aug. 6, 10, 26, 1853. It is probable that Bennett talked to Soulé when he was in New York en route to Europe in July 1853. See Amos A. Ettinger, *The Mission to Spain of Pierre Soulé, 1853–1855* (New Haven, 1932), 157, 169, 175.

37. Bennett to Franklin Pierce, Dec. 15, 1852, Franklin Pierce Papers, Library of Congress. Bennett denied that he had sought the French mission in *NYH*, Jan. 22, 1854. See the discussion in Fermer, *Bennett and the Herald*, 84–85, and in John Tebbel and Sarah Miles Watts, *The Press and the Presidency from George Washington to Ronald Reagan* (New York, 1985), 154–55.

38. *NYH*, Oct. 9, 16, Nov. 15, 19–21, Dec. 17, 1853; Ettinger, *Mission to Spain of Soulé*, 317. The Senate refused to confirm Sanders's appointment.

39. *NYH*, Mar. 9, 13, 20, 22, 24, 26, Apr. 27, May 3, 11, 27, 29, 31, June 3, 19, July 4, 1854.

40. *NYH*, Oct. 22, 1854. Managing editor Hudson was receiving information about Cuba from New Yorkers who had visited there (Hudson Diary, Oct. 26, 1854, Hudson Papers).

41. Ettinger, *Mission to Spain of Soulé*, 375–76; *NYH*, Oct. 18, 22, 26–31, Nov. 7, 11, 18, 1854. Pierce's biographer calls the *Herald*'s version of the conference "strained," and Buchanan's biographer describes it as "garbled." See Roy F. Nichols, *Franklin Pierce, Young Hickory of the Granite Hills*, rev. ed. (Philadelphia, 1958), 358; Klein, *President James Buchanan*, 240.

42. Ettinger, *Mission to Spain of Soulé*, 405.

43. *NYH*, Mar. 13, 14, 18 (quote), 21, 24, 26, 28, 30, Apr. 2, 1855.

44. *NYH*, Apr. 3, 9–11, 15, 30, May 25, June 28, July 9, Oct. 17, 1855.

45. *NYH*, Nov. 16, 1857, Feb. 21, 28, Mar. 2, 6, 18–23, June 2, 7, Aug. 22, 1858.

46. *NYH*, Sept. 3, Oct. 6, 8, 12, Nov. 23, 24, 26, Dec. 8, 10, 27, 30, 31, 1858, Jan. 17–20, 22, 25–29, Feb. 1–3, 5, 7, 10, May 14, 1859.

47. *NYH*, July 1, Oct. 25 (quote), 1851, July 2, 3, 1852.

48. *NYH*, Jan. 20, 21, 1853, Mar. 20, July 11, Aug. 27, Sept. 8, 9, Oct. 7, Dec. 19, 23, 1855.

49. *NYH*, Oct. 2, 3, Nov. 5, 12, 13, 30, Dec. 13, 15, 18, 1855, Jan. 15, 16, 26, Feb. 14, Mar. 14, 17, 1856.

50. *NYH*, Apr. 2, 10, 1856.

51. *NYH*, Apr. 17, 18, 30, May 1, 2, 5, 6, 8, 9, 12, 13, June 3, 1856.

52. *NYH*, Oct. 20, 21, 23, Nov. 18, 21, 22, 25–27, 29, 1856.

53. *NYH*, Dec. 1, 14, 15, 20, 22, 1856, Jan. 12, 15, 16, 25–29, Apr. 4–8, May 1, 2, 19, 29, 30, June 1, July 14, Nov. 6, 10, 14, Dec. 2, 16, 17, 31, 1857, Jan. 9, Apr. 9, 20, Dec. 12–14, 1858.

54. *NYH*, Oct. 7, 1859, Sept. 20, 28, Oct. 4, 1860.

55. *NYH*, Sept. 2, 1850, Sept. 1, 1852, Jan. 14, 1853, Sept. 5, Oct. 8, 1855. For a discussion of the *Herald*'s impact in England, see Wilbur D. Jones, *The American Problem in British Diplomacy, 1841–1861* (Athens, Ga., 1974), 112–13.

56. *NYH*, Aug. 23, 1852, Jan. 14, 1853, Sept. 5, Oct. 8, 1855.

57. Nevins and Thomas, eds., *Diary of Strong*, 2:425–26.

58. Merk, *Manifest Destiny and Mission*, 193.

59. Hamilton and Crouthamel, "A Man for Both Parties," 474–75.

5 – National Issues

1. *Springfield* (Mass.) *Daily Republican*, Dec. 9, 1859, quoted in George S. Merriam, *The Life and Times of Samuel Bowles*, 2 vols. (New York, 1885), 1:257–58.

2. In 1839, for example, the *Herald* covered the *L'Amistad* case with two special correspondents and printed an engraving of the captured slaves (*NYH*, Sept. 2, 9–14, 23, Oct. 2, 4, 1839). The random sample is *NYH*, weeks of May 5, 1840, May 5, 1845, May 5, 1850, May 5, 1855, May 5, 1860.

3. *NYH*, Sept. 30, Dec. 3, 5, 1835.

4. *NYH*, May 13, 1845, May 21, 1853, May 8, 1855. Bennett also believed in the racial inferiority of the Indians and the Chinese (*NYH*, Jan. 7, 28, May 8, 1856).

5. *NYH*, Sept. 19, 20, 1843, Jan. 3, 1846, July 4, 1858, Jan. 19, 1859, Jan. 29, Feb. 6, 1860.

6. *NYH*, Jan. 21, 1859, Apr. 1, 1860. The same argument was made by George Fitzhugh in *Cannibals All! or, Slaves without Masters* (Richmond, Va., 1857). The *Herald*, Jan. 5, 1860, in a long article about fugitive slave settlements in Ontario, Canada, concluded that "the fugitive slaves go into Canada as Beggars, and the mass of them commit larceny and lay in jail until they become lowered and debased, and ready for worse crimes."

7. *NYH*, July 23, Oct. 28, 1849, Feb. 16, 1860. A *Herald* reporter covering an Alabama slave auction early in 1860 wrote that the slaves did not appear "to have the slightest cause for grief or complaint." They were "happier and less concerned about their situation than three-quarters of the white people clustered about them" (*NYH*, Feb. 16, 1860).

8. *NYH*, June 18, 1844, Dec. 15, 1854, Nov. 15, 1857, Nov. 9, 1859, Jan. 15, 16, 28, Feb. 18, 25, 28, 29, Mar. 2, 5, 7, 8, 10, 14, Apr. 12, 1860.

9. *NYH*, Aug. 10, 1856, Aug. 26, 1859, Jan. 5, Mar. 26, Oct. 25, 28, 29, 1860.

10. *NYH*, Mar. 21, Apr. 9, 1856, Apr. 1, July 29, 1857, Mar. 2, 6, July 9 (quote), 1858, Aug. 6, 1859, Feb. 16, Mar. 6, 8, 1860.

11. *NYH*, Mar. 3, 10 (quote), Apr. 11, 12, 21, 1857, July 23, Nov. 6, 13, 1858, Jan. 10, 1859.

12. *NYH*, Aug. 31, Sept. 5, 11, 16, Oct. 17, Dec. 22–24, 1835, Jan. 11, May 23, Dec. 20, 1838, Oct. 13, 1841, July 18, Aug. 12, 1845, Mar. 17, Oct. 17, 1847, May 6, Oct. 8, Nov. 4, 1850.

13. *NYH*, Oct. 17, 19, 1835, May 28, Oct. 20 (quote), 1838. Lorman Ratner, *Powder Keg: Northern Opposition to the Abolitionists, 1831–1840* (New York, 1968), 37–38, 78, calls Bennett and Webb "the leading proponents of the idea of an abolitionist conspiracy."

14. *NYH*, Oct. 27, 1835, Oct. 21, 1836, Jan. 6, Nov. 27, 1837.

15. *NYH*, Apr. 30, May 1, Oct. 20, 1846, Apr. 8, 1855, Sept. 8, 1860.

16. Tebbel and Watts, *The Press and the Presidency*, 96–119.

17. *NYH*, Nov. 23, Dec. 9, 1846, Jan. 20, Feb. 17, Sept. 29, Nov. 28, Dec. 6, 1847, Mar. 16, Apr. 6, Nov. 9, 1848. Nevins, *Ordeal of the Union*, 1:210, claims that Bennett met Taylor at Niagara Falls in 1840, liked him, and for that reason supported him. This is confirmed in a letter from Bennett to Taylor written after the election and quoted in Tebbel and Watts, *The Press and the Presidency*, 135.

18. *NYH*, July 10, 29, Nov. 21, 28, Dec. 1, 3, 29, 1849, Jan. 13, 21, 23, 27, 28, 30, 31, 1850.

19. *NYH*, Feb. 5, 7, 14, Mar. 5, 6, 8, 9, 13, 14, 21, Apr. 5, 8, 11, May 11, 12, 26, June 2, 5, 8, July 1, Aug. 1, 2, Sept. 2, 7, 1850. In apportioning credit for the passage of the compromise, the *Herald* did not mention Stephen A. Douglas. Occasionally, when it appeared that the compromise would not pass, Bennett supported the extension of the Missouri Compromise line to the Pacific (*NYH*, May 29, 1850).

20. *NYH*, June 6, 7, 29, Nov. 3–5, 1852, Sept. 22, Oct. 10, 11, 13, 31, Dec. 2, 1853.

21. *NYH*, Feb. 17, 19, 28, Aug. 25, 1851, Mar. 1, Aug. 9, 1852, May 27–29, 1854, Mar. 10, Apr. 9, Oct. 30, 1855, Dec. 4, 1858, Mar. 25, 1860.

22. *NYH*, Jan. 24, 29, Feb. 9, 15, 16, May 10, 23, 24, 27, Oct. 25, 1854. Quote from

Jan. 10, 1854. The *Herald* and the *Journal of Commerce* were the only New York City papers to support the Kansas-Nebraska Act (Nevins, *Ordeal of the Union*, 2:131).

23. *NYH,* Apr. 20, 29, May 2-7, 13, June 13, Sept. 15, Dec. 5, 9, 21, 1855, Feb. 19, May 26, July 1, 3, 4, 1856.

24. *NYH,* May 23 (quote), 27, 30, 31, June 2, 3, 7, 1856.

25. *NYH,* Aug. 22-24, 26, Oct. 11, 1856.

26. *NYH,* Jan. 9, 13, 19, 24, 27, Feb. 1, 15, 23, 27, Mar. 1, 16, 17, Apr. 21, 30, May 27, June 26, July 25, 28, Sept. 6, 13, 25, Oct. 2, 5, Nov. 6, 1855, Feb. 24, 1856.

27. *NYH,* Feb. 27, Mar. 2-4, 22, May 6, June 4, 7, 8, 1856. See Phillip G. Auchampaugh, "Political Techniques — 1856, or Why the Herald Went for Fremont," *Western Political Quarterly* 1 (1948): 243-51, and Fermer, *Bennett and the Herald,* 92-99.

28. *NYH,* June 10-12, 19, 1856.

29. *NYH,* June 20, 24, 30, July 10, 13, 19, 28, 31, Aug. 2, 11, 15, Oct. 1, 3, 14, 15, 21, 1856.

30. *NYH,* Nov. 1, 5-8, Dec. 20, 1856. Buchanan wrote to Bennett two weeks before the election to "rejoice that our former friendly relations are about to be restored" (Buchanan to Bennett, Oct. 20, 1856, in John Bassett Moore, ed., *The Works of James Buchanan,* 12 vols. [Philadelphia, 1908-11], 10:95). On the reconciliation see Tebbel and Watts, *The Press and the Presidency,* 162-65, which quotes extensively from the correspondence between Bennett and Buchanan.

31. *NYH,* Mar. 8, 15, Apr. 14, 1857. Bennett said later (*NYH,* May 5, 1859) that he regarded the decision as *obiter dicta* and not binding.

32. *NYH,* Apr. 2, 5, 10, June 23, 24, July 8, Sept. 11, Nov. 9, Dec. 13, 17, 1856, Jan. 10, Feb. 1, Mar. 19, 27, Oct. 26, 27, Nov. 1, 2, 7, 10, 18, 20, 1857.

33. *NYH,* Nov. 21, 25, 28, Dec. 2, 10, 11, 13, 15, 18, 30, 1857.

34. *NYH,* Jan. 1, 3-7, 12, 13, 26, Feb. 5, 6, Mar. 5, 15, 19, 24, Apr. 1, 4, 7, 8, 18, May 1, 2, 1858.

35. *NYH,* Nov. 26, 28, Dec. 1-13, 1859. Bennett opposed the election as House Speaker of anyone who had endorsed the book.

36. *NYH,* Oct. 18-24, 27-31, Nov. 1-8, Dec. 2, 1859. The *Charleston Courier* quoted the *Herald* to reassure the South that northern opinion did not support John Brown's raid (Stephen A. Channing, *Crisis of Fear: Secession in South Carolina* [New York, 1970], 85-86). The *Herald*'s reporter for the trial was a Charlestown, Va., resident, a cousin of the local newspaper editor, who got himself hired as a guard at the jail, which gave him a chance to speak to Brown. At the execution he drove the undertaker's wagon on which Brown rode to the gallows. See Bernard A. Weisberger, *Reporters for the Union* (Boston, 1953), 67-68.

37. *NYH,* Jan. 16, June 1, 1855, Aug. 13, 17, 18, Nov. 30, Dec. 1, 12, 15, 1856, Feb. 26, Apr. 30, May 15, June 9, July 9 (quote), Aug. 5, 12, 19, Sept. 18, 1857, May 13, 14, July 21, Aug. 26, 31, Dec. 21, 1858, Mar. 29, Apr. 7, May 14, 18, 24, 26, June 10, July 10, Sept. 1, 1859.

38. *NYH,* Feb. 18, July 11, 1857, Aug. 26, May 8, Sept. 11, 13, 20, Oct. 11, 13, Nov. 16, 17, 29, Dec. 3, 16, 28, 29, 1858, Feb. 11, June 7, 9, 13, 14, July 8, Aug. 9, 13, 14, 17, 20, Sept. 12, 19, Nov. 11, Dec. 14, 15, 18, 30, 1859, May 7, 10, 13-15, 1860.

39. *NYH,* Mar. 10, Apr. 4, Aug. 5, 1858, July 3, 9, 19, 29, Dec. 2, 4, 8, 1859, Jan. 2, 24, 25, Feb. 2, 21, 25, 28, Mar. 31, 1860.

40. *NYH,* Apr. 24-30, May 1-8, 19-27, 30, June 2, 5, 8, 11, 17, 21-25, 30, July 1, 1860. Quotes from May 19, 30. The *Herald* had attacked Lincoln as a fanatic during the 1858 debates with Douglas, and it had ridiculed the Cooper Union speech in early 1860 (*NYH,* July 3, 14, 16, Sept. 15, 27, 30, 1858, Feb. 29, Mar. 12, 1860).

41. *NYH,* July 2, 3, 6, 7, 10, 11, 18, 19, 21, 26, 27, Aug. 2, 7–11, 15, 16, 21, 23, 24, 26, 28, 30, Sept. 19, Oct. 1, 3, 5, 11, 13, 21, 23, 24, 27, Nov. 4, 5, 1860.

42. *NYH,* Nov. 7, 10, 13, 14, 16–27, Dec. 3–9, 18, 21, 24, 28, 31, 1860, Feb. 5, Mar. 7, Apr. 11, 1861. On Dec. 28, 1860, there was a large front-page map of Charleston harbor; on Dec. 31, a diagram of Fort Sumter. Channing, *Crisis of Fear,* 74–75, points out that South Carolina editors used the *Herald*'s advocacy of peaceable secession to demonstrate the probability of northern acquiesence in secession.

43. *NYH,* Feb. 1, Apr. 29, 1861. See Howard R. Floan, "The New York *Evening Post* and the Antebellum South," *American Quarterly* 8 (1956): 243–53, for the treatment of the South by a Democratic paper with free-soil leanings.

44. Channing, *Crisis of Fear,* 84–85; Merriam, *Samuel Bowles,* 1:257–58; Thomas H. Baker, *The Memphis Commercial Appeal: The History of a Southern Newspaper* (Baton Rouge, 1971), 35; Allan Nevins, *The Emergence of Lincoln,* 2 vols. (New York, 1950), 158. In Pensacola and Richmond *Herald* reporters were almost lynched by angry mobs. Bennett deprecated this "reign of terror" in the South (*NYH,* Jan. 4, 12, 1860; Lucy M. Salmon, *The Newspaper and Authority* [New York, 1923], 274).

45. Nevins, *Emergence of Lincoln,* 1:431; Nevins, *Ordeal of the Union,* 2:490–91; James Buchanan to Bennett, June 18, Dec. 20, 1860, in Moore, ed., *Works of Buchanan,* 10:434, 11:69–70, 165–66.

46. Allan Nevins, *The War for the Union,* 4 vols. (New York, 1959–71), 4:137; Nevins, *Emergence of Lincoln,* 2:291. See Abraham Lincoln to George G. Fogg, Aug. 16, 29, 1860, in Roy M. Basler, ed., *The Works of Abraham Lincoln,* 8 vols. (New Brunswick, 1953), 4:96–97, 102.

47. *NYH,* Feb. 28, 1838.

48. Marvin Meyers, *The Jacksonian Persuasion: Politics and Belief* (Stanford, 1957), 1–23.

49. *NYH,* Aug. 31, Sept. 11, 16, Nov. 7, 1835. Quotes from Sept. 11, 16.

50. *NYH,* Feb. 10 (quote), Mar. 14, June 18, 1836.

51. *NYH,* June 24, 28, Sept. 20 (quote), 26, Nov. 29, 1836, Jan. 2, 4, 1837.

52. *NYH,* Jan. 6, 7, 10, 11, 1837.

53. *NYH,* Jan. 30, Feb. 2, 3, 1837.

54. *NYH,* Mar. 20, 30, 31, Apr. 4, 5, 7, 1837. The standard account is Reginald C. McGrane, *The Panic of 1837* (Chicago, 1924). He uses several New York newspapers in his research, but never the *Herald.* Samuel Rezneck, "Social History of an American Depression, 1837–1843," *American Historical Review* 40 (1935): 662–87, credits *Niles' Register* with warning in April of approaching panic but fails to note the *Herald*'s early warnings.

55. *NYH,* May 3, 1837; Bray Hammond, *Banks and Politics in America from the Revolution to the Civil War* (Princeton, 1957), 560.

56. *NYH,* May 9–13, 15, 17–20, 29, June 5, 12, 14, 15, July 1, 3, 7, 21, 1837.

57. *NYH,* July 31, Aug. 15, Sept. 5, 6, 9, 1837.

58. *NYH,* Oct. 7, 1837.

59. *NYH,* Nov. 13, 1837, Feb. 6, 26, 1838.

60. *NYH,* Dec. 5, 15, 17, 1838.

61. *NYH,* Oct. 10, 12, 14, 15, 19, 1839.

62. *NYH,* Jan. 27 (quote), Feb. 8, 1840.

63. *NYH,* Apr. 30, 1841.

64. *NYH,* May 31, June 12, 1841.

65. *NYH,* June 15, 18, 24, July 30, 31, Aug. 5, 6, 9–12, 16, 1841.

66. *NYH,* Aug. 26, 27, Sept. 11–14, Nov. 27, 1841.

67. *NYH,* Dec. 24, 27, 29, 1841, Jan. 10–13, 19, 1842.

68. *NYH,* Dec. 20, 1841.

69. *NYH,* Mar. 28, Aug. 10, 11, 1842.

70. *NYH,* July 26, 1845, Mar. 7, Apr. 4, 1846.

71. *NYH,* July 18, Nov. 13, 1844, July 24, Sept. 10, 1845, Feb. 14, 16, Apr. 7, 8, July 30, 1846.

72. *NYH,* Feb. 26, Mar. 1, 3, 12, Apr. 5, July 9, 1855, Jan. 6, 23, Nov. 30, 1856, Mar. 6, 1857.

73. *NYH,* Feb. 6, 7, 1847, Mar. 4, 6, 1855, Feb. 7, Mar. 19, May 30, July 23, 1858, Feb. 17, 1860.

74. *NYH,* July 17, Sept. 11, 28, 1846, June 14, 1847, May 23, 1849.

75. *NYH,* Aug. 29, 1849, Apr. 11, 1854, July 3, 9, Sept. 7, Dec. 7, 8, 10, 25, 1856.

76. *NYH,* Feb. 9, 18, 20, 21, 23, 25, 27, Apr. 22, 1857, Apr. 23–25, Aug. 3, 8, 1858.

77. *NYH,* Apr. 9, 1855, Dec. 4, 1858.

78. *NYH,* Nov. 11, 1841, Jan. 17, 1852, Mar. 27, 1855, Mar. 25, 28, Apr. 12, 21, 1858, Jan. 5, Sept. 4, 9, 1859, Jan. 4, 1860.

79. *NYH,* Mar. 1, 1850, Mar. 1, Aug. 9, 1852.

80. *NYH,* Jan. 20, 1856, Mar. 6, 1858, Feb. 3, 1859, Mar. 25, May 12, 17, 1860.

81. *NYH,* Jan. 4, 6, 8, 15, 17, 20, 27, Feb. 25, May 1, 7, July 1, Aug. 7, Sept. 10, Oct. 2, 8, 19, 20, 22, 28, Nov. 4, 5, 1855. Standard accounts of the Panic of 1857 are George W. VanVleck, *The Panic of 1857: An Analytical Study* (New York, 1943), and Samuel Rezneck, "The Influence of Depression upon American Opinion, 1857–1859," *Journal of Economic History* 2 (1942): 1–23. In contrast to McGrane's study of the Panic of 1837, which never used the *Herald,* VanVleck uses it as a source more than any other newspaper.

82. *NYH,* July 8, 9, Oct. 18, 24, Nov. 13, 15, Dec. 9, 12, 13, 18, 1856, Jan. 3, 5, 6, 11, 13, 15, 22, 23, 30, 1857.

83. *NYH,* Feb. 11, 12, 21, Mar. 18, 19, 28, May 5, 21–23, 25, June 12, 1857.

84. *NYH,* June 27, 1857.

85. *NYH,* July 18, Aug. 4, 12, 14, 18, 1857; Nevins, *Emergence of Lincoln,* 1:182.

86. *NYH,* Aug. 25–27, 1857. Rezneck, "Influence of Depression," 1, points out the *Herald*'s early warnings.

87. *NYH,* Aug. 26, Sept. 1–4, 7, 10, Dec. 13, 1857.

88. *NYH,* Sept. 2, 1857.

89. *NYH,* Sept. 3, 14, 26, 28–30, Oct. 2, 4, 5, 7, 9, 11, 12, 14–16, 26, 28, 1857.

90. *NYH,* Sept. 29, Oct. 2, 8, 10, 15, 21, 22, 25, Nov. 2, 6, 8, 1857, Apr. 2, 3, 5, Oct. 18, 23, Nov. 27, 1858.

91. *NYH,* Nov. 20, 23–28, Dec. 3, 6, 14, 20, 22, 26, 1858.

92. *NYH,* Jan. 6, Feb. 7, Oct. 14, 1858, Apr. 26, 1859.

93. *NYH,* Jan. 10, 19, 28, Feb. 2, July 24, 1860.

94. *NYH,* Oct. 3, 30, Nov. 14, Dec. 7, 1860.

6—Monitor of New York

1. Gunther Barth, *City People: The Rise of Modern City Culture in Nineteenth-Century America* (New York, 1980), 59.

2. *NYH,* July 22, Dec. 17–22, 24, 1835, Feb. 10, 1836.

3. D. B. Tyler, *Steam Conquers the Atlantic* (New York, 1939), 56–64; *NYH,* Aug. 4, 1842, May 1, 1859.

4. *NYH*, May 9, 1837.

5. Francis Brown, *Raymond of the Times* (New York, 1951), 69–72; *NYH*, Jan. 20, May 2, 7–16, Sept. 29, 30, 1849.

6. *NYH*, June 1, 1849, Feb. 28, Mar. 7, 9, 10, 13, 14, 20, 22, 1855, Oct. 4–6, 12, 17, 1856.

7. Fermer, *Bennett and the Herald*, 72–73.

8. *NYH*, Feb. 25, Mar. 4, 29, Apr. 1, 1857.

9. *NYH*, Feb. 4, 8–10, 13–17, 1837, Jan. 12, 1838.

10. *NYH*, Aug. 12–14, 1855, Apr. 6, 1856, Dec. 4, 1858.

11. *NYH*, July 18, 1838, Apr. 24, 1859, May 5, 1856, Jan. 13, 14, 1855, Dec. 21, 1856, Sept. 16, 1858.

12. *NYH*, June 14, 1836. For ample documentation of Bennett's hostility to unions, see Wilentz, *Chants Democratic,* 286–94.

13. *NYH*, Sept. 23, Nov. 28, 1835, Feb. 24, 26, 27, 1836. Bennett was still attacking the gas monopoly and supporting protest meetings against its rates in 1850 (*NYH*, Jan. 13, 1850).

14. *NYH*, Aug. 6, 30, 31, Sept. 1–9, 1855, Jan. 30, Feb. 9, 10, 18, 23, Mar. 17, 18, 23, 28, Apr. 4, June 21, 1856, Sept. 7, 1857, Nov. 13, 23, 27, 1859, Feb. 21, Aug. 1, Sept. 9, 12–15, 1860. Between 1854 and 1865 there were 1,413 railroad and 324 steamboat accidents in New York, with 7,576 fatalities (*NYH*, Dec. 31, 1865).

15. *NYH*, June 6, July 1, 3, 9, 17, 27, Aug. 12, 1849. See Charles E. Rosenberg, *The Cholera Years: The United States in 1832, 1849, and 1866* (Chicago, 1962).

16. *NYH*, June 4, 1855, Feb. 12, 13, 24, 26, Mar. 6, 8, 27, 30, 1856, Jan. 29, 1857, Feb. 1, 5, Mar. 16, 22, May 6, 15, 19, 20, 23, 26, 1859, Feb. 23, Mar. 1–3, 1860.

17. *NYH*, May 3, 1853, July 24, 1855, Jan. 21, Feb. 15, Mar. 11, June 11, 1856, Jan. 21, 1857, May 19, 22, 31, June 11, July 14, 1858, June 21, Nov. 13, 1859, Feb. 15, Mar. 6, July 30, 1860. See Ian R. Stewart, "Politics and the Park: The Fight for Central Park," *New-York Historical Society Quarterly* 61 (1977): 124–55.

18. *NYH*, June 22–25, 1835, Aug. 23, 1839, Feb. 29, 1840, May 6, Nov. 12, 18, 1841, Nov. 4, 1843; John W. Pratt, "Governor Seward and the New York City School Controversy, 1840–1842: A Milestone in the Advance of Nonsectarian Public Education," *New York History* 42 (1961): 351–64; Glyndon G. Van Deusen, "Seward and the School Question Reconsidered," *Journal of American History* 52 (1965): 313–19.

19. *NYH*, Mar. 25–31, Apr. 1–10, May 9 (quote), 19–25, July 8–10, 1844.

20. *NYH*, July 17, Aug. 17, 1844, Jan. 4, Mar. 12, 13, 1847, Feb. 27, Apr. 14, Aug. 8, 1849, Nov. 27, 1851. See Barth, *City People,* 107–8, on the role of the press in assimilation of immigrants.

21. *NYH*, July 3, 10, 12–15, 17, 21, 28, Sept. 4, 12–14, 16, 18, 25, Oct. 2, 1859, June 10, 13, Oct. 4, 5, 1860.

22. *NYH*, Sept. 25, 1835, Mar. 1, July 18, 1839, July 2, 1857.

23. *NYH*, Apr. 24, 26, May 4, July 1, 1839, Feb. 18, 21, Mar. 5, 6, May 1, Sept. 8, 1840. The series on banking began on Feb. 24, 1840.

24. *NYH*, Sept. 16, 1835, July 4, 1836.

25. *NYH*, Jan. 9, 1849, Apr. 15, Sept. 6, 1850. See Ira M. Leonard, "The Politics of Charter Revision in New York City, 1845–1847," *New-York Historical Society Quarterly* 62 (1978): 43–70.

26. *NYH*, June 8, 1853, Feb. 7, 9, 18, Sept. 25, 30, Oct. 10, 12, Nov. 12, Dec. 4, 5, 1855.

27. *NYH*, Feb. 6, Nov. 14, 28, Dec. 30, 1856, Jan. 31, Feb. 6, 21, Mar. 8, Apr. 4, 5, 9, 10, 17, May 22–26, 28, June 1, 5, 8, 9, 11, 13–15, 18–20, 22, July 25, 26, 1857.

28. *NYH,* Jan. 16, Feb. 17, 19, 20, 25, 28, Mar. 7, 8, May 3, 4, 6, 14, 24, 25, 28, June 3, 6, 9, 28, July 13, Aug. 25, 30, Sept. 28, Nov. 3, 19–21, 24, 27, 1858, July 26, 29, Aug. 5, 8, 25, 1859, Nov. 23, 25, 1860.

29. *NYH,* Dec. 21, 1858, Jan. 7, 9, 11, Feb. 18, 24, Apr. 4, 8, 10, 12, 14, 16, May 3, Oct. 22, 1859, Jan. 13, June 16, 18, Nov. 10, 1860. For an elaboration of the apathy argument, see Amy Bridges, *A City in the Republic: Antebellum New York and the Origins of Machine Politics* (Cambridge, 1984).

30. *NYH,* July 20, Sept. 9, 21, 1836. See James F. Richardson, *New York City Police: Colonial Times to 1901* (New York, 1970).

31. *NYH,* Jan. 2, 9, 1843, Jan. 6, 1851, Feb. 16, 21, 1853.

32. *NYH,* Feb. 27, Mar. 16, 17, 19, 21, 25, Apr. 3, Dec. 8, 16, 1855, Apr. 10, 11, 1856.

33. *NYH,* Apr. 17, 20, 23, 25, May 19–21, June 17, 1857. A good treatment is James F. Richardson, "Mayor Fernando Wood and the New York Police Force, 1855–1857," *New-York Historical Society Quarterly* 50 (1966): 5–40.

34. *NYH,* July 15, 16, 20–23, Aug. 3, 4, Oct. 20, 23, Nov. 23, 24, 27, 29, 1857.

35. *NYH,* Jan. 3, Apr. 5, 25, 1858, Mar. 5, 6, 8, 11, June 12, 1859, June 9, Sept. 8, 1860.

36. *NYH,* Mar. 22, Apr. 5, 12, 13, 1839, Jan. 1, Feb. 19, 24, Mar. 25–27, Apr. 4, 11, 14, 15, Aug. 21, 22, 1840.

37. *NYH,* Oct. 8, 12–14, Nov. 6, 1850, Feb. 10, 1853; Samuel A. Pleasants, *Fernando Wood of New York* (New York, 1948), 32.

38. *NYH,* Jan. 3, 1855.

39. *NYH,* Jan. 4, 5, 8, 12, 21, Feb. 2, Mar. 26, 31, May 27, June 8, July 2, Aug. 14, Sept. 4, 1855, Jan. 5, 1856.

40. *NYH,* Sept. 3, 4, 27–30, Oct. 9, 11, 15, 23, 28, 30, 31, Nov. 2–4, 6, 8, 12, 1856.

41. *NYH,* Dec. 2, 1856, Jan. 6, 7, 15, Oct. 17, Nov. 11–13, 16, 17, 22, 30, Dec. 1, 3, 6, 1857. For an analysis of Wood's popularity, see Mushkat, *Tammany,* 297.

42. *NYH,* Jan. 4, 6, 7, Sept. 26, 28, Nov. 3, 5, 8, 10, 11, Dec. 1, 3, 5, 8, 1858.

43. *NYH,* Sept. 1, 2, Oct. 6, Nov. 1, 7–11, 15, 18, 20–22, 26–30, Dec. 1, 3–9, 1859, Jan. 2, 4, 6, Nov. 15, Dec. 2, 4, 6, 1860; Mushkat, *Tammany,* 318–19. For the Russell appointment, see Fermer, *Bennett and the Herald,* 77–78.

44. *NYH,* Oct. 26, Nov. 4, 22, Dec. 2, 1836, Nov. 4, 11, 28, Dec. 4, 11, 1837, Oct. 3, 19, 20, 24, 25, 29, Nov. 3, 5, 8, 9, 1838. Bennett did give lukewarm support to Van Buren for president in 1836 and to Marcy, who was elected governor.

45. *NYH,* Sept. 6, Nov. 4–8, 1839, Aug. 4, 15, Nov. 4–7, 9, 1840, Jan. 7, 1841. On Jan. 8 Bennett offered a $100 reward to anyone who could prove that he had read Seward's message from beginning to end at one sitting. This was raised to $500 on Jan. 9.

46. *NYH,* Oct. 4, 18, 19, 25, 26, 29, 30, Nov. 1–5, 1841.

47. *NYH,* Sept. 8, 1842.

48. *NYH,* Sept. 12, Nov. 9–11, 1842, Jan. 5, 1843, Apr. 24, 1844, Jan. 9, 10, 1845.

49. *NYH,* Nov. 5–8, 1845. For the antirent issue see David M. Ellis, *Landlords and Farmers in the Hudson-Mohawk Region, 1790–1850* (Ithaca, 1946), 225–312, and Henry Christman, *Tin Horns and Calico* (New York, 1945).

50. *NYH,* Dec. 10–12, 16, 1839, Jan. 1–3, 1845.

51. *NYH,* Mar. 25, 28, Apr. 1, 1845.

52. *NYH,* Sept. 12, 22, Oct. 13, 14, 1845, Jan. 7, 8, 1846.

53. *NYH,* Sept. 25, Oct. 8, Nov. 3–6, 1846.

54. *NYH,* Sept. 25, Oct. 8, Nov. 3–6, 1845.

55. *NYH,* Jan. 3, 4, 1844, May 20, June 4, 1845; Edward P. Cheyney, "The Antirent Movement and the Constitution of 1846," in Alexander C. Flick, ed., *The History of the State of New York,* 10 vols. (New York, 1933-37), 6:283-321.

56. *NYH,* Sept. 18-20, Nov. 7, 1845, May 1, 1846.

57. *NYH,* Nov. 7, 8, Dec. 27, 1848, Jan. 5, 25, 26, 28, 30, 31, Feb. 3, Oct. 24, 1849.

58. *NYH,* Mar. 22, 24, 27, Sept. 26, 29, 30, Oct. 1, 1850, Oct. 18, 1851.

59. *NYH,* Oct. 21, 23, Nov. 1, 3, 4, 6-8, 1850.

60. *NYH,* Mar. 21, 27, July 6, 1851.

61. *NYH,* Apr. 3, 1852.

62. *NYH,* Nov. 3-5, 1852, July 13, 14, Aug. 2, 10, 1853.

63. *NYH,* Sept. 27, Oct. 2, 3, 7, 9, 26-28, 30, 31, Nov. 1, 8-20, 1854.

64. *NYH,* Jan. 3, 8, 10, 12, Feb. 3, 7, 1855.

65. *NYH,* Aug. 1, 1851, Jan. 27, 30, Feb. 1, Apr. 3, 1852, Mar. 24, Apr. 1, 2, 1854.

66. *NYH,* Apr. 10, 12, 15, 16, 18-20, 22, 24, 26, 28, May 1, 2, 9, 13, 16, June 5, 6, 14, 15, 25, July 2, 3, 6, 7, 10, 12-14, 20, 29, Aug. 10, Sept. 1, 4, 17, 29, 30, 1855, Mar. 26, 1856.

67. *NYH,* Mar. 26, 27, 30, Apr. 16, 1855.

68. *NYH,* Aug. 3, 5, 18, 22, 25, 28, 31, Sept. 1, 6, 7, 25, 28, Oct. 1, 2, 1855.

69. *NYH,* Oct. 30, 31, Nov. 6-9, 1855, Jan. 17, Apr. 11, July 14, 17, 19, 24, 26, 29, Sept. 16, 19, 20, 24, 26, Oct. 1, 2, 7, 12, 26, Nov. 3, 6, 1856.

70. *NYH,* Jan. 31, Mar. 21, 27, Aug. 19, 23, 27, 30, 31, Sept. 6, 9, 1857.

71. *NYH,* Sept. 12-18, 25, Oct. 1, 4, Nov. 2-5, 12, 1857.

72. *NYH,* Nov. 11, 1841, Jan. 15, 1852, Mar. 27, 1855, Mar. 25, 28, Apr. 12, 21, 1858, Jan. 5, Sept. 4, 9, 1859, Jan. 4, 1856.

73. *NYH,* Apr. 8, 15, May 27, 28, July 22, 27, 31, Sept. 10, 16-18, 22-24, 26, 28, 30, Nov. 1-4, 1858. A peripheral issue in the election was a proposition to call a state constitutional convention. Bennett supported this idea, hoping for changes that would provide municipal home rule, the appointment of city judges, voter registration, and a four-year term for governor. The proposal lost (*NYH,* Apr. 20, July 26, Aug. 15, Nov. 2, 15, 1858).

74. *NYH,* Jan. 17, 18, Apr. 20, June 3, 4, 16, 17, Aug. 2, 3, Sept. 7-16, 21, Oct. 1-5, Nov. 2, 7-9, 1859.

75. *NYH,* Nov. 10, 1859, Jan. 1, 9, Mar. 4, 10, 13, 15, 20, 24, Apr. 2, 11, 18, 19, May 3, 5, 8, 1860.

76. *NYH,* July 3, Aug. 12, 17, 18, Sept. 8 (quote), Oct. 13, Nov. 2, 1860.

7 — Covering the Civil War

1. Hudson Diary, Jan. 19, 1861, Hudson Papers. There is a good sketch of Hudson in Louis Starr, *Bohemian Brigade* (New York, 1954), 16-17.

2. *NYH,* May 16, 1844; "Fragmentary Chronicles of Frederic and Elizabeth Woodward Hudson 1817 to 1876 with Some Earlier Family History," compiled by Woodward Hudson, 3 vols., Hudson Papers; Hudson Diary, July 1, 1851, Hudson Papers.

3. "Fragmentary Chronicles"; Hudson Diary, Jan. 19, Mar. 8, July 3, 5, 1851, Oct. 23, 1852, Oct. 1, 1853, June 3, 1854, July 10, 1855, Jan. 25, 1861, Hudson Papers.

4. *New York Leader,* May 7, 1859, clipping in Hudson Papers.

5. Hudson Diary, Jan. 12, 1851; "Fragmentary Chronicles," Hudson Papers.

6. Starr, *Bohemian Brigade,* 16-17; Sylvanus Cadwallader, *Three Years with Grant,* ed. Benjamin P. Thomas (New York, 1953), 197.

7. Hudson Diary, Jan. 28, Feb. 1, May 29, June 2, 3, 6, 1851, Feb. 7, 22, 25, Apr. 26, 28, May 9, 10, 15, Aug. 14, Oct. 10, 17, Nov. 18, 24, 1854, Jan. 1, 9, 12, 1855, Hudson Papers.

8. Starr, *Bohemian Brigade,* 63–67. The quote is from Tebbel and Watts, *The Press and the Presidency,* 182.

9. *NYH,* Jan. 1–17, 19, 21–23, 26, 27, 1861.

10. *NYH,* Jan. 27–31, Feb. 1–9, 1861.

11. *NYH,* Feb. 11, 13, 19–23, 25–27, Mar. 2, 1861; Nevins and Thomas, eds., *Diary of Strong,* 3:105.

12. *NYH,* Mar. 4–31, Apr. 1–6, 1861.

13. *NYH,* Apr. 7–12, 1861; Nevins and Thomas, eds., *Diary of Strong,* 3:117–18.

14. *NYH,* Apr. 13, 1861; Starr, *Bohemian Brigade,* 19; Nevins and Thomas, eds., *Diary of Strong,* 3:119.

15. *NYH,* Apr. 14, 1861; Starr, *Bohemian Brigade,* 24–25.

16. *NYH,* Apr. 15, 16, 1861; Nevins and Thomas, eds., *Diary of Strong,* 3:121–22.

17. *New York Times,* Apr. 16, 17, 1861; Fermer, *Bennett and the Herald,* 187–88.

18. *NYH,* Apr. 17–23, 25, 29, May 5, 1861.

19. Glyndon G. Van Deusen, *Thurlow Weed: Wizard of the Lobby* (Boston, 1947), 275. Weed's account is in *Autobiography of Thurlow Weed,* ed. Harriet A. Weed (Boston, 1883), 615–19. See also Harry J. Carman and Reinhard H. Luthin, *Lincoln and the Patronage* (New York, 1943), 122–25; Abraham Lincoln to Salmon P. Chase, May 6, 1861, in Basler, ed., *Works of Lincoln,* 4:357; and the extended discussion in Fermer, *Bennett and the Herald,* 195–98.

20. Buchanan to Bennett, May 11, 1861; Buchanan to J. B. Henry, May 17, 1861; Edwin M. Stanton to Buchanan, July 16, 1861, all in Moore, ed., *Works of Buchanan,* 9:165–66, 191–93, 210–11.

21. Press coverage of the Civil War is the most heavily researched topic in the history of American journalism. Four good books deal with northern reporting: Andrews, *North Reports the Civil War;* Emmett Crozier, *Yankee Reporters, 1861–1865* (New York, 1956); Starr, *Bohemian Brigade;* and Weisberger, *Reporters for the Union.* Three *Herald* correspondents published their memoirs: Cadwallader, *Three Years with Grant;* Thomas W. Knox, *Camp-fire and Cotton-field: Southern Adventure in Time of War* (New York, 1865); and Villard, *Memoirs.* Others wrote shorter accounts: W. F. G. Shanks, "How We Get Our News," *Harper's New Monthly Magazine* 34 (Mar. 1867): 511–22; Townsend, "Recollections and Reflections"; and Henry Villard, "Army Correspondence," *Nation* 1 (July 20, 27, Aug. 3, 1865): 79–81, 114–16, 144–46.

22. Andrews, *North Reports the Civil War,* lists the *Herald* correspondents on pp. 751–59. Three *Herald* reporters died in the war (Weisberger, *Reporters for the Union,* 128). Quotes from Knox, *Camp-fire and Cotton-field,* 20, 24.

23. Villard, *Memoirs,* 1:153–54, 173, 217.

24. Thomas W. Knox to Bennett, June 28, 1862, L. A. Whitely to Bennett, Sept. 9, 1862, Bennett Papers. Some of the wartime letters to the *Herald* in the Bennett Papers at the Library of Congress are reprinted in "Federal Generals and a Good Press," *American Historical Review* 39 (1933–34): 284–97.

25. Quote in Starr, *Bohemian Brigade,* 90–91; Andrews, *North Reports the Civil War,* 20–21.

26. Cadwallader, *Three Years with Grant,* 99, 200; Starr, *Bohemian Brigade,* 192.

27. Weisberger, *Reporters for the Union,* 130–34; Andrews, *North Reports the Civil War,* 71–72.

28. The connection with Mrs. Lincoln is discussed and documented in Fermer, *Bennett and the Herald,* 215–16.

29. Andrews, *North Reports the Civil War,* 40, 48–49; Hudson, *Journalism in the United States,* 483.

30. Andrews, *North Reports the Civil War,* 6, 20–21.

31. Weisberger, *Reporters for the Union,* 125.

32. *NYH,* July 1, 4, 6, 13, 17, 1861. On July 8 a map of Missouri appeared on the front page.

33. *NYH,* July 18–23, 1861; Villard, *Memoirs,* 1:200. There were front-page maps of the Manassas area on July 19 and 21.

34. *NYH,* July 24, 25, 28, Aug. 6, 1861.

35. *NYH,* July 10, Aug. 8, 9, 14, 15, Sept. 1–6, 8, 1861. Andrews, *North Reports the Civil War,* 119–34, is a good account of the war in the Missouri theater.

36. *NYH,* Sept. 1–3, 20, 24, Oct. 3, 14, 16, Nov. 1, 8, 1861; S. P. Bascom to Bennett, Oct. 6, 1861, Bennett Papers.

37. *NYH,* Sept. 12, Oct. 18, Dec. 11, 1861, Jan. 3, 4, 6, 1862.

38. M I [Malcolm Ives] to Bennett, Jan. 15, 1861 [1862], Confidential, Bennett Papers.

39. M I to Hudson, Jan. 16, 1861 [1862], Confidential; M I to Bennett, Jan. 27, 1862, Private & Confidential, Bennett Papers.

40. M I to Bennett, Jan. 29, Feb. 8, 1862; S. P. Hanscom to Hudson, Feb. 4, 1862, Private, Bennett Papers; *NYH,* Feb. 11, 14, May 21, 1862.

41. *NYH,* Feb. 10, 21, 22, 24, 1862; S. P. Hanscom to Bennett, Feb. 16, 26, 1862, Bennett Papers.

42. *NYH,* Feb. 1862 (e.g., Feb. 13), Mar. 19, 20, 1862.

43. Andrews, *North Reports the Civil War,* 227.

44. *NYH,* Mar. 10–14, 1862; William H. Stiner to Hudson, Apr. 12, 1862, Bennett Papers.

45. *NYH,* Apr. 25, 28, 29, May 1, 10, 1862; Andrews, *North Reports the Civil War,* 233–43.

46. *NYH,* Sept. 7, 1861, Feb. 2, 6, 8, 13, 16–19, 22, Mar. 29, Apr. 6, 1862. Maps of the Corinth area appeared on the front page on Mar. 29 and Apr. 6.

47. *NYH,* Apr. 9–11, 1862; Andrews, *North Reports the Civil War,* 177–79; Starr, *Bohemian Brigade,* 81–85.

48. *NYH,* May 4, 23, 31, June 1, 1862; Andrews, *North Reports the Civil War,* 185–86.

49. *NYH,* July 7–9, 13, 1862, Jan. 8, 9, 15, 16, Mar. 24, 1863; Thomas W. Knox to Bennett, June 28, Aug. 19, 1862, Private, Bennett Papers; Abraham Lincoln to "To Whom It May Concern," Mar. 20, 1863, in Basler, ed., *Works of Lincoln,* 6:142–43; Thomas W. Guback, "General Sherman's War on the Press," *Journalism Quarterly* 36 (1959): 171–76. John F. Marszalek, *Sherman's Other War* (Memphis, 1981), is an exhaustive account of Sherman's press relations.

50. *NYH,* Sept. 3, 28, Oct. 10, 11, 13, 15, 1862; Finley Anderson to Hudson, Feb. 10, 1863, Private, Thomas W. Cash to Hudson, Mar. 5, 1863, Bennett Papers; Andrews, *North Reports the Civil War,* 404.

51. *NYH,* Nov. 27, Dec. 7, 1862, Jan. 1, 3–7, 9, 10, 1863; Andrews, *North Reports the Civil War,* 305–14.

52. *NYH,* Mar. 12–15, 1862; Hanscom to Bennett, Feb. 27, 1862, Bennett Papers.

53. Weisberger, *Reporters for the Union,* 138–53.

54. Quoted in Andrews, *North Reports the Civil War,* 192.

55. *NYH,* Apr. 8-12, 14, 21, 28, 30, May 5, 6, 8-13, 1862; *Daily Missouri Republican* (St. Louis), Apr. 28, 1862, quoted in Andrews, *North Reports the Civil War,* 684.

56. Andrews, *North Reports the Civil War,* 197; L. A. Whitely to Bennett, May 28, 1862, Bennett Papers, complaining about the censorship.

57. *NYH,* May 20, 24, 26, 27, 29, 1862; Whitely to Bennett, May 28, 1862, Bennett Papers; Andrews, *North Reports the Civil War,* 200.

58. *NYH,* June 2, 5, 11, 1862; Andrews, *North Reports the Civil War,* 204-6. The *Herald* (June 7, 10, 12, 1862) was still concerned about the threat to the Shenandoah Valley and the inept Union command there.

59. *NYH,* June 15, 16, 26, 27, July 1-4, 6-10, 1862.

60. *NYH,* July 4, 1862; Andrews, *North Reports the Civil War,* 214, 689-90.

61. *Cincinnati Daily Gazette,* Sept. 4, 1862, quoted in Andrews, *North Reports the Civil War,* 690.

62. *NYH,* July 11, 13, 14, 16, 20, 29, 31, Aug. 3-6, 12-15, 19, 21, 1862; Whitely to Bennett, June 17, July 29, 1862, Bennett Papers; Townsend quoted in Andrews, *North Reports the Civil War,* 265.

63. *NYH,* Aug. 23-27, 29-31, Sept. 1-8, 1862.

64. *NYH,* Sept. 6, 7, 9-12, 14-21, 23, 1862; Whitely to Hudson, Sept. 10, 1862, Bennett Papers; Andrews, *North Reports the Civil War,* 282.

65. *NYH,* Oct. 1, 2, 16-18, 21, 22, 24-26, Nov. 5, 8, 1862; A. B. Talcott to Hudson, Oct. 19, 1862, Bennett Papers.

66. *NYH,* Nov. 10, 11, 13, 14, 17, 19, 21, 22, 1862.

67. *NYH,* Nov. 23 (front-page map of Fredericksburg area), Dec. 1, 8, 9, 12-19, 24-26, 1862.

68. *NYH,* Dec. 14, 1862; Meade quoted in Andrews, *North Reports the Civil War,* 335; Gen. David B. Birney to Bennett, Mar. 28, 1864, Bennett Papers.

69. *NYH,* Jan. 10, 12, 14, 23, 24, 27, 29, 31, Mar. 14, Apr. 3, 6, 9, 10, 14, 1863; W. C. Barry to Hudson, Dec. 28, 1862, S. M. Carpenter to Hudson, Jan. 21, Feb. 2, 1863, Bennett Papers.

70. *NYH,* Apr. 30, May 2-10, 1863.

71. *NYH,* May 22, 27, 31, June 2, 11, 13, 15-22, 24, 26, 27, 1863.

72. *NYH,* June 29, 30, July 1-4, 6, 7, 1863, The *Herald* did not publish on July 5 because of the holiday.

73. *NYH,* July 7, 8, 1863; Andrews, *North Reports the Civil War,* 428-31; Starr, *Bohemian Brigade,* 171.

74. *NYH,* May 10, 17-20, 23-29, 31, June 3, 7-10, 14, 21, 27, July 8, 15, 25, 1863. On May 25 the *Herald* prematurely reported the surrender of the city.

75. *NYH,* Sept. 3 (front-page map of Tennessee), 5, 6, 8, 19, 20, 21-27, 29, 30, Oct. 1, 3, 22, 23, 1863.

76. *NYH,* Nov. 19, 25-30, 1863.

77. *NYH,* Mar. 6, 7, 9-11, 18, 22-24, Apr. 12-16, 1864.

78. Cadwallader, *Three Years with Grant,* 167-70, 220-21; Cadwallader to Hudson, May 3, 1864, Bennett Papers; Andrews, *North Reports the Civil War,* 585-86.

79. Cadwallader, *Three Years with Grant,* 197-98; Andrews, *North Reports the Civil War,* 74-75.

80. *NYH,* Apr. 28, 29, May 6-10, 1864; Cadwallader to Hudson, May 3, 1864, Whitely to Bennett, May 5, 1864, Confidential, Bennett Papers; Cadwallader, *Three Years with Grant,* 185-97; Andrews, *North Reports the Civil War,* 527-37.

81. Cadwallader, *Three Years with Grant,* 197-98; Andrews, *North Reports the Civil War,* 537; Starr, *Bohemian Brigade,* 276. Cadwallader's conspicuous display was good for

business. The *Herald* sold eleven thousand copies daily, at ten cents each, in the Army of the Potomac.

82. *NYH*, May 11-18, 22-27, 29-31, June 1, 1864.

83. *NYH*, June 2, 3, 6, 16, 18, 20-22, 28, 1864; Whitely to Hudson, May 22, 1864, Bennett Papers.

84. *NYH*, July 4-19, Sept. 21-25, Oct. 2, 5, 21, 22, 1864; Finley Anderson to Hudson, Sept. 10, 1864, Private, Bennett Papers. The *Herald*'s Francis C. Long scored a beat with the earliest news of Early's retreat (Andrews, *North Reports the Civil War*, 603).

85. *NYH*, Aug. 1-4, 23, 25, Sept. 19, 30, Oct. 1, 3, 9, 1864, Jan. 6, 8, 15, 22, 26, 28, Mar. 2, 1865.

86. *NYH*, Mar. 7, 11, 13, 18, 27, 28, 30, 31, Apr. 1-11, 1865.

87. William H. Stiner to Hudson, Apr. 21, May 30, 1864, Bennett Papers; William H. Merriman to Gen. Benjamin Butler, Nov. 5, 1864, quoted in Andrews, *North Reports the Civil War*, 666; Weisberger, *Reporters for the Union*, 159-61.

88. *NYH*, Dec. 29-31, 1864, Jan. 11, 12, 16, 18, 19, 1865; Andrews, *North Reports the Civil War*, 616-17.

89. *NYH*, July 8, 15, 17, 20, 21, 23, 26, Aug. 5, Sept. 3-5, 1864; Andrews, *North Reports the Civil War*, 552-56.

90. *NYH*, Aug. 6, 10, 14, 15, 29, 1864; Thomas M. Cook to Hudson, Nov. 3, 1864, Bennett Papers; Andrews, *North Reports the Civil War*, 572.

91. *NYH*, Oct. 19, Nov. 11, 12, 15, 19, 20, 22, 23, 26, 28, Dec. 2, 3, 5, 18, 22, 23, 1864.

92. *NYH*, Dec. 13-17, 19, 20, 22, 26, 27, 1864, Jan. 12, Feb. 5, 12, 13, 15-22, 27, Mar. 2, 8, 13, 15, 16, 20, 27, 30, Apr. 23-25, 29, 1865.

8 – War and Postwar Politics

1. *NYH*, Apr. 7, 1865.

2. For example, *NYH*, Mar. 9, 1865, Feb. 20-25, 1864.

3. *NYH*, May 22, June 1-4, July 31, 1861.

4. *NYH*, Nov. 17-21, 1861.

5. *NYH*, Dec. 16, 17, 19, 20, 21, 1861. D. P. Crook, *The North, the South, and the Powers, 1861-1865* (New York, 1974), 114, argues that Bennett "had been recruited by Seward."

6. *NYH*, Jan. 6, 7, Oct. 10, 19, 1862.

7. *NYH*, Nov. 30, Dec. 2, 26, 1862.

8. Crook, *The North, the South, and the Powers*, 282.

9. *NYH*, Oct. 13, Nov. 30, 1861, July 2, 3, 7, 30, Oct. 12, 1863.

10. *NYH*, Jan. 4, 12, Feb. 27, July 8, 15, 17, 24, 1864, Jan. 25, 27, Feb. 28, Mar. 13, 22, Aug. 1, 1865.

11. *NYH*, Aug. 26, 1865.

12. *NYH*, Aug. 1, 1865.

13. *NYH*, Feb. 8, Dec. 14, 1868, Jan. 28, 1870.

14. *NYH*, Sept. 1, 3, 20, 24, Oct. 3, 14, 16, Nov. 1, 8, 1861.

15. *NYH*, Jan. 8, 13, Feb. 25, 1862.

16. *NYH*, Mar. 7-9, Apr. 1, 3, 5, 1862.

17. *NYH*, Mar. 22, 31, Apr. 4, 1862; Weisberger, *Reporters for the Union*, 161-68.

18. *NYH*, May 17, 18, 20, 21, June 28, 1862; Lincoln to Bennett, May 21, 1862, in Basler, ed., *Works of Lincoln*, 5:225. Bennett sent Lincoln a fawning response, calling Stanton "a gentleman and patriot of whom I have a high opinion" (ibid., 226n).

19. *NYH*, July 13, 14, 16, 17, 21, 1862. A separate state of West Virginia was denounced

as unconstitutional at the same time. Whitely wrote from the Washington bureau in near hysteria about the adverse effect of emancipation on army morale (Whitely to Bennett, Sept. 9, 1862, Confidential, Bennett Papers).

20. *NYH,* Sept. 23-29, Oct. 19, 20, 23, 1862. Again Whitely reported from Washington about the effect of the proclamation on the army: "The air is thick with revolution. . . . The sentiment throughout the army seems to be in favor of a change of dynasty" (Whitely to Bennett, Sept. 24, 1862, Confidential, Bennett Papers).

21. *NYH,* Jan. 1, 3, 20, Feb. 4, Apr. 24, 1863.

22. *NYH,* July 9, 11, Aug. 2, 1863, Jan. 9, 24, Feb. 1, 1864.

23. *NYH,* Feb. 6, 11, 13, Apr. 8, 9, 30, May 3, Aug. 1, Dec. 5, 1864, Jan. 7, 13, 15, Feb. 1, 2, 1865.

24. *NYH,* Mar. 1, 1865.

25. *NYH,* Feb. 17, Mar. 1, 1862, July 10, Aug. 25, Oct. 8, 1863.

26. *NYH,* Dec. 10, 11, 1863, Jan. 31, 1864.

27. *NYH,* May 6, July 5, 10, Aug. 6, 1864.

28. *NYH,* Apr. 12-14, 1865.

29. *NYH,* Sept. 18, Oct. 16, 1865, June 15, Oct. 2, Nov. 8, 1866; Fermer, *Bennett and the Herald,* 297-310. For a survey of the *Herald's* relations with Johnson see Marguerite Hall Albjerg, "The New York Herald as a Factor in Reconstruction," *South Atlantic Quarterly* 46 (1947): 204-11. There is much information about the *Herald* in Hans L. Trefousse, *The Radical Republicans: Lincoln's Vanguard for Racial Justice* (New York, 1968), and Forrest G. Wood, *Black Scare: The Racist Response to Emancipation and Reconstruction* (Berkeley, 1968).

30. *NYH,* Aug. 11, 13, 17, 24, 1861.

31. *NYH,* June 22, 1862, on the railroad; June 23, July 2, 1862, on the tariff; Sept. 14, Dec. 5, 10, 1861, Jan. 4, 1862.

32. *NYH,* Jan. 15, 17, Aug. 2, 9, 10, Nov. 4, 1862.

33. *NYH,* July 9, 24-26, 29, Nov. 28 (quote), 1862.

34. *NYH,* Sept. 13, Oct. 1, 1861, Jan. 8, July 11, 27, 29, Sept. 6, 26, Oct. 5-7, 11, 13-20, 24, 25, 29-31, Nov. 1, 2, 4-6, 8, 1862; Sidney D. Brummer, *Political History of New York State during the Period of the Civil War* (New York, 1911), 203. Bennett's support of Seymour did not last very long. By summer Bennett had turned on Seymour because of the draft riots and because the governor rejected his advice on appointments. See Bennett to Seymour, Jan. 2, 1863, Fairchild Collection, New-York Historical Society, and Stewart Mitchell, *Horatio Seymour of New York* (Cambridge, Mass., 1938), 305.

35. *NYH,* Dec. 1-3, 21-23, 27, 31, 1862, Jan. 5, Feb. 3, 11, 23, 24, 27, Mar. 2, May 23, 26, June 12, 1863. Although the *Herald* was critical of the Copperheads (e.g., Apr. 4, 8, 1863), it urged the release of their arrested leader Clement L. Vallandigham and opposed arbitrary arrests (*NYH,* May 20, 22, 1863).

36. *NYH,* Aug. 12-18, 20, Oct. 15, 1863; Whitely to Hudson, Oct. 12, Nov. 29, 1863, both Confidential, Thomas W. Knox to Bennett, Oct. 22, 1863 (warning from St. Louis of Chase's popularity in the West), Bennett Papers.

37. *NYH,* Dec. 15-31, 1863, Jan. 3, 4, 6, 8, 10, 12-17, 21, 22, 26, 29, 30, 1864; William G. Shanks to Bennett, Dec. 18, 1863, Private and Confidential, Bennett Papers; Nevins and Thomas, eds., *Diary of Strong,* 3:383.

38. *NYH,* Jan. 7, 11, 15, 16, 21, 24, Feb. 1, 3, 22, 26, 27, Mar. 2, 5, 7, 11, 25, 1864.

39. *NYH,* Apr. 2-4, 7, 9, 11, 12, 25, 27, May 2, 20, 1864.

40. *NYH,* May 8, 16, 28, 29, 31, June 2, 1864.

41. *NYH,* June 4, 5, 7-13, July 1-4, 1864.

42. *NYH,* July 17, 18, 24, Aug. 23, 26, 29, Sept. 3, 4, 6, 9, 1864; Finley Anderson to Hudson, Sept. 10, 1864, Private, Bennett Papers.

43. *NYH,* Sept. 14, 15, 20, 23, 24, 30, Oct. 5, 6, 11, 15, 22, 1864.

44. *NYH,* Oct. 25, 27-29, 31, Nov. 7, 8, 1864; Nevins, *War for the Union,* 4:126.

45. *NYH,* Nov. 9-11, 17-20, 1864. Bennett did not support Seymour's reelection, accusing him of being a Copperhead. Instead, he backed Republican victor Reuben Fenton, despite Fenton's radical leanings (*NYH,* Sept. 26, Nov. 13, 1864, Jan. 4, 7, 1865).

46. Lincoln to Bennett, Feb. 20, 1865, Bennett to Lincoln, Mar. 6, 1865, in Basler, ed., *Works of Lincoln,* 8:307, 308n.

47. David Quentin Voigt, "'Too Pitchy to Touch'—President Lincoln and Editor Bennett," *Abraham Lincoln Quarterly* 6 (1950): 139-61, was the first to document the charges from the newly opened Robert Todd Lincoln Collection at the Library of Congress. The definitive treatment is Fermer, *Bennett and the Herald,* 281-96, which quotes extensively from the relevant Wakeman and Bartlett letters. John J. Turner, Jr., and Michael D'Innocenzo, "The President and the Press: Lincoln, James Gordon Bennett and the Election of 1864," *Lincoln Herald* 76 (1974): 63-69, questions the value of the *Herald's* neutrality. Lincoln received only 33 percent of the vote in New York City, the second smallest proportion in nineteen northern cities. The *Herald* did not comment on the offer until Apr. 29, 1865, after Lincoln's death.

48. *NYH,* Oct. 16, 18, Nov. 22, Dec. 4, 7, 8, 14, 1864, Jan. 5, 10, 1865. Bennett's choice for chief justice was Maryland conservative Reverdy Johnson.

49. *NYH,* Mar. 4, 5, 1865.

50. *NYH,* Apr. 15-May 5, 1865.

51. *NYH,* Apr. 17, 1865.

52. *NYH,* Apr. 16-18, May 4, 5, 19, July 10, 1865.

53. Tebbel and Watts, *The Press and the Presidency,* 187; Fermer, *Bennett and the Herald,* 236-44, quotes from 238, 241. The standard work on the riots is Adrian Cook, *The Armies of the Street* (Lexington, Ky., 1974).

54. *NYH,* July 6, 1863, for Seymour's speech; July 7, 1863, for attack on Seymour; July 11, 13, 1863. Bennett's support of the draft is in Bennett to Lincoln, Aug. 11, 1862, Oct. 26, 1863, Abraham Lincoln Papers, Library of Congress.

55. *New York Times,* July 15, 1863; *New York Tribune,* July 15, 17, 1863; *NYH,* July 1 (quote), 14-30, 1863.

56. U.S. Department of Internal Revenue receipts, cited in Albjerg, "New York Herald as a Factor in Reconstruction," 205; *NYH,* Apr. 5, 1865; Weisberger, *Reporters for the Union,* 128. Its five rivals were the *Times, Tribune, Evening Post, Sun,* and *World.*

57. *NYH,* July 10, 1861, Sept. 26, 1863; Nevins and Thomas, eds., *Diary of Strong,* 4:86.

58. Hudson Diary, Apr. 9, 24, 1866, Mar. 29, 30, Apr. 15, July 17, 25, 1867; Henry J. Raymond to Hudson, Apr. 13, 1867, Hudson Papers.

59. There is no good biography of the younger Bennett. See Allan Nevins, "James Gordon Bennett [Jr.]," *DAB,* 2:199-202. For a summary of the various anecdotal biographies stressing his outrageous personal behavior, see Piers Brendon, *The Life and Death of the Press Barons* (New York, 1983), 19-36.

60. LaWanda Cox and John H. Cox, *Politics, Principle, and Prejudice, 1865-1866: Dilemma of Reconstruction America* (Glencoe, Ill., 1963), 88-95, 100; Andrew Johnson to Bennett, Oct. 6, 1865, cited in ibid., 252n.

61. *NYH,* May 3, Oct. 12, 15, 31, 1865, Mar. 17, 28, 1866; Eric L. McKitrick, *Andrew Johnson and Reconstruction* (Chicago, 1960), 56-57.

62. *NYH*, Jan. 29, Feb. 11, Apr. 23, 25, June 23, Aug. 18, Sept. 3, 17, 1866. See McKitrick, *Andrew Johnson and Reconstruction*, 364-67, and Patrick W. Riddleberger, *1866: The Crucial Year Revisited* (Carbondale, 1979), 203, 245-46.

63. *NYH*, June 12, Sept. 4, 1866.

64. *NYH*, Sept. 6, 8, 10, 12, 14, 19, 27-29, 1866; Riddleberger, *1866*, 225.

65. *NYH*, Aug. 13 (quote), Sept. 9, Oct. 10, 19, Nov. 4, 6, 1867, Dec. 9, 1868.

66. *NYH*, Feb. 8, 28, Apr. 29, 1868; Nevins and Thomas, eds., *Diary of Strong*, 4:191.

67. *NYH*, May 13, 1867, May 6-8, 31, June 3, 9, 11, 12, 1868; Nevins and Thomas, eds., *Diary of Strong*, 4:188, 220; Alexander C. Flick and G. S. Lobrano, *Samuel J. Tilden* (New York, 1939), 167.

68. *NYH*, July 6, Aug. 21, Oct. 15, Nov. 7, 1868; Nevins and Thomas, eds., *Diary of Strong*, 4:224.

9 – Bennett in Retrospect

1. Nevins and Thomas, eds., *Diary of Strong*, 4:428. For details on Bennett's illness and death, see *NYH*, June 2, 1872. He died in the late afternoon on June 1.

2. *New York Times*, June 14, 1872. *NYH*, June 14, 1872, reprinted accounts of the funeral from all the city papers. Bennett was buried in the Green-Wood Cemetery in Brooklyn. *New York Sun*, June 3, 1872, has details of the will. Bennett's widow received the mansion on Fifth Avenue and other real estate; his daughter Jeanette, aged eighteen, got the Washington Heights property; James, Jr., received the *Herald* and other New York City real estate.

3. Nevins and Thomas, eds., *Diary of Strong*, 4:430.

4. *NYH*, June 4, 5, 8, 1872, reprinted dozens of obituary notices from newspapers around the country. With few exceptions, they were uncritical.

5. *Sun*, June 3, 1872; *NYH*, June 4, 5, 8, 1872.

6. *New York Evening Express*, June 3, 1872; *Sun*, June 3, 1872; *New York Evening Mail*, June 3, 1872; *Philadelphia Post*, June 3, 1872.

7. *Tribune*, June 3, 1872. The page 1 story, continuing on pages 4 and 8, was headed: "A GREAT JOURNALIST DEAD."

8. *NYH*, June 2, 1872.

9. *NYH*, June 3, 1872.

10. *NYH*, June 10, 1872. Hudson probably wrote the piece.

11. See William J. Thorn, "Hudson's History of Journalism Criticized by His Contemporaries," *Journalism Quarterly* 57 (1980): 99-106.

12. *New York Evening Post*, Feb. 6, 1873; *New York World*, Jan. 10, 1873; *Times*, Jan. 4, 1873; *Tribune*, Jan. 10, 1873. Obituaries in *Evening Post*, Oct. 22, 1875; *World*, Oct. 22, 1875; *Times*, Oct. 22, 1875.

13. *Tribune*, June 3, 1872.

14. *NYH*, June 3, 1872.

15. Leonard I. Gappelberg, "M. M. Noah and the Evening Star: Whig Journalism, 1833-1840" (Ph.D. dissertation, Yeshiva Univ., 1970), chap. 3; Sarna, *Jacksonian Jew*, 98-117.

16. Hudson, *Journalism in the United States*, 470.

17. Dan Schiller, *Objectivity and the News: The Public and the Rise of Commercial Journalism* (Philadelphia, 1981), 15-17.

18. Ibid., 46.

19. Ibid., 50-65. Schiller points out that Judge Edwards, who was trying the case, was

also in the process of trying and convicting twenty journeymen tailors for a conspiracy to resist wage reductions. The *Herald* sided with the journeymen at the same time that it was charging a conspiracy against the innocent Robinson.

20. Alexander Saxton, "Problems of Class and Race in the Origins of the Mass Circulation Press," *American Quarterly* 36 (1984): 211–34, quotes from 212, 221.

21. Schudson, *Discovering the News,* 43–60, quotes from 44, 60.

22. Ibid., 51–56, quoting *NYH,* May 20, 1835, Apr. 13, 1840.

23. Merk's views are discussed above in chapter 4.

24. Richard Hofstadter, "The Paranoid Style in American Politics," in *The Paranoid Style in American Politics and Other Essays* (New York, 1965), 3–40; David B. Davis, *The Slave Power Conspiracy and the Paranoid Style* (Baton Rouge, 1869); Davis, ed., *The Fear of Conspiracy: Images of Un-American Subversion from the Revolution to the Present* (Ithaca, 1971).

25. *Tribune,* June 3, 1872.

Bibliographical Essay

The chapter notes indicate the relevant sources and secondary materials used in this study in enough detail to make a complete bibliographic listing unnecessary. Even a casual glance at the notes will demonstrate that Bennett's daily newspaper, the *New York Herald,* was the most important source. For another view I have read closely the *Morning Courier and New York Enquirer* of his rival, James Watson Webb, and scattered issues of other New York daily newspapers. Bennett, like most mid-nineteenth-century newspaper editors, was not very careful about preserving his correspondence, especially that dealing with the mundane daily functioning of his paper. He communicated with his staff and colleagues orally, and his public posture was on record in the *Herald's* editorial columns.

Manuscript materials dealing with Bennett are scant. The largest collection of Bennett letters is in the Nicholas Biddle Papers at the Library of Congress, and most of them are from the years before the *Herald* was established. The other sizable collection is the James Gordon Bennett Papers at the Library of Congress, dealing with the Civil War years. (Some of these have been published as "Federal Generals and a Good Press," *American Historical Review* 39 (1934): 284-97.) There are other Bennett manuscripts in the following collections:

James Gordon Bennett, Diary of a Journey through New York . . . June 12–Aug. 18, 1831, New York Public Library
Luther Bradish Papers, New-York Historical Society
James Wright Brown Collection, New-York Historical Society
John M. Clayton Papers, Library of Congress
Fairchild Collection of Horatio Seymour Manuscripts, New-York Historical Society
Azariah C. Flagg Papers, New York Public Library
Simon Gratz Collection, Historical Society of Pennsylvania
Greer Collection, Historical Society of Pennsylvania
Frederic Hudson Papers, Concord, Massachusetts, Public Library
William L. Marcy Papers, Library of Congress
Miscellaneous Manuscripts, New-York Historical Society
Miscellaneous Papers, New York Public Library
Levi Woodbury Papers, Library of Congress

There is also significant Bennett material in several published sources: Allan Nevins, ed., *The Diary of Philip Hone, 1828–1851,* 2 vols. (New York, 1927); Allan Nevins and Milton H. Thomas, eds., *The Diary of George Templeton Strong,* 4 vols. (New York, 1952); Roy M. Basler, ed., *The Works of Abraham Lincoln,* 8 vols. (New Brunswick, N.J., 1953); and John Bassett Moore, ed., *The Works of James Buchanan,* 12 vols. (Philadelphia, 1908–11.)

Of the older studies of Bennett, [Isaac C. Pray], *Memoirs of James Gordon Bennett and His Times* (New York, 1855), is valuable but must be used with care. Don C. Seitz, *The James Gordon Bennetts, Father and Son* (Indianapolis, 1928), and Oliver Carlson, *The Man Who Made News, James Gordon Bennett* (New York, 1942), are anecdotal, as is the recent Piers Brendon, *The Life and Death of the Press Barons* (New York, 1983), chap. 2, "Satan and Son." Although it is over a century old, one of the more substantial analyses of Bennett is James Parton, "The New York Herald," *North American Review* 102 (Apr. 1866): 373–419. There is a short account of the Bennett ancestry of the *Herald Tribune,* drawn from secondary sources, in Richard Kluger, *The Paper: The Life and Death of the New York Herald Tribune* (New York, 1986). Douglas Fermer, *James Gordon Bennett and the New York Herald: A Study of Editorial Opinion in the Civil War Era, 1854–1867* (New York, 1986), is a superb study of Bennett's editorials on national politics during the Buchanan and Lincoln administrations. My own earlier appraisals are in James L. Crouthamel, "The Newspaper Revolution in New York, 1830–1860," *New York History* 45 (1964): 91–113, and "James Gordon Bennett, the New York *Herald,* and the Development of Newspaper Sensationalism," *New York History* 54 (1973): 294–316.

The most reliable general history of the press is Edwin Emery and Michael Emery, *The Press and America,* 5th ed., (Englewood Cliffs, N.J., 1984). Alfred McClung Lee, *The Daily Newspaper in America* (New York, 1937), has a wealth of information not available elsewhere. Invaluable because of his close connection to Bennett and the *Herald* is Frederic Hudson, *Journalism in the United States from 1690 to 1872* (New York, 1873). Helen MacGill Hughes, *News and the Human Interest Story* (Chicago, 1940), is insightful. Charles H. Levermore, "The Rise of Metropolitan Journalism, 1800–1840," *American Historical Review* 6 (1900–1901): 446–65, and Elwyn B. Robinson, "The Dynamics of American Journalism from 1787 to 1865," *Pennsylvania Magazine of History and Biography* 61 (1937): 435–45, are still useful. The best brief treatment of the nineteenth-century city newspaper is Gunther Barth's essay "The Metropolitan Press" in his *City People: The Rise of Modern City Culture in Nineteenth-Century America* (New York, 1980). Standard histories of two of the *Herald*'s local rivals are Allan Nevins, *The Evening Post: A Century of Journalism* (New York, 1922), and Frank M. O'Brien, *The Story of the Sun* (New York, 1918). A comparative perspective of English newspapers contemporary with the *Herald* is provided in Lucy Brown, *Victorian News and Newspapers* (Oxford, 1985). John Tebbel and Sarah Miles Watts, *The Press and the Presidency* (New York, 1985), contains much of value but its usefulness is limited by a lack of documentation.

Bennett's contemporaries in New York journalism are each the subject of a sketch in the *Dictionary of American Biography*. Some of them also have modern biographies: Francis Brown, *Raymond of the Times* (New York, 1951); James L. Crouthamel, *James Watson Webb: A Biography* (Middletown, Conn., 1969); Isaac Goldberg, *Major Noah: American-Jewish Pioneer* (Philadelphia, 1936); Jonathan D. Sarna, *Jacksonian Jew: The Two Worlds of Mordecai Noah* (New York, 1981); and Glyndon G. Van Deusen, *Horace Greeley: Nineteenth Century Crusader* (Philadelphia, 1953).

Three provocative recent interpretations of the emergence of the popular press and Bennett's role are Michael Schudson, *Discovering the News: A Social History of American Newspapers* (New York, 1978); Dan Schiller, *Objectivity and the News: The Public and the Rise of Commercial Journalism* (Philadelphia, 1981); and Alexander Saxton, "Problems of Class and Race in the Origins of the Mass Circulation Press," *American Quarterly* 36 (1984): 211-34. I prefer the analyses of the role of the popular press in Frederick Merk, *Manifest Destiny and Mission in American History: A Reinterpretation* (New York, 1963), and *The Monroe Doctrine and American Expansionism* (New York, 1966).

The *Herald's* importance to Civil War reporting has been studied by J. Cutler Andrews, *The North Reports the Civil War* (Pittsburgh, 1955); Emmett Crozier, *Yankee Reporters, 1861-1865* (New York, 1956); Louis Starr, *Bohemian Brigade* (New York, 1954); and Bernard A. Weisberger, *Reporters for the Union* (Boston, 1953). Some of the *Herald* reporters wrote autobiographical accounts: Sylvanus Cadwallader, *Three Years with Grant,* ed. Benjamin P. Thomas (New York, 1953); Thomas W. Knox, *Camp-fire and Cotton-field: Southern Adventure in Time and War* (New York, 1865); Henry Villard, *Memoirs of Henry Villard: Journalist and Financier, 1835-1900* 2 vols. (Boston, 1904); W. F. G. Shanks, "How We Get Our News," *Harper's New Monthly Magazine* 34 (Mar. 1867): 511-22; and George Alfred Townsend, "Recollections and Reflections," *Lippincott's Monthly Magazine* 38 (Nov. 1886): 515-24. The *Herald's* problems with General Sherman are discussed in Thomas H. Guback, "General Sherman's War on the Press," *Journalism Quarterly* 36 (1959): 171-76, and John F. Marszalek, *Sherman's Other War* (Memphis, 1981).

The specialized studies dealing with Bennett and the *Herald* that I found most useful are Marguerite Hall Albjerg, "The New York *Herald* as a Factor in Reconstruction," *South Atlantic Quarterly* 46 (1947): 204-11; Phillip G. Auchampaugh, "Political Techniques – 1856, or Why the Herald Went for Fremont," *Western Political Quarterly* 1 (1948): 243-51; E. Maurice Bloch, "The American Art-Union's Downfall," *New-York Historical Society Quarterly* 37 (1953): 331-59; D. P. Crook, *The North, the South, and the Powers, 1861-1865* (New York, 1974); Wallace B. Eberhard, "Mr. Bennett Covers a Murder Trial," *Journalism Quarterly* 47 (1970): 457-63; Anna Kasten Nelson, "Secret Agents and Security Leaks: President Polk and the Mexican War," *Journalism Quarterly* 52 (1975): 9-15, 98; Nils Gunnar Nilsson, "The Origin of the Interview," *Journalism Quarterly* 48 (1971): 707-13; Marvin Olasky, "Advertising Abortion during the 1830s and 1840s: Madame Restell

Builds a Business," *Journalism History* 13 (1986): 49–55; William J. Thorn, "Hudson's History of Journalism Criticized by His Contemporaries," *Journalism Quarterly* 57 (1980): 99–106; John J. Turner, Jr., and Michael D'Innocenzo, "The President and the Press: Lincoln, James Gordon Bennett and the Election of 1864," *Lincoln Herald* 76 (1974): 63–69; David Quentin Voigt, "'Too Pitchy to Touch'—President Lincoln and Editor Bennett," *Abraham Lincoln Quarterly* 6 (1950): 139–61; and Arnold Whitridge, "Anglo-American Trouble-Makers: J. G. Bennett and J. T. Haldane," *History Today* 6 (Feb. 1956): 88–95.

The more useful of the specialized studies dealing broadly with technology and the news are T. H. Giddings, "Rushing the Transatlantic News in the 1830s and 1840s," *New-York Historical Society Quarterly* 42 (1958): 47–59; Oliver Gramling, *A.P.: The Story of News* (New York, 1940); Harold A. Innis, *The Bias of Communication* (Toronto, 1961); Richard B. Kielbowicz, "News Gathering by Mail in the Age of the Telegraph: Adapting to a New Technology," *Technology and Culture* 28 (1978): 26–41; Frederick B. Marbut, *News from the Capital: The Story of Washington Reporting* (Carbondale, 1971); Calder M. Pickett, "Technology and the New York Press in the 19th Century," *Journalism Quarterly* 37 (1960): 398–407; William S. Pretzer, "The Quest for Autonomy and Discipline: Labor and Technology in the Book Trades," *Proceedings of the American Antiquarian Society* 96 (1986): 85–131; Victor Rosewater, *History of Cooperative Newsgathering in the United States* (New York, 1940); Richard A. Schwartzlose, "Harbor News Association: The Formal Origin of the AP," *Journalism Quarterly,* 45 (1968): 253–60, and "Early Telegraphic News Dispatches: Forerunners of the AP," *Journalism Quarterly* 51 (1974): 595–601; Donald L. Shaw, "At the Crossroads: Change and Continuity in American Press News, 1820–1860," *Journalism History* 8 (1981): 38–50; and Robert L. Thompson, *Wiring a Continent: The Telegraph Industry in the United States* (Princeton, 1947).

Index

www.ingramcontent.com/pod-product-compliance
Lightning Source LLC
Chambersburg PA
CBHW011203090426
42742CB00019B/3388